THE CLASSICS OF WESTERN SPIRITUALITY
A Library of the Great Spiritual Masters

President and Publisher
Kevin A. Lynch, C.S.P.

EDITORIAL BOARD

Native North American Spirituality of the Eastern Woodlands

SACRED MYTHS, DREAMS, VISIONS, SPEECHES, HEALING FORMULAS, RITUALS AND CEREMONIALS

EDITED
BY
ELISABETH TOOKER

PREFACE
BY
WILLIAM C. STURTEVANT

PAULIST PRESS

Cover Art—

The artist, Norval Morriseau, was born in 1931 in Beardmore, Ontario on the North Shore of Lake Superior. His first exhibition in 1961 was a sensational success and he was acclaimed the leader of a new and dynamic school of art. A member of the Royal Academy of Art, he has painted murals for the Canadian Pavilion at EXPO '67 and has been the subject of cover stories by *Time* Magazine and *Maclean's* Magazine. A number of films, books and articles have been produced on the subject of this gifted Ojibway visionary and shaman. Awarded the Order of Canada in 1979, Mr. Morriseau's paintings hang in most of the major galleries and corporate boardrooms of Canada and the United States, including the National Gallery of Canada and the National Museum of Man.

"Either Norval Morriseau is painting the documentary truth about another reality, another parallel universe, in which case he is a cosmonaut of inner space, or else he is a great triumph of the artistic imagination and a great artist. Heads or tails, Norval wins." These words by a critic sum up the vision world of Norval, in which color mirrors the inner reality of the astral or soul plane. "I transmit its harmonies through my brushes into the physical plane. These otherworld colors are reflected in the alphabet of nature, a grammar in which the symbols are plants and animals, birds, fishes, earth and sky. I am merely a channel for the spirit to utilize," Mr. Morriseau says, "and it is needed by a spirit-starved society."

9/01

Design: Barbini, Pesce & Noble, Inc.

Copyright © 1979 by Paulist Press, Inc.

Library of Congress
Catalog Card Number: 79-66573

ISBN: 0-8091-2256-1

Published by Paulist Press
997 Macarthur Boulevard
Mahwah, New Jersey 07430

www.paulistpress.com

Printed and bound in the United States of America

Replacement

Contents

Acknowledgments

I am indebted to William C. Sturtevant for writing the chapter on Southeastern Indian formulas and to Ives Goddard for providing a new translation of the Delaware text appearing in Frank G. Speck's *A Study of the Delaware Indian Big House Ceremony* (Publications of the Pennsylvania Historical Commission vol. 2, 1931).

Other texts appearing in this volume are from the following sources, whose authors and publishers merit the gratitude of those who would seek to better understand the ways and thought of these Indians.

Cherokee texts
> Jack Frederick Kilpatrick and Anna Gritts Kilpatrick, *Notebook of a Cherokee Shaman*, Smithsonian Contributions to Anthropology, vol. 2, no. 6, 1970.
>
> James Mooney, *The Sacred Formulas of the Cherokee*, in the Seventh Annual Report of the Bureau of American Ethnology, 1891.

Creek texts
> Frank G. Speck, *Ceremonial Songs of the Creek and Yuchi Indians*, University of Pennsylvania Anthropological Publications, vol. 1, no. 2, 1911.

Delaware texts
> M.R. Harrington, *Religion and Ceremonies of the Lenape*, Indian Notes and Monographs, Museum of the American Indian, Heye Foundation, vol. 19, 1921.

Fox texts
> Truman Michelson, *Fox Miscellany*, Bureau of American Ethnology Bulletin 114, 1937.

Iroquois texts
> Wallace L. Chafe, *Seneca Thanksgiving Rituals*, Bureau of American Ethnology Bulletin 183, 1961.
>
> J.N.B. Hewitt, *Iroquoian Cosmology—Second Part*, in the Forty-third Annual Report of the Bureau of American Ethnology, 1928.
>
> Arthur C. Parker, *Seneca Myths and Folk Tales*, Buffalo Historical Society Publications, vol. 27, 1923.

Menominee texts
> Leonard Bloomfield, *Menomini Texts*, American Ethnological Society Publication 12, 1928.
>
> Alanson Skinner, *Associations and Ceremonies of the Menomini Indians*, American Museum of Natural History Anthropological Papers, vol. 13, no. 2, 1913.

Montagnais-Naskapi texts
> Frank G. Speck, *Naskapi*, Norman: University of Oklahoma Press, 1935.

Penobscot texts
> Frank G. Speck, *Penobscot Shamanism*, in American Anthropological Association Memoir 6, 1919.

Winnebago texts
> Paul Radin, *The Autobiography of a Winnebago Indian*, University of California Publications in American Archaeology and Ethnology, vol. 16, no. 7, 1920.
>
> Paul Radin, *The Winnebago Tribe*, in the Thirty-seventh Annual Report of the Bureau of American Ethnology, 1923.

The quotations from A. Irving Hallowell's "Ojibwa Ontology, Behavior, and World View" in Stanley Diamond, *Culture in History: Essays in Honor of Paul Radin*, New York: Columbia University Press are reprinted by permission of the publisher.

Author of the Preface
WILLIAM C. STURTEVANT is Curator of North American Ethnology at the Smithsonian Institution and Adjunct Professor of Anthropology at Johns Hopkins University. He took his undergraduate work at the University of California at Berkeley and his Ph.D. at Yale University, and has done field work among the Seminole Indians in Florida and the Iroquois of Oklahoma and New York State. Author of a number of articles on Indian culture, history, and languages, he is currently General Editor of the 20-volume *Handbook of North American Indians*.

The Editor of this Volume
ELISABETH TOOKER is an anthropologist specializing in the study of North American Indian cultures and history and in the religions of non-Western peoples. She received her B.A. and Ph.D. from Radcliffe College and M.A. from the University of Arizona, and has done field work among the Indians of the American Southwest and the Iroquois of New York State. Her publications include *An Ethnography of the Huron Indians, 1615-1649* (Bureau of American Ethnology, 1964), *The Iroquois Ceremonial of Midwinter* (Syracuse University Press, 1970), *The Indians of the Northeast: A Critical Bibliography* (Indiana University Press, 1978) and a number of articles on North American Indians. She served as Coordinator for the Six Nations Chapters in the Northeast volume of *Handbook of North American Indians* (Smithsonian Institution, 1978) and author of some chapters in this volume. She has taught at the University of Buffalo and Mount Holyoke College and since 1965 at Temple University where she is now Professor of Anthropology. During the academic year 1978-79 she was Visiting Professor of Anthropology at the State University of New York at Albany.

Foreword

This volume concerns the religious beliefs and practices of the Indians of eastern United States and Canada. It is a subject that has received too little attention, and of the descriptions that have appeared in the literature, only a small portion prints accounts by the Indians themselves and that often in relatively inaccessible scholarly anthropological monographs. Thus, one present objective is to make a sampling of these texts available to the general reader.

A number of the texts were originally recorded in native languages and then translated into English. With the exception of the Delaware texts, which have been retranslated especially for this volume by Ives Goddard, the translations used are those originally published. However, they have been somewhat edited for readability and consistency of spelling and punctuation.

Such texts are not available for all the aspects of religious life of any one Indian people. Nor are they available for all Indian peoples of the eastern part of the North American continent. Many of those that are, are from Indians of the Great Lakes region: Winnebago, Fox, Menominee, and Iroquois. Despite these limitations, however, much may be learned about Eastern Woodland Indian religions from a perusal of these texts. It is with the hope that they will, and that understanding of these peoples will be increased, that they are presented here.

Preface

The North American Indians lived in spiritual worlds very different from those of Western cultures. The differences between Christianity, Islam, and Judaism are minor compared to the difference between any one of those religions and the religion of any North American Indian society. North American Indian religions do bear a family resemblance to each other, just as the religions derived from the ancient Near East are similar from a world-wide perspective. But there were and still are many unique Native American societies, each with a distinctive culture. In aboriginal America there developed several hundred separate world views with associated ritual systems and applications to everyday life. Within major geographical regions these cultures were broadly similar, so that it is reasonable to collect in one volume expressions of spiritual beliefs and practices from many of the societies of the Eastern Woodlands. Yet each society within the Eastern Woodlands was different, and the religions of the Naskapi and the Cherokee, for example, or even of the Penobscot and the Winnebago, were probably more different than the Christianity of England differs from the Islam of Egypt.

Certain themes were shared over much of the Eastern Woodlands, and are reflected in the organization of this volume. But the scarcity of suitable texts has forced an unbalanced representation both of the full distribution of these themes, and of well-rounded accounts of the religion of any society. For these one must go to the anthropological literature. There one can find how widespread were the great cosmological themes, the reliance on visions and dreams, the notion of some sort of pervasive supernatural "power," the importance of song and dance, the varying concepts of the afterlife, the nature and domains of spiritual beings, as well as more specific elements such as the spiritual importance of tobacco and the preservation of sacred objects in "medicine bundles." Each of these societies also possessed a rather well integrated system of religious beliefs and ritual practices that related to such important matters as the annual economic round (with major differences between hunting and agricultural peoples), health, the stages of individual lives, and warfare.

Selecting Eastern Indian spiritual texts and explaining them for modern English-reading audiences present great problems, some of them insoluble. Our customary categories do not fit. It is not easy to decide what is spiritual as opposed to secular, what is ritual as opposed to mere customary behavior, what is religion as opposed to proto-science or philosophy. As Tooker explains, such oppositions distort Indian reality.

There are other difficulties. Native Americans were not People of the Book, and are not today to the extent that they are participants in more or less traditional Indian religions. Not only did they not write, and thus had no books, but there were very few standardized sacred texts (and commentaries on them) that were distinct from what was said and done in specific rituals or to fill practical needs, and rarely was any effort made to preserve the exact wording unchanged (an extremely difficult thing with purely oral transmission). When writing was introduced from the outside it was not normally used to record sacred texts for use within the society; only the Cherokees invented their own writing system, and evidently only Cherokee religious specialists made a practice of writing texts in their own language for their own use.

So most of the texts we have were collected by anthropologists and linguists in an attempt to record and understand cultures very different from their own; they are not texts written by believers for their own use. The quality of the available texts varies tremendously. Some seem to be quite accurate records of what was said in a purely Indian context. Others have been shortened or expanded, by either the sources or the recorders and translators (or both, in collaboration), because the texts as actually used would be quite incomprehensible across the cultural barrier. Still other texts are descriptions for outsiders of what was said, done, and thought, cast in forms that would have been unnecessary between participating believers of the Indian religion.

None of the texts represents explanations and justifications of spiritual beliefs for the purpose of convincing outsiders of their unique validity as opposed to other religious beliefs and practices, for no traditional North American Indian religion was proselytizing. Participants seem not to have thought that they had unique access to the truth nor that they had a religious duty to persuade others to change to their own forms of spirituality. One result is that it is difficult to find didactic texts that lay out a system of belief in an organized way intended to be comprehensible to non-believers; such texts normally were produced only in response to anthropologists' questioning, and the interest of scholars is different (and thus tends to draw a different response) from that of potential converts to a religion explicitly seeking adherents.

Not only was cultural translation and modification necessary to give us access to these texts. As we read them in English, we should bear in mind that this is not their original language. And translation from an oral text in an Indian language to a written one in English is a larger, more difficult transformation than turning a written text in Aramaic or classical Greek or Arabic into modern English. The first consideration is how the text in the Indian language was recorded. In this volume we have examples of several methods. The text may have been written down by a speaker of the Indian language. But how at ease was he with writing in his own language, especially to record an essentially oral text? What was the intended audience of the written text? What were the motives of the writer? If the text was spoken, it may have been mechanically reproduced. Modern tape recorders can capture a long text with a high (but not perfect) degree of accuracy. But the wax cylinders sometimes used seventy-five years ago had to be replaced every few minutes (interrupting the speaker), had very low fidelity, and rapidly wore out during replaying. Until the widespread use of tape recorders (at first wire recorders) beginning about 1950, often the best method for recording a text was dictation—where much depended on the speed and skill of the writer, and the patience of the speaker.

Once produced, how was the text translated? The simplest and least accurate method is to use an interpreter who translates orally, with no record being made of the original text. Use of an interpreter working from a written text is a better method. Reference to a repeatedly replayed tape recorded version or use of a taped version with dictation and explanation added is even better. The best available translations were made in the latter manner by a scientific linguist who had detailed knowledge of the grammar and semantics of the Indian language and worked with consultants who understood well the original texts and were trained at analysis. In this volume probably only the text of the Seneca Thanksgiving Address, translated by Wallace L. Chafe, meets these high standards. But the Menominee texts translated by the linguist Leonard Bloomfield must be nearly as good, even though Bloomfield worked without recording equipment. Paul Radin's Winnebago texts are very carefully prepared and no doubt approach the preceding in adequacy. J. N. B. Hewitt well understood the structure and semantics of Iroquoian languages, but tended to carry these over into his English translations in a manner that somewhat obscured the content. It is clear from this and other examples that another important variable, perhaps more difficult to assess, is the literary style of the English version and its appropriateness to the style of the original. Here is the classical and ultimately insoluble problem of all translations, made even more difficult when translating from Indian languages whose styles are so different from those of European languages. For the Eastern Woodland Indians we do not yet have the ideal translations, which would require a fully bilingual, trained translator, skilled in literary English, who also has a deep understanding of the original text and its religious contexts. In fact, given the rapid disappearance of Native languages and the lack of competent speakers trained in linguistics, anthropology, and literature, we will probably never have such ideal translations.

Perhaps it can be said that the more accurate the translation, the less comprehensible it will be without thorough knowledge of the culture from which the original text was extracted. That is why Tooker's introductions to and comments on the texts are essential. She has chosen from the best translations, so she must supply some of their cultural contexts—they cannot stand alone. Yet, paradoxically, the better we understand the spiritual expressions in this volume the less relevant they are for our own spiritual concerns. As we begin to discern the exotic and complicated world views illustrated here, the attitudes and the understandings of the original speakers appear so different from our own that the most we can hope for is a beginning at understanding and appreciating them in their own terms. Our assumptions and understandings are so different that attempts to adopt traditional Native American spirituality must result in such drastic adaption, such severe reinterpretation to fit our conceptions of reality, that they no longer reflect the ancient Indian religions. The principal message here is probably the great variety of human spirituality, the very different results human societies reach after thousands of years of coping with human problems.

Most of the texts presented here were recorded fifty to more than seventy-five years ago. Even at those times, many of the people who provided them were among the last who could have done so, for the rituals even then were often moribund or extinct and most members of their communities were not followers of the old ways. So the spiritual expressions that follow are in large part reflections of worlds that have not been fully operative for a century or a century and a half. Yet long before 1850 all the Indian societies of the Eastern Woodlands had been heavily influenced directly as well as indirectly by the customs, the beliefs, and the military and economic motives imported from Europe beginning about 1600. These texts are fully Indian but they cannot be fully aboriginal, even though

PREFACE

Tooker has avoided those that contain obvious Christian elements and those that are central to the new Indian religions that repeatedly arose as reformers' reactions to the cultural and social disruptions of Indian societies caused by the massive European invasions.

Over the last half century, since these texts were collected, the changes in Eastern Indian spiritual beliefs and the associated rituals have probably been greater than those over the preceding three hundred years. The old beliefs and practices have been replaced by those taught by Christian missionaries, or have been replaced or strongly affected by various new Indian religions, especially the Peyote religion of the Native American Church and, among the Iroquois, the Good Message of the prophet Handsome Lake. Where the more traditional religions have persisted, as they have among some Eastern Indian societies, they have usually come to fill much more restricted roles in individual daily lives and are applicable in far fewer contexts than they were. They have also been modified, usually simplified, both in the number of constituent elements and in the complexity of the philosophical structure.

Scores of Indian communities descended from aboriginal Eastern Woodland societies persist today along the coastal plain from Labrador to Florida, around the Great Lakes, in the North Carolina mountains, in eastern Oklahoma, and elsewhere. These communities are socially distinct and usually clearly viable as such into the foreseeable future, but they are culturally much different from what they were when the texts in this volume were collected among them. Increasing formal education, the spread of English at the expense of the Native languages, the continuing pressures of Christian missionaries, the influence of the modern mass media (especially television), the improvement of roads and other means of communication, the loss of economic self-sufficiency with the concomitant integration of community members into the occupational system of the surrounding society—all these and other causes have resulted in a marked decline of the specific forms of spirituality represented in this volume. The Delaware Big House collapsed long ago, Winnebago men no longer yearn for battle, but

PREFACE

Cherokee physicians still cure with ancient charms and many modern Iroquois believe that their participation in the Four Sacred Ceremonies is pleasing to the Creator.

William C. Sturtevant

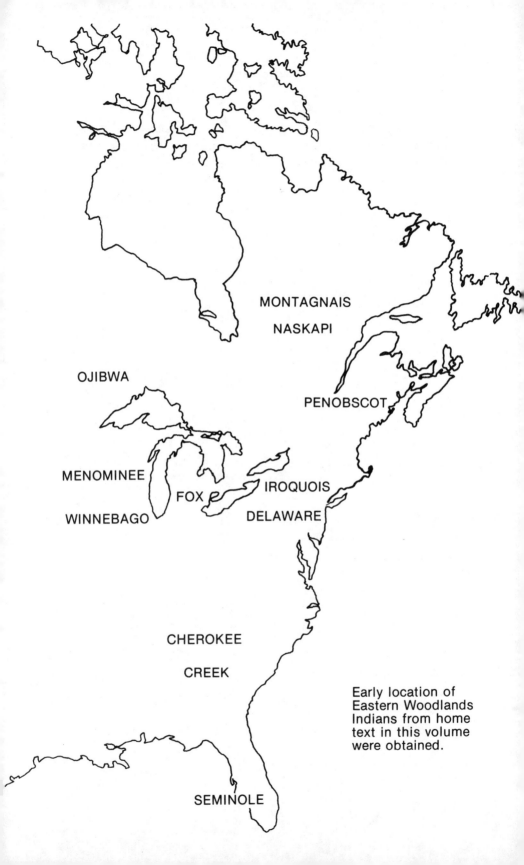

MONTAGNAIS

NASKAPI

OJIBWA

PENOBSCOT

MENOMINEE

FOX   IROQUOIS

WINNEBAGO   DELAWARE

CHEROKEE

CREEK

Early location of
Eastern Woodlands
Indians from home
text in this volume
were obtained.

SEMINOLE

Introduction

1. An Overview

The Indians of eastern North America have long fascinated the Western world—a fascination that began in the sixteenth century when Europeans first began to have some knowledge of them and that has continued to the present day. Because of this, a considerable literature describing their life and culture now exists—the result of the curiosity and industry of explorers, missionaries, early settlers, government officials, travelers, anthropologists, and others. Relatively little of this literature, however, records in the words of the Indians themselves their beliefs and practices, and of this amount, only a very small fraction was written down by the Indians for their own use. The greater bulk of the literature consists of texts recorded by anthropologists in the first decades of this century, and it is from these writings that the present selection has been made.

For the most part, these texts originally appeared in scholarly anthropological publications with limited distribution, so the general reader often did not know of their existence and continued to hold the erroneous notion that Indians were and are incapable of producing such works. But just as in recent decades the artistic qualities of the objects manufactured by members of the world's numerous and varied cultures are increasingly appreciated in our own, so also has the time come for increased appreciation of their verbal productions—for what Daniel G. Brinton noted in 1883 is still true:

> Time and money are spent in collecting remains in wood and stone, in pottery and tissue and bone, in laboriously collating isolated words, and in measuring ancient constructions. This is well, for all these things teach us what manner of men made up the indigenous race, what were their powers, their aspirations, their mental grasp. But closer to very self, to thought and being, are the connected expressions of men in their own tongues. The monuments of a nation's literature are more correct mirrors of its mind than any merely material objects.[1]

And, further,

> The time has long since passed, at least among thinking men, when the religious legends of [other] races were looked upon as trivial fables, or as the inventions of the Father of Lies. They are neither the one nor the other. They express, in image and incident, the opinions of these races on the mightiest topics of human thought, on the origin and destiny of man, his motives for duty and his grounds of hope, and the source, history and fate of all external nature. Certainly the sincere expressions on these subjects of even humble members of the human race deserve our most respectful heed, and it may be that we shall discover in their ... narrations gleams of a mental light which their proud Aryan brothers have been long in coming to, or have not yet reached.[2]

One reason that few such texts have been collected is, of course, the time and effort, not to mention talent, required

---

1. Daniel G. Brinton, *Aboriginal American Authors and their Productions* (Philadelphia, 1883), p. 59.
2. Daniel G. Brinton, *American Hero-myths* (Philadelphia: H. C. Watts, 1882), pp. vii–ix.

INTRODUCTION

both to record them in languages so different from those we are most familiar with and to translate them into English. Not only are the Indian words themselves apt to refer to unfamiliar concepts, but also ideas quite different from those of English occur in the grammars of these languages. As a result, all the difficulties of translation are compounded and, more than is usual in translation, the English text distorts the meaning of the original. Nonetheless, perhaps some insight into the world of Indian peoples can be gained from a perusal of these translations, and with the insights so gained the way cleared a little more for interest in and publication of the detailed, linguistically annotated treatment these texts deserve.

The translators of the texts presented here did not attempt to recast Indian statements into poetical or literary forms familiar to English readers and hence some of the distortion introduced by such efforts has been avoided. Nonetheless, the translations do vary in style; some are more literal than others, which accounts for some of the apparent differences between the religions here discussed.

As a partial corrective, it is well to remember that the concerns, religious and otherwise, of these peoples are not ours and that our own views of them are often colored by our own interests. One such is quite nationalistic. After the American Revolution the newly independent nation, lacking any history of its own, turned to the Indians to fill this lack. If Britain had its megalithic Stonehenge, America also had its own archaeological monuments: the imposing and mysterious mounds of the Midwest. If England had its kings, the United States had its Indian chiefs, equal in bravery and villainy, whose exploits could be recalled and names recited as a kind of litany of the past.

Then, too, beginning in earlier centuries, those peoples Europeans found already residing in lands they "discovered," as they slowly roused themselves from the slumber brought on by the fall of Rome and cut their ties to other parts of the world, seemed to them by the Age of Enlightenment to be representatives of the past. The discoverers, like other peoples of the world, regarded only themselves as "real human beings"

3

and those of other cultures as, if in fact human, not quite so human. But unlike others, Europeans have been concerned as to whether these differences resulted from the progress of their own civilization over the course of time, with bettering of all aspects of life, including religious practice and belief, or a degeneration, a slow decay into corruption and debasement. In either case, history was regarded as having lessons to teach—if only it were studied—and the search began for such lessons as could be extracted from the very early history of man as evidenced in the customs of "primitive peoples." The perspective to be gained from such a consideration was great. As Andrew Lang depicted it:

> The student of this lore can look back and see the long trodden way behind him, the winding tracks through marsh and forest and over burning sands. He sees the caves, the camps, the villages, the towns where the race has tarried, for shorter times or longer, strange places many of them, and strangely haunted, desolate dwellings and inhospitable. But the scarce visible tracks converge at last on the beaten ways, the ways to that city whither mankind is wandering, and which it may never win. We have a foreboding of a purpose which we know not, a sense as of will, working, as we would not have worked, to a hidden end.[3]

These concerns are with us yet, exerting their influence in many varied and often subtle ways. Some still search for and see in the beliefs and practices of other peoples evidence of the benefits of "civilization" and a guide for how not to act and what not to believe. Others search for and find in the same data guides for improvement of their lives and evidence of a better way, a way often thought to be simpler, stripped of the complexities of modern life.

But the lives of these so-called primitive peoples may well be no more or no less complicated than our own, and their concerns no more or no less profound. What is certain is that they are different, and that the extent to which they are so is

---

3. Andrew Lang, *Adventures among Books* (London: Longmans, Green, 1905), p. 37.

often obscured by a facile readiness to assume that every practice and belief means exactly what it means in our society.

This assumption has led to notions that other peoples cannot make abstractions or make fewer abstractions than we do. However, this is not the case. They have merely chosen to attend to somewhat different matters, and by so doing to organize their worlds differently. They have made different abstractions, and consequently their intellectual world is quite unfamiliar to us, for even in particulars their beliefs do not have precisely comparable meanings to beliefs in ours.

Unfortunately, scholars have paid relatively little attention to these differences and to their philosophic import. Until they do, the philosophic musings of the people themselves—for in all societies individuals ponder on their world and their place in it—will make little sense, and so be recorded. As of now, only most rarely have such reflections of primitive peoples—these peoples who until recently have not had a written language because they did not need it—been committed to paper.

Of the material available, what is closest to these religious reflections and perhaps even more basic to the understanding of religious beliefs are the long accounts Indians have given whites of religious practice—for it is in the ritual that many beliefs deemed most important are either repeated or alluded to. For this reason, many of the texts given here are accounts of ritual practice.

Also important are the great sacred traditions, which we—in our arrogance—usually term "myths" as if others regard them with the same disbelief we do. These are not the tales so avidly collected by folklorists, which comprise so many library volumes, but the long accounts of that time in the past when the world was new and of what happened then, including the creation of things and beings that still exist. Some of these incidents may be told separately rather as if they were tales, but the myth as a whole is a statement of basic cosmological beliefs.

These beliefs and practices, the myths and rituals of the many Indian peoples of eastern North America, are rich and varied, and can only be sampled in a volume such as this. But it should not be presumed that a larger selection would answer many of the questions left undiscussed in these texts. People tend to talk about what interests them, not about what is of interest to those of other cultures. And, for this reason, some greater understanding of the nature of these religions is to be gained not by seeking in these texts answers to questions we presume to be universal ones, but by paying attention to what is not said as well as to what is—for as has been noted each culture has elected to attend to certain matters while ignoring others and therefore classifying observed and felt phenomena in a way that is to some degree unique to it. It is the all too frequent failure to recognize that each culture is a system, complete in itself, that has led to the notion that these religions are crude and unintelligible.

2. Note on Selection and Editing of the Texts

The selection of texts to represent the religions of the Indians of eastern North America has been guided by availability, for unfortunately such materials are not available for many groups.

An attempt has been made throughout to use those texts in which Indians describe their beliefs and rituals—the materials available that most closely resemble our religious texts. However, folktales—of which there are numerous volumes—are omitted in favor of a selection of longer and more sacred myths.

Some effort has been made to describe and illustrate a few themes that recur in the religions of various Indian peoples of the region rather than attempting an exhaustive survey of all the varieties of these beliefs and practices. Neither have those of relatively recent origin been included such as, for example, the teachings of the various prophets who sought to introduce reforms in religious practice in the last several centuries. However, it should not be supposed that the beliefs and practices here described represent only those of pre-Columbian times.

The texts have been edited to varying degrees, and an

indication of the extent of the editing is given in the first footnote accompanying each text. Subsequent footnotes containing explanations of words and beliefs and practices that may be unfamiliar to the general reader are provided by the translator and, on occasion, by the editor. The source of the notes is given in the first footnote accompanying each text.

In editing these texts, the author has been guided by the following: Indian words have generally been eliminated; although familiarity with such words is essential for a more complete understanding, they are more distracting than illuminating to the general reader. Also, certain stylistic features that result from very literal translation of the texts have been eliminated, although enough remains to give the reader some sense of how very different the structures of these languages are. Biblical forms such as "thee" and "thou" have been rendered into modern English. Punctuation and spelling have been standardized throughout.

3. The People

The Indians of eastern North America were not one people as the term "Indian" might imply. Rather, a number of peoples occupied the region, each speaking its own language and having its own customs and traditions.

Each of these peoples was composed of small local groups who, speaking the same language, felt a special kinship to each other and in times of trouble might call on each other for help. Thus, for example, in times of war a number might unite against a common enemy or otherwise engage in some common political action. It was this propensity, in part, that has led to the characterization of these groups as "tribes." But most of the groups so termed did not have a formal and centralized political organization. Members of these larger nationalities were not ruled by a tribal council of chiefs. In fact, even the idea that chiefs could rule was an alien one. As early European observers noted, chiefs did not govern by coercion; their power was not the absolute power of European monarchs. Their power was that of persuasion, and the extent of their influence rested on this ability. Each group was small in number and occupied a large territory. It had neither the need nor necessity for more despotic forms of government. But although not states such as have become familiar in recent centuries, they were nonetheless nations.

Because political ties so often rested on language, the most convenient listing of the groups in the region is a linguistic one. Such a classification is also a cultural listing, for people speaking the same language are apt to share similar beliefs and customs, including those relative to religion. This is so partly because language facilitates exchange of new ideas and partly because certain ideas are embedded in the language itself.

Language similarities and differences also provide the basis for a more inclusive classification of the peoples of the area. Those peoples speaking closely related languages, that is, languages relatively recently differentiated from a common ancestral one, are also apt to have similar cultures. And, although the cultures of peoples speaking more distantly related languages are apt to be quite different, linguistic similarities afford a convenient means of identifying them. These similarities and differences are the basis on which the large language families are identified. There are four such important language families in eastern North America: Algonquian, Iroquoian, Siouan, and Muskogean. Muskogean may be very distantly related to Algonquian, and Siouan to Iroquoian, but Muskogean and Algonquian give no evidence of being related to Siouan and Iroquoian.

The northern part of the area, what is now the eastern half of Canada, was occupied by Algonquian-speaking groups including the Algonkin proper (a small group after which the language family is named), Montagnais-Naskapi, Ottawa, Cree, and Ojibwa (also called Chippewa). Speakers of other Algonquian languages lived in the east coast region extending from the St. Lawrence River to North Carolina. They include the Micmac, Maliseet (Malecite), Passamaquoddy, Penobscot, Abenaki, Pennacook, Massachuset, Narraganset, Mahican, Delaware, and Nanticoke. Still others lived in the upper Great Lakes–Ohio River area. They include the Menominee, Sauk,

INTRODUCTION

Fox, Kickapoo, Potawatomi, Miami, Illinois, and Shawnee. In the lower Great Lakes region lived a number of Iroquoian-speaking groups including the five Iroquois tribes proper (Mohawk, Oneida, Onondaga, Cayuga, and Seneca), Huron, Petun, Neutral, Erie, and Susquehannock. Others, including the Cherokee and Tuscarora, lived in the Southeast. To the south lived some speakers of Muskogean languages such as Creek, Chickasaw, Choctaw, Hitchiti, Yamasee, and Apalachee. There were also some Siouan speakers in the southeast region, such as the Catawba and Tutelo. Another Siouan-speaking group, the Winnebago, lived in the upper Great Lakes region, an area otherwise occupied by those who spoke Algonquian language.

As even this partial listing indicates, the history of the region is long and complex, if incompletely understood. It is evident, however, from both the archaeological and ethnographic record that the Indian cultures of eastern North America were influenced by those of Mexico. These influences are most apparent in the Southeast and less so among the Great Lakes Indians such as the Winnebago and Iroquois. They were scarcely felt at all among the northernmost Indians, and the way of life of these peoples remained largely one that was probably more characteristic of the whole region before agriculture and other ideas from Mesoamerica had been adopted.

Unfortunately, too little is known about Indian religious beliefs and practices to trace in any detail the nature and course of this Mesoamerican influence. The archaeological record, however, indicates that some "temples" similar to those in Mexico and elsewhere in Mesoamerica were built in the Southeast and that some of the activity in these ceremonial centers was also derived from southern practice. Further north, though such temples were not built, there are tantalizing fragments of information suggesting that Mesoamerican religions influenced these religions more than might first appear. But at present few conclusions can be drawn from the scanty data available.

Better known are the changes that followed on European discovery of America. The first impact was that of epidemics. The peoples of the New World lacked the immunities of those in the Old, immunities that had been built up over the course of thousands of years to a number of diseases there. As a result, the Indian populations were decimated by a series of epidemics that began in the sixteenth century after only the briefest contacts with whites and continued in succeeding centuries.

Other changes followed on more intensive contact with Europeans. The great riches that attracted Europeans to the northern part of the region were not gold, as in Mesoamerica, but furs. In exchange for furs, Europeans could offer various manufactured goods, particularly metal objects (including guns) that Indians wanted—goods they soon became dependent on. One result was a series of wars between Indians—each group attempting to gain or maintain a share of this trade—and these wars, combined with those between England and France, resulted in more deaths, further reducing the population of some Indian groups and leading to the extinction of others.

Still other wars were fought between Indians and white settlers for the land itself. Before the American Revolution, such wars were confined to the land east of the Appalachians, but after the revolution, they were extended to the west as white settlers spilled over the mountains in search of more land. At the same time, sentiment grew for the removal of all Indians still living east of the Mississippi River to lands west of it. A half century later, the removal of Indians to lands west of the Mississippi was well underway, and when completed left behind only a few communities of Indians living in the East.

Here and there in this region, some Indians not only survived epidemics and wars, but also, despite three centuries of Christian proselytizing, kept up their traditional religious beliefs and practices into the twentieth century. It was to these groups that ethnographers seeking to record Indian ways went in the first decades of the century, and among other information collected the texts reprinted here. But when they began doing so, they found that the record for the region as a whole undoubtedly would remain incomplete. Information on many of the Indians who were living or had lived on the East Coast and in the South was fragmentary. Disease, war, migration, and long contact with whites had so radically changed their way of life that little or nothing of their old religious belief and practice remained. However, in areas of the North old beliefs existed alongside Christianity and in places in the Great Lakes region other Indian peoples still followed the religious teachings of their ancestors.

But even for these peoples the record is incomplete. Few have had the time, inclination, and ability to put texts on paper. Chance has also played a role: In some instances, an Indian and a white interested in doing so happened to meet; in other instances, not. In fact, given all the circumstances, we are probably fortunate to have as many Indian descriptions of their religious practices and beliefs as we do.

For these reasons, the following is not a representative survey of the religions of the Indians of eastern North America. Rather, it is merely a survey of the available data, much of which pertains to the Indians of the Great Lakes region. Nonetheless, it may serve to give some insight into the worlds of all the Indians of the East.

4. Beings-Other-Than-Human

If Europeans found the peoples of the New World as strange as their cultures were numerous, they also found their religions at least equally incomprehensible. Something of the difficulty involved is illustrated in the report written in 1634 by the French Jesuit missionary Father Paul Le Jeune of his conversation with a Montagnais Indian on the subject:

> "You see," I said, "what love I bear you; I have not only left my own country, which is beautiful and very pleasant, to come into your snows and vast woods, but I have also left the little house we have in your lands to follow you and learn your language. I cherish you more than my brothers, and have left them for love of you. It is he who has made all who has given me this affection for you. He created the first man from whom we are all descended, and as we have the same father, we are all brothers and ought to acknowledge the same Lord and the same chief. We all ought to believe in him and obey his will."

INTRODUCTION

The Indian, interrupting me, said in a loud voice, "When I see him, I will believe in him and not until then. How are we to believe in him whom we do not see?"

I answered, "When you tell me that your father or one of your friends has said something, I believe what he has told you, supposing that he is not a liar although I have not seen him. Then, too, you believe there is a manitou and you have never seen him. You believe also that there are Spirits of the Light and you have not seen them."

"Others have seen them," he replied.

"You could not tell," I said, "either when, how, in what way, or in what place they were seen. But I, I can tell you the names of those who have seen the Son of God upon earth, when they saw him and in what place, what they have done, and in what countries they have been."

"Your God," he answered, "has not come to our country, and that is why we do not believe in him. Make me see him and I will believe in him."

"Listen to me and you will see him," I said. "We have two kinds of sight: the sight of the eyes of the body and the sight of the eyes of the soul. What someone sees with the eyes of the soul may be just as true as what he sees with the eyes of the body."

"No," he said. "I see nothing except with the eyes of the body, except while sleeping, and you do not approve our dreams."

"Hear me to the end," I replied. "When you pass a deserted house and see still standing the circle of poles, the floor covered with pine boughs, and the fire still smoking, is it not true that you know positively and you see clearly that Indians have been there, that the poles and other things you leave when you break camp are not brought together by chance?"

"Yes," he answered.

"Now I say the same. When you see the beauty and grandeur of this world—how the sun continuously turns round without stopping, how the seasons follow each other in their time, and how perfectly all the stars maintain their order, you clearly see that men have not made these wonders and that they do not govern them. There must be someone more noble than man who has built and who rules

INTRODUCTION

this grand mansion. It is he whom we call God, who sees all things and whom we do not see. But we shall see him after death and shall be forever happy with him if we love and obey him."

"You do not know what you are talking about," he replied. "Learn to talk and we will listen to you."[1]

In succeeding centuries, the impediments encountered by Le Jeune in understanding Indian religious conceptions have not vanished, as witnessed by the scholarly debate in this century regarding the meaning of the word *manitou*[2] mentioned by Le Jeune—a word that occurs not only in Montagnais but also in other Algonquian languages and is perhaps the most central religious conception in the beliefs of these Indians.

An early and one of the most important discussions of this word is contained in the article "The Algonkin Manitou" by William Jones, himself a Fox Indian as well as anthropologist. In it, Jones concludes that manitou is "an unsystematic belief in a cosmic, mysterious property which is believed to be existing everywhere in nature."[3] He further states that this property is impersonal, although this "becomes obscure and confused when the property becomes identified with objects in nature" (such objects may also be called manitou) and that it "manifests itself in various forms."[4]

Something of these latter qualities of manitou can be seen in an example given by Jones—a comment by a Fox Indian on his experience in a sweat house, a special house heated by hot stones and so inducing a sweat. This Fox Indian said:

> Often one will cut one's self over the arms and legs, slitting one's self through the skin. It is done to open up many passages for the manitou to pass into the body. The

---

1. Reuben Gold Thwaites, ed., *The Jesuit Relations and Allied Documents*, 73 vols. (Cleveland: Burrows Bros., 1876–1901), 7: 99–103, with some modification.
2. Also spelled "manito" and "manitu."
3. William Jones, "The Algonkin Manitou," *Journal of American Folk-Lore, 18* (1905): 190.
4. Ibid.

manitou comes from the place of its abode in the stone. It becomes roused by the heat of the fire, and proceeds out of the stone when water is sprinkled on it. It comes out in the steam, and in the steam it enters the body wherever it finds entrance. It moves up and down and all over inside the body, driving out everything that inflicts pain. Before the manitou returns to the stone it imparts some of its nature to the body. That is why one feels so well after having been in the sweat lodge.[5]

This characterization of manitou is similar to that offered earlier by Alice Fletcher of the Siouan word *wakanda:* a mysterious power or permeating life that also has the implied power to bring to pass, a power that pervades all things and is possessed of a quality similar to the willpower of man.[6] By way of illustrating these ideas, Fletcher offered a description given her by an old Dakota Indian of this power that animates all things, always moving and filling the sky and earth:

Every thing as it moves, now and then, here and there, makes stops. The bird as it flies, stops at one place to rest in its flight, and at another to build its nest. A man when he goes forth stops when he wills, so the mysterious power has stopped. The sun, the moon, the four directions, the trees, the animals, all mark where it has stopped. The Indian thinks of all these places ... and sends his prayers to reach the mysterious power where it has stopped.[7]

About the same time, J. N. B. Hewitt, the Tuscarora Indian anthropologist, suggested that the meaning of the Iroquoian word *orenda* was similar to both wakanda and manitou. As Hewitt defined it, orenda is "a hypothetic potence or potentiality to do or effect results mystically,"[8] and, by way of

---

5. Ibid., p. 184. See also below, chap. 7, note 11.
6. Alice C. Fletcher, "The Emblematic Use of the Tree in the Dakotan Group," *Proceedings of the American Association for the Advancement of Science for 1896* (1897), pp.5–6.
7. Ibid., p. 6.
8. J.N.B. Hewitt, "Orenda and a Definition of Religion," *American Anthropologist* 4 (1902): 38.

illustrating the concept, he gave meanings of various Iroquoian words.[9] For example: A shaman is one whose orenda is great, powerful. A fine hunter is one whose orenda is fine, superior in quality. When a hunter is successful in the chase, it is said he baffled or thwarted the orenda of the quarry. But if a hunter is unsuccessful, it is said the game foiled or outmatched the hunter's orenda. If a person defeats another in a game of chance or skill, it is said that he thwarted or overcame the orenda of his opponent. When a storm is brewing, it is said that the storm maker is making or preparing its orenda. When the storm clouds appear to be ready, it is said that the storm maker has finished or prepared its orenda. A prophet is one who habitually puts forth or effuses his orenda and thereby learns the secrets of the future. The orenda of shy animals and birds—those difficult to snare or kill—is said to be acute or sensitive. In fact, anything whose orenda is reputed or believed to have been instrumental in obtaining some food or in accomplishing some purpose is said "to possess orenda."[10]

As Hewitt elsewhere summarized it, orenda is "the force, principle, or magic power" assumed by the Iroquois "to be inherent in every body and being of nature and in every personified attribute, property, or activity, belonging to each of these and conceived to be the active cause or force, or dynamic energy, involved in every operation or phenomenon of nature, in any manner affecting or controlling the welfare of man." It is conceived of as "immaterial, occult, impersonal, mysterious in mode of action, limited in function and efficiency, and not at all omnipotent, local and not omnipresent, and ever embodied or immanent in some object, although it was believed that it could be transferred, attracted, acquired, increased, suppressed, or enthralled by the orenda of occult ritualistic formulas endowed with more potency."[11]

Not long after Fletcher's, Jones' and Hewitt's work, the

---

9. Most words in the Iroquoian languages are composed of several meaningful parts (morphemes). Hewitt is here analyzing a number of these "sentence-words" that contain the morpheme "orenda."

10. Condensed from Hewitt, "Orenda and . . . Religion," pp. 38–39.

11. Hewitt, "Orenda," *Bureau of American Ethnology Bulletin* 30, vol. 2 (1910): 147.

INTRODUCTION

most noted and influential anthropologist of the time, Franz Boas, could summarize Indian religious concepts concerning individuals as follows:

> The fundamental concept bearing on the religious life of the individual is the belief in the existence of magic power, which may influence the life of man, and which in turn may be influenced by human activity. In this sense magic power must be understood as the wonderful qualities which are believed to exist in objects, animals, men, spirits, or deities, and which are superior to the natural qualities of man. This idea of magic power is one of the fundamental concepts that occur among all Indian tribes. It is what is called *manito* by the Algonquian tribes; *orenda*, by the Iroquois; *sulia*, by the Salish; *naualak*, by the Kwakiutl, and *tamanoas*, by the Chinook. Notwithstanding slight differences in the signification of these terms, the fundamental notion of all of them is that of a power inherent in the objects of nature which is more potent than the natural powers of man. This idea seems adequately expressed by our term "wonderful"; and it is hardly necessary to introduce an Indian term, as has often been attempted.[12]

These ideas were given further popularity by Ruth Benedict's chapter "Religion" in *General Anthropology*, a book edited by Boas and designed to serve as a textbook in anthropology. Remarking on the concept of "supernatural," she noted:

> The striking fact about this plain distinction between the religious and the nonreligious in actual ethnographic recording is that it needs so little recasting in its transfer from one society to another. No matter into how exotic a society the traveler has wandered, he still finds the distinction made and in comparatively familiar terms. And it is universal. There is no monograph in existence that does not group a certain class of facts as religion, and there are no records of travelers, provided they are full enough to warrant such a judgment, that do not indicate this category.

12. Franz Boas, "Religion," *Bureau of American Ethnology Bulletin* 30, vol. 2 (1910): 366.

INTRODUCTION

This category, moreover, is commonly made explicit in language. There are several terms that have been widely used in discussions of religion. Three of these, in three different American Indian languages, are *manitou, orenda,* and *wakan,* and they have all the same range. They are all terms for supernatural power. They do not mean specifically a supernatural person—that is, a god—though *manitou* may be used in this sense without further composition, and *wakan* when it is used with the adjective "great." The Great Wakan is now the Siouan term for the Christian God, just as Great Manitou is the Algonquian term. . . . *Manitou* . . . means either supernatural power in the abstract, or a Supernatural Power. It has other extensions of meaning. A *manitou* means not only a supernatural being but a holy man, a religious practitioner. In ordinary speech the term is constantly recurring, too, in the sense of "wonderful," "surprising." A traveler comes upon fine high-bush cranberries on the prairie and they are *manitou;* Coyote, in the tales, sees a piece of dung he does not recognize, and it is *manitou.* This simple meaning of "wonderful" underlies all its extensions however it is used.

This fundamental meaning of *manitou* is kept even more explicitly in the case of the Siouan term *wakan.* It is used in essentially the same range of meanings as the Algonquian *manitou,* but there are a large number of words in Dakota that have been made with the term *wakan* and that have become fossilized, and the essential meaning of "*wakan*" in these uses is clearly not "sacred" or "holy," but "wonderful."[13]

And, further:

The fundamental concept that is represented by these native terms is the existence of wonderful power, a voltage with which the universe is believed to be charged. This voltage is present in the whole world in so far as it is considered supernatural, whether it is regarded as animate or inanimate. A stick or a stone is *wakan* and is used as an

---

13. Ruth Benedict, "Religion," in *General Anthropology*, ed. Franz Boas (Boston: D. C. Heath, 1938), pp. 628–629.

amulet; a place, and is used as a sacred grove; a formula, and by faithful repetition it will accomplish what is inaccessible to the techniques of everyday routine. Or it may be persons of particular attainments or in particular circumstances that are *wakan:* a seer who can foretell events or bring about wonderful cures, a warrior who has killed an enemy, a menstruating woman, the dead. Different civilizations regard as *wakan* different objects or aspects of life, sometimes in narrowly limited designated objects, sometimes very unsystematically, almost pantheistically. They are at one only in the universal recognition of the existence of this wonderful power. Always, moreover, the manipulation of this wonderful power, and the beliefs that grow out of it, are religion. They are elaborated by specifically religious techniques.[14]

Authors of new textbooks often base part of their presentation on material in older ones, and by so doing, give material in these older works even wider dissemination. Such occurred in the case of Benedict's characterization of the concepts of manitou, wakan, and orenda; it has come to be the standard one through repetition in a number of textbooks, including recent ones.

But not all concurred with this interpretation. Most significantly, Paul Radin did not. As he wrote:

> I was fortunate enough to work among the Winnebago and Ojibwa, where the belief in *wakanda* and *manito* is strongly and characteristically developed. In both tribes the term always referred to definite spirits, not necessarily definite in shape. If at a vapor-bath the steam is regarded as *wakanda* or *manito,* it is because it is a spirit transformed into steam for the time being; if an arrow is possessed of specific virtues, it is because a spirit has either transformed himself into the arrow or because he is temporarily dwelling in it; and, finally, if tobacco is offered to a peculiarly shaped object, it is because either this object belongs to a spirit, or a spirit is residing in it. The terms *wakanda* and

---

14. Ibid., p. 630.

manito are often used in the sense of "sacred." If a Winnebago tells you that a certain thing is *waka* (i.e., sacred),
further inquiry will elicit from him the information that it
is so because it belongs to a spirit, was given by a spirit, or
was in some way connected with a spirit. It is possible that
Dr. Jones, Miss Fletcher, and Mr. Hewitt interpreted a
certain vagueness in the answer, or a certain inability (or
unwillingness) to discuss objects that were regarded as *manito* or *wakanda*, as pertaining to the nature of sacred. In
addition to the connotation of "sacred," *wakanda* and *manito*
also have the meaning "strange," "remarkable," "wonderful," "unusual," and "powerful," without, however, having
the slightest suggestion of "inherent power," but having
the ordinary sense of those adjectives.[15]

But why did such scholars as Fletcher, Jones, and Hewitt
reach the conclusions they did? Having reviewed their statements Radin concluded that "quite apart . . . from the fact that
there is abundant evidence to show that they have generally
approached the subject from a preconceived European metaphysical viewpoint (whether they have done this consciously or
not is immaterial), the premises of which it is legitimate to
examine, we are compelled to reject their data because they
have confused interpretations with facts."[16]

From present-day perspective, it is clear that students of
Indian religion such as Fletcher, Jones, and Hewitt were
caught up with the concerns of their time, one of the most
prominent being the origin of all religion, and that this concern influenced their interpretation of Indian religious belief
and practice. The search at the time was for the one or few
religious ideas that could be considered the foundation of all
religions and hence representative of man's earliest religious
belief. This is evident in some of Fletcher's statements that
precede her discussion of wakanda. For example, she states that
"Indian religions seem to have been subject to the same laws

---

15. Paul Radin, "Religion of the North American Indians," *Journal of American Folk-Lore* 27 (1914): 349–350.
16. Ibid., p. 349.

that governed the development and growth of religions on the eastern continent."[17] She states further that traces of this similar history can be found in Indian religions such as Siouan ones: "for, penetrating beneath the varied forms of their religious rites, we come upon a few fundamental conceptions or thoughts, the most dominant of which perhaps is the idea of the all-permeating presence of what we call life, and that this life is the same in kind, animating all natural forms and objects alike with man himself."[18]

But it was Edward B. Tylor's earlier formulation that came to dominate studies of the so-called primitive religions. Also seeking "a rudimentary definition of religion," the "essential source" of religion, he proposed "as a minimum definition of religion, the belief in Spiritual Beings"[19]—a belief he termed "animism." And he found animism in all religions: "Animism characterizes tribes very low in the scale of humanity, and thence ascends, deeply modified in its transmission, but from first to last preserving an unbroken continuity, into the midst of high modern culture."[20] Although Tylor's theory regarding the origin of animism—he found it in the presumed reflection of primitive man on the difference between a living body and a dead one and on the shapes that appear in dreams and visions—has long since been disregarded, the term animism in the sense he coined for it has become part of English vocabulary and a number of religions, perhaps rather too facilely, are still characterized as being "animistic."

Fletcher also used the term, but her opinions regarding its origin differed from those of Tylor:

> There is no reason to think that at any time in the past, it was possible for the idea of animism, or for any other idea, to have fallen into the mind of every savage simultaneously, as a cloud-burst drenches the plain. Ideas have ever made their way as they do now, slowly, and by being

---

17. Fletcher, "Emblematic Use," p. 4.
18. Ibid., p. 5.
19. Edward B. Tylor, *Primitive Culture* (London: John Murray, 1873), 2: 8.
20. Ibid., p. 10.

communicated and talked over. The idea of animism is a very remarkable one. It has been so built into the mind of the race, that it is difficult to imagine a time when it was not; and yet there was such a time, a time when man stood dumbly wondering at the birds and beasts, assailed like himself by hunger, and finding food from the same supply; at the alternation of day and night; and at the destructive and vivifying effects of the storm. But these wondering observations were like so many disconnected fragments until some thoughtful mind caught the clue that led to the bold and clarifying thought, that all things were animated by a common life, and that man was not alone upon the earth with strange and alien creatures, but was surrounded by forms replete with life like his own, and therefore of his kindred.[21]

A somewhat similar opinion was held by Jones. As he wrote:

The essential character of Algonkin religion is a pure, naive worship of nature. In one way or another associations cluster about an object and give it a certain potential value; and because of this supposed potentiality, the object becomes the recipient of an adoration. The degree of the adoration depends in some measure upon the extent of confidence reposed in the object, and upon its supposed power of bringing pleasure or inflicting pain. The important thing with the individual is the emotional effect experienced while in the presence of the object, or with an interpreted manifestation of the object. The individual keeps watch for the effect, and it is the effect that fills the mind with a vague sense of something strange, something mysterious, something intangible. One feels it as the result of an active substance, and one's attitude toward it is purely passive.[22]

But such hypotheses as these—wonder at nature or the emotional effect of an object in nature on the individual—may be only one result of the influence Radin noted of "a precon-

---

21. Fletcher, "Emblematic Use," p. 5.
22. Jones, "Algonkin Manitou," p. 183.

ceived European metaphysical viewpoint" on the interpretation of Indian religions, and it must not be supposed that because an individual identified as an Indian wrote in such a vein that such a description is free of Western metaphysical notions. It may be that the Indians were little affected by such considerations. Le Jeune's attempt to convince the Montagnais of the existence of God by reference to the wonders of nature quoted above seems to have failed—although undoubtedly not just for this reason.

In the discussions that raged at the turn of the century regarding the origin of religion, the data on Indian religions provided evidence for another important feature thought to be characteristic of the earliest religions—animatism. As defined by R. R. Marett,[23] *animatism* is the attribution of life, or, better, supernatural power to inanimate objects. Marett was not, of course, the first to note that not all fundamental religious beliefs can be subsumed under the notion of *animism*—belief in spiritual beings—and that an object can be regarded as having supernatural power without being considered as animated by a spirit. (The concept of animatism is conveniently illustrated by attitudes toward the lucky rabbit's foot. Such a rabbit's foot is not regarded as deriving its power from a spirit that resides in it, that is, from any notion of animism. Rather, it derives its power from a belief in animatism—pure supernatural power being attributed to it.) But it was Marett's term for the phenomenon that came into general use—perhaps, in part, because he noted that native concepts such as wakan, orenda, and manitou were evidence that such an idea existed in other, "simpler" religions. As a result, textbooks came routinely to liken the concepts of manitou, orenda, and wakan to animatism.

Radin's critique of earlier writers on the subject of manitou and wakan was little noticed until A. Irving Hallowell returned to it in an article published in 1960.[24] By this time,

---

23. *The Threshold of Religion* (London: Methuen, 1909).
24. A. Irving Hallowell, "Ojibwa Ontology, Behavior, and World View," in *Culture in History: Essays in Honor of Paul Radin*, ed. Stanley Diamond (New York: Columbia University Press, 1960), pp. 19–52.

interest in the origin of religion and the related matter of defining the fundamental character of all religions of the world had long since declined. Attention had turned to the differences between the various religions of the world—although it was assumed that all such religions had similar functions, that is, satisfied the same psychological and social needs—and how religious beliefs and practices constituted part of the unique world view of each people. It was in this context that Hallowell took up again the meaning of the word manitou, particularly as it was used among the Algonquian-speaking Ojibwa.

Hallowell pointed out that the "person" category of beings in the various cultures of the world is not limited to human beings, but also includes supernatural beings. Further, in Algonquian languages a grammatical distinction is made between nouns of the so-called animate and inanimate classes. But as is so often the case in respect to such categories, the classification sometimes seems arbitrary to us. For example, Hallowell notes, "substantives for some, but not all—trees, sun-moon (*gízis*), thunder, stones, and objects of material culture like kettle and pipe—are classified as 'animate.' "[25] Further, this classification is bound up with behavior toward these "animate" objects that in part rests on actual experience. This accounted, Hallowell thought, "for the fact that what we view as material, inanimate objects—such as shells and stones—are placed in an 'animate' category along with 'persons' which have no physical existence in our world view."[26]

Hallowell's discussion of Ojibwa ideas regarding stones may help clarify this matter:

> Since stones are grammatically animate, I once asked an old man: Are *all* the stones we see about us alive? He reflected a long while and then replied, "No! But *some* are." This qualified answer made a lasting impression on me. And it is thoroughly consistent with other data that indicate that the Ojibwa are not animists in the sense that they dogmatically attribute living souls to inanimate objects

25. Ibid., p. 23.
26. Ibid., p. 24.

such as stones. The hypothesis which suggests itself to me is that the allocation of stones to an animate grammatical category is part of a culturally constituted cognitive "set." It does not involve a consciously formulated theory about the nature of stones. It leaves a door open that our orientation on dogmatic grounds keeps shut tight. Whereas we should never expect a stone to manifest animate properties of any kind under any circumstances, the Ojibwa recognizes, *a priori*, potentialities for animation in certain classes of objects under certain circumstances. The Ojibwa do not perceive stones, in general, as animate, any more than we do. The crucial test is experience. Is there any personal testimony available? In answer to this question we can say that it is asserted by informants that stones have been seen to move, that some stones manifest other animate properties, and . . . Flint is represented as a living personage in their mythology.[27]

The vagueness, then, that Jones noticed regarding the application of the word manitou may not be the result of "an unsystematic belief" or confusion of the property of an object with the object containing that property, but the result of the difficulty in translating the perceptions of members of one culture to those of another—each culture being a consistent and logical whole, although resting on different basic principles and premises. At least, that is implied in Hallowell's analysis.

Similarly, some of the seemingly peculiar features of Algonquian mythology become less so when viewed from this perspective. Myths are not about fictitious or necessarily fabulous characters, but about past lives of "persons," including importantly persons of the other-than-human-type. Here Hallowell's observations regarding the Western notions of "natural" and "supernatural" so basic in many discussions of religion (including those of Benedict and others quoted above) are pertinent:

27. Ibid., pp.24–25.

INTRODUCTION

In formal definitions of myth . . . the subject matter of such narrative often has been said to involve not only fictitious characters but "supernatural persons." This latter appellation, if applied to the Ojibwa characters, is completely misleading, if for no other reason than the fact that the concept of "supernatural" presupposes a concept of the "natural." The latter is not present in Ojibwa thought. It is unfortunate that the natural-supernatural dichotomy has been so persistently invoked by many anthropologists in describing the outlook of peoples in cultures other than our own. . . .

To the Ojibwa, for example, *gízis* (day luminary, the sun) is not a natural object in our sense at all. Not only does their conception differ; the sun is a "person" of the other-than-human class. But more important still is the absence of the notion of the ordered regularity in movement that is inherent in our scientific outlook. The Ojibwa entertain no reasonable certainty that, in accordance with natural law, the sun will "rise" day after day. In fact, *Tcakábec*, a mythical personage, once set a snare in the trail of the sun and caught it. Darkness continued until a mouse was sent by human beings to release the sun and provide daylight again. . . .

We may infer that, to the Ojibwa, any regularity in the movements of the sun is of the same order as the habitual activities of human beings. There are certain expectations, of course, but, on occasion, there may be temporary deviations in behavior "caused" by other persons. Above all, any concept of *impersonal* "natural" forces is totally foreign to Ojibwa thought.[28]

Further, persons-other-than-human do not always have a human appearance. Such beings may or may not exhibit outward anthropomorphic features. Again, as Hallowell summarizes it:

My Ojibwa friends, I discovered, were as puzzled by the white man's conception of thunder and lightning as natural phenomena as they were by the idea that the earth

---

28. Ibid., pp. 28–29.

is round and not flat. I was pressed on more than one occasion to explain thunder and lightning, but I doubt whether my somewhat feeble efforts made much sense to them. Of one thing I am sure: My explanations left their own beliefs completely unshaken. This is not strange when we consider that, even in our naturalistic frame of reference, thunder and lightning as perceived do not exhibit the lifeless properties of inanimate objects. On the contrary, it has been said that thunder and lightning are among the natural phenomena which exhibit some of the properties of "person objects." Underlying the Ojibwa view there may be a level of naive perceptual experience that should be taken into account. But their actual construct departs from this level in a most explicit direction: Why is an avian image central in their conception of a being whose manifestations are thunder and lightning? Among the Ojibwa with whom I worked, the linguistic stem for bird is the same as that for Thunder Bird *(pinésī; pl. pinésīwak)*. Besides this, the avian characteristics of Thunder Birds are still more explicit. Conceptually they are grouped with the hawks, of which there are several natural species in their habitat.

What is particularly interesting is that the avian nature of the Thunder Birds does not rest solely on an arbitrary image. Phenomenally, thunder does exhibit "behavioral" characteristics that are analogous to avian phenomena in this region. According to meteorological observations, the average number of days with thunder begins with one in April, increases to a total of five in midsummer (July) and then declines to one in October. And if a bird calendar is consulted, the facts show that species wintering in the south begin to appear in April and disappear for the most part not later than October, being, of course, a familiar sight during the summer months. The avian character of the Thunder Birds can be rationalized to some degree with reference to natural facts and their observation.[29]

A characteristic not unrelated to this seeming ambiguity of outward appearance is the ability of both beings-other-than-human and human beings to change shape, that is, to metamor-

29. Ibid., pp. 31–32.

phose. Animals may transform into other animals, and humans, both living and dead, may take on the form of animals while their vital part remains unchanged. Such instances of metamorphosis are reported to have taken place in contemporary times as well as in myths. Also not unrelated to this idea is the attention paid to dreams:

> Since . . . dream visitors are other-than-human "persons" possessing great power, it is to be expected that the experiences of the self in interaction with them will differ from those with human beings in daily life. Besides this, another assumption must be taken into account: When a human being is asleep and dreaming, his *òtcatcákwin* (vital part, soul), which is the core of the self, may become detached from the body (*mīyó*). Viewed by another human being, a person's body may be easily located and observed in space. But his vital part may be somewhere else. Thus, the self has greater mobility in space and even in time while sleeping. This is another illustration of the deceptiveness of appearances.[30]

In summary, then:

> Speaking as an Ojibwa, one might say: all other "persons"—human or other than human—are structured the same as I am. There is a vital part which is enduring and an outward appearance that may be transformed under certain conditions. All other "persons," too, have such attributes as self-awareness and understanding. I can talk with them. Like myself, they have personal identity, autonomy, and volition. I cannot always predict exactly how they will act, although most of the time their behavior meets my expectations. In relation to myself, other "persons" vary in power. Many of them have more power than I have, but some have less. They may be friendly and help me when I need them but, at the same time, I have to be prepared for hostile acts, too. I must be cautious in my relations with other "persons" because appearances may be deceptive.[31]

---

30. Ibid., p. 41.
31. Ibid., p. 43.

INTRODUCTION

"Persons," then, cause events in the Ojibwa world. Impersonal forces are not major determinants. And this helps explain some of the ambiguities in the earlier definitions of the word manitou. Manitou "may be considered as a synonym for a person of the other-than-human class."[32] The term merely seems to connote an impersonal, magical, or supernatural force because, lacking beliefs identical to the Ojibwa regarding the characteristics of persons other than human, we interpret their nature in terms of our own cultural premises, and so regard them as impersonal forces.

One such preconception so influencing the misinterpretation of the nature of these beings has been suggested by Radin in a discussion of Winnebago beliefs:

> The reason why, in our opinion, so many ethnologists have apparently misinterpreted the nature of *wak'a^n* is due to the fact that when something that, from the European viewpoint, is immaterial and inanimate, like vapor, light, movement, etc., is called *wak'a^n*, then it seems difficult for them to imagine that it can be so except by virtue of some intimate connection with a definite spirit, and if that can not be demonstrated, then the only solution left is to fall back upon the "magic power" idea. By doing this they clearly show that for them the test of individualization is corporeality of a fairly definite kind, dependent mainly upon visual sensations.[33]

In talking with Winnebagos, Radin found:

> It was soon quite clear that the Winnebago did not base their test of the existence of a spirit on the presence or absence of corporeality; in other words, upon such sense perceptions as sight and hearing. It is because we Europeans do insist that the presence or absence of corporeality is the test of reality or unreality that we have been led to make the classification into personal and impersonal. But the

---

32. Ibid., p.44.
33. Paul Radin, *The Winnebago Tribe*, Annual Report of the Bureau of American Ethnology 37 (1923), p. 283.

Winnebago apparently does not insist that existence depends upon sense perceptions alone. He claims that what is thought of, what is felt, and what is spoken, in fact, anything that is brought before his consciousness, is a sufficient indication of its existence and it is the question of the existence and reality of these spirits in which he is interested. The question of their corporeality is of comparative unimportance and most of the questions connected with the personal or impersonal nature of the spirits do not exist.[34]

Thus,

To the average Winnebago the world is peopled by an indefinite number of spirits who manifest their existence in many ways, being either visible, audible, felt emotionally, or manifesting themselves by some sign or result. From a certain point of view, all the spirits demonstrate their existence by the result, by the fact that the blessings they bestow upon man enable him to be successful, and this holds just as much for the spirit who manifests himself in the most intangible, emotional manner as for that one who is visible to man.[35]

In summary, then, the world of the Indian—both spiritual and otherwise—is not to be understood by assuming that it is like ours, and some of these differences are apparent in the texts that follow. But this is not to say that an attentive perusal of these texts will produce a complete understanding of these Indian worlds—for, as Hallowell has noted, "even at best our comprehension of the belief system of a primitive people remains on the intellectual level. We never learn to feel and act as they do. Consequently we never fully penetrate their . . . behavioral world. We never *wear* their culturally tinted spectacles; the best we can do is to try them on."[36]

---

34. Ibid., pp. 283–284. In this and the following quotation it can be seen why it is sometimes said that in these Indian religions stress is placed on wishing, on the power of thought.

35. Ibid., pp. 283–284.

36. A. Irving Hallowell, *The Role of Conjuring in Saulteaux Society* (Philadelphia: University of Pennsylvania Press, 1942), p. 3.

INTRODUCTION

These considerations also warn against a too-literal reading of the texts. Too often facile comparisons of such texts to more familiar religious traditions have been made with the result that symbols of no great importance to the Indians themselves are elevated to the stature of cosmic universals while matters of great moment to them are ignored and relationships that underlie their belief and actions overlooked. This is an area too little explored, but the experience of ethnographers such as those who recorded the texts here reproduced suggests that the task is not as easy as is generally supposed.

I. Cosmology

Some description of the nature of the worlds in which the various Indian peoples live and how these worlds originated is given in their great cosmological myths—the sacred traditions that are comparable to the Christian Bible and to the sacred books of other faiths as well as to Western secular scientific accounts. As has been noted, it is unfortunate that these narratives are usually termed "myths" in English—for they are based on no less acute observations of nature nor do they reflect any less intellectual effort than do the sacred and secular texts of the high civilizations of the Old Word.

Nonetheless, there are differences in the form of these descriptions. In large, politically centralized societies, particularly those heavily dependent on trade and hence dependent also on writing systems (small societies have little need for such a means of communication; face-to-face oral exchange suffices), there is apt to be considerable interest in having a single text against which other, presumably more defective accounts may be measured. Such an interest is lacking in small societies such as those of North American Indians. In these societies, each individual's knowledge is measured against the knowledge of others rather than against written knowledge potentially the property of anyone, and those individuals recognized as possessing the most extensive information are regarded as the best authorities. As a result, the versions given by different individuals or even the same individual at different times are apt to be different in some respects. But in these societies, these differences are not regarded as troublesome. Authenticity is not judged by rote accuracy. Some variation is expected and even welcomed, and a particular account is judged accurate if the principal matters customarily mentioned are recounted in a manner familiar to the listeners.

Circumstances surrounding the occasion may also affect the length of the account, what is included, and how much detail is given. If the listeners are willing, the telling of the cosmological myth may take days. But it is not required that it be recounted at such a length, and the version given at any particular time may be considerably shorter. Then, too, parts of the account may be told separately, rather as incidents described in the Bible may be told as tales from it.

These considerations mean that the desiderata of such texts in our society cannot be met. It is not possible to present a single text, authoritative in all its details. Nor is it possible here to follow what would be the more appropriate mode of presentation—the inclusion of a number of such accounts as told by different individuals. Space limitations would preclude doing so even if such accounts were available. Unfortunately, they usually are not. Only rarely have the longer versions of Indian cosmological myths been recorded and translated into English. Most of those that have appeared—and they are not numerous—are relatively short, and hence give a meager portrayal of the cosmological ideas involved.

Unfortunately, too, for a number of eastern North American Indian peoples either no such texts or only a few incidents from the longer versions have been recorded. As a result, no proper comparison of these cosmologies can be made here. Although it is evident that some of the themes and incidents of the myths of one group of Indians are apt also to be found in the myths of others, the data are as yet inadequate (and may remain so) for more than a cursory and misleading summary.

For these reasons, only some illustration of these accounts

can be given here. The examples chosen are two Iroquois accounts. One is a relatively short version of the cosmological myth; the other, an extract from a long version.

But statements regarding cosmology are not confined to these accounts of the origin and early eras of the cosmos. Perhaps more important to the average person, because they are more often repeated, are certain speeches in the ritual that refer to aspects of this cosmology. By far the most frequently given speech of this type among the Iroquois is the Thanksgiving Speech, or Address. For this reason, one example of this speech is also given here.

Iroquois Cosmological Myths

Cosmological myths, of course, are composed of a number of incidents. In the Iroquois myths, a series of three major events is typically included. First comes some description of the sky world and the people living there, and how the wife of the chief of this world above came to fall from it. The next part recounts how the animals below, when they saw her falling, dived into the water and, finding dirt there, put it on turtle's back to create the earth. The third part includes a description of how this woman gave birth to a daughter who when grown gave birth to twin sons, the older of which was the "good twin" who created things useful to man and the younger, the "evil twin" bent on destruction of his brother's work.

As might be expected, some of these incidents or motifs appear in the mythologies of other Indian peoples. One such is that of the twin brothers, although not necessarily symbolizing creation and destruction. Another is the earth-diver segment, that is, an account of the animals diving into the water, one of whom finds mud, which expands to become the earth.

Nonetheless, the Iroquoian myth contains a number of quite Iroquoian features. For example, the customs of people in the sky world resemble those of the Iroquois later on the earth below. Even the reasons often given for the chief's pushing his wife through the hole in the sky world is Iroquoian. By Iroquois custom, fulfillment of a dream could cure a sick individual and sometimes it was necessary that the content of the dream be guessed by another before it was fulfilled and so the individual cured. Now, in the myth, it is often said that the chief of the sky world was ill and that he dreamed that in order to become well again his wife should be pushed out of the sky world, and it is further said in some accounts that he asked the people to guess his dream before it was fulfilled, and so a cure effected.

Other parts are not so easily understood. It is difficult, for example, to know why the younger twin is regarded as evil or to know why his grandmother, the woman who fell from the sky, is also so regarded—although facile psychological explanations come to mind. On the other hand, the earth does bear some resemblance to a large turtle floating on water: The North American continent is largely surrounded by water and is ridged with mountains and valleys that bear some very general similarity to a turtle's carapace.

Of the various aspects of concern in this myth, two are worthy of special mention here. One is the division between the world above and the world below—a matter given attention in the first parts of the myth and, as will be seen, the most basic division in the Thanksgiving Address. The other is the conflict between creation and destruction, which is symbolized in the cosmological myth in the exploits of the Twin Brothers and, as will be seen, is a central theme of the Iroquois yearly ritual cycle.

Both these concerns are evident in the two accounts given here, the relatively short one from the Senecas (the westernmost of the five Iroquois tribes) and the excerpt from a long version from the Onondagas (the most centrally located of the tribes of the Iroquois Confederacy). But as has been noted, the differences between these two versions are not so much those between two tribes as between two tellers: Different versions from the same tribe exhibit as much variation as those from different tribes. They illustrate, then, not differences in belief between two distinct peoples having similar languages and customs, but differences ordinarily discerned in the accounts of different narrators.

They also illustrate differences that are introduced by the form of translation, differences of translation style rather than substance. The Seneca version is a very free, consciously literary translation; the Onondaga excerpt, although here somewhat edited, is a much more literal one reflecting more accurately Iroquois phrasing.

A Seneca Cosmological Myth[1]

Beyond the dome we call the sky there is another world. There in the most ancient of times was a fair country where lived the great chief of the up-above-world and his people, the celestial beings. This chief had a wife who was very aged in body, having survived many seasons.

In that upper world there were many things of which men of today know nothing. This world floated like a great cloud and journeyed where the great chief wished it to go. The crust of that world was not thick, but none of these men beings knew what was under the crust.

In the center of that world there grew a great tree that bore flowers and fruits and all the people lived from the fruits of the tree and were satisfied. Now, moreover, the tree bore a great blossom at its top, and it was luminous and lighted the world above, and wonderful perfume filled the air the people breathed. The rarest perfume of all was that which resembled the smoke of sacred tobacco and this was the incense greatly loved by the great chief. It grew from the leaves that sprouted from the roots of the tree.

The roots of the tree were white and ran in four directions. Far through the earth they ran, giving firm support to the tree. Around this tree the people gathered daily, for here the Great Chief had his lodge where he dwelt. Now, in a dream he was given a desire to take as his wife a certain maiden who was very fair to look upon. So, he took her as his wife, for when he had embraced her he found her most pleasing. When he had eaten the marriage bread he took her to his lodge, and to his

1. Arthur C. Parker, *Seneca Myths and Folk Tales*, Buffalo Historical Society Publications 27 (1923), pp. 59–73, with slight modification. All notes mine.

surprise found that she was with child. This caused him great anger and he felt himself deceived, but the woman loved the child, which had been conceived by the potent breath of her lover when he had embraced her. He was greatly distressed, for this fair Mature Flowers[2] was of the noblest family.

He, the Ancient One,[3] fell into a troubled sleep and a dream commanded him to have the celestial tree uprooted as a punishment to his wife and as a relief for his troubled spirit.[4] So on the morrow he announced to his wife that he had a dream and could not be satisfied until it had been divined. Thereupon she "discovered his word," and it was that the tree should be uprooted.

"Truly you have spoken," said Ancient One, "and now my mind shall be satisfied." And the woman, his wife, saw that there was trouble ahead for the sky world, but she too found pleasure in the uprooting of the tree, wishing to know what was beneath it. Yet did she know that to uproot the tree meant disaster for her, through the anger of Ancient One against her.

It so happened that the chief called all his people together and they endeavored to uproot the tree, it being deep-rooted and firm. Then did the chief grow even more angry, for Mature Flowers had cried out that calamity threatened and nobody would avert it. Then did the chief himself embrace the tree and with a mighty effort uprooted it, throwing it far away. His effort was tremendous, and in uprooting the tree he shook down fruits and leaves. Thereafter he went into his lodge and entered into the apartment where his wife, Mature Flowers, lay moaning that she too must be satisfied by a look into the hole. So the chief led her to the hole made by uprooting the tree.

He caused her to seat herself on the edge of the hole and

---

2. This is the English translation of her name.

3. I.e., Tharonhiawagon, "He Who Grasps the Sky" or Sky-Holder.

4. As has been noted, fulfillment of a dream could cure an ill individual, and sometimes it was (and is) regarded as necessary that this dream (that is, the "desire" or "desires" expressed in the dream) be guessed before it was fulfilled, that is, the ritual or other action indicated by the dream performed.

peer downward. Again his anger returned against her, for she said nothing to indicate that she had been satisfied. Long she sat looking into the hole until the chief in rage drew her blanket over her head and pushed her with his foot, seeking to thrust her into the hole and be rid of her. As he did this she grasped the earth at her side and gathered in her fingers all manner of seeds that had fallen from the shaken tree. In her right hand she held the leaves of the plant that smelled like burning tobacco, for it grew from a root that had been broken off. Again the chief pushed the woman, whose curiosity had caused the destruction of the greatest blessing of the up-above-world. It was a mighty push, and despite her hold upon the plant and upon the ground, she fell into the hole.

Now, this hole had penetrated the crust of the upper world and when Mature Flowers fell she went far down out of sight and the chief could not see her in the depths of the darkness below. As she fell she beheld a beast that emitted fire from its head. It is said that as she passed by him he took out a small pot, a corn mortar, a pestle, a marrow bone, and an ear of corn and presented them to her, saying, "Because you have thus done, you shall eat by these things, for there is nothing below, and all who eat shall see me once and it will be the last."

Now it is difficult to know how this Fire Beast can be seen, for he is of the color of the wind and is of the color of anything that surrounds it, though some say he is pure white.

Hovering over the troubled waters below were other creatures, some like and some unlike those that were created afterward. It is said by the old people that in those times lived the spirits of the Wind, the Defending Face, the Thunder, and the Heavy Night. There were also what seemed to be ducks upon the water and these also saw the descending figure.

The creature-beings knew that a new body was coming to them and that here below there was no abiding place for her. They took council together and sought to devise a way to provide for her.

It was agreed that the duck-creatures should receive her on their interknit wings and lower her gently to the surface below. The great turtle from the under-world was to arise and make his broad back a resting place. It was as had been agreed and the woman came down upon the floating island.

Then did the creatures seek to make a world for the woman and one by one they dived to the bottom of the water seeking to find earth to plant upon the turtle's back. A duck dived but went so far that it breathed the water and came up dead. A pickerel went down and came back dead. Many creatures sought to find the bottom of the water but could not. At last the creature called Muskrat made the attempt and succeeded only in touching the bottom with his nose, but this was sufficient, for he was enabled to smear it [the mud] upon the shell and the earth immediately grew, and as the earth-substance increased so did the size of the turtle.

After a time the woman, who lay prone, aroused herself and released what was in her hands, dropping many seeds into the folds of her garment. Likewise she spread out the earth from the heaven world she had grasped and thus caused the seeds to spring into germination as they dropped from her dress.

The root of the tree that she had grasped she sunk into the soil where she had fallen and this too began to grow until it formed a tree with all manner of fruits and flowers and bore a luminous orb at its top by which the new world became illuminated.

Now in due season Mature Flowers[5] lay beneath the tree and to her a daughter was born. She was then happy, for she had a companion. The girl grew rapidly until very soon she could run about. It was then the custom of Mature Flowers to say: "My daughter, run about the island and return telling me what you have seen."

Day by day the girl ran around the island and each time it became larger, making her trips longer and longer. She observed that the earth was carpeted with grass and that shrubs and trees were springing up everywhere. This she reported to her mother, who sat beneath the centrally situated great tree.

---

5. Parker here and in the remainder of this selection uses "Sky-Woman," as he notes, "for convenience only." This appellation has been changed to "Mature Flowers."

COSMOLOGY

In one part of the island there was a tree on which grew a long vine and upon this vine the girl was accustomed to swing for amusement and her body moved to and fro giving her great delight. Then did her mother say, "My daughter, you laugh as if being embraced by a lover. Have you seen a man?"

"I have seen no one but you, my mother," answered the girl, "but when I swing I know someone is close to me and I feel my body embraced as if with strong arms. I feel thrilled and I tingle, which causes me to laugh."

Then did Mature Flowers look sad, and she said, "My daughter, I know not now what will befall us. You are married to Wind, and he will be the father of your children. There will be two boys."

In due season the voices of two boys were heard speaking, and the words of one were kind and he gave no trouble, but the words of the other were harsh and he desired to kill his mother. His skin was covered with warts and boils and he was inclined to cause great pain.

When the two boys were born, Elder One made his mother happy but when Warty One was born he pierced her through the arm pit and stood upon her dead body. So did the mother perish, and because of this Mature Flowers wept.

The boys required little care but instantly became able to care for themselves. After the mother's body had been arranged for burial, Mature Flowers saw the elder one, whom she called Good Mind, approach, and he said, "Grandmother, I wish to help you prepare the grave." So he helped his grandmother, who continually wept, and deposited the body of his mother in a grave. Then the grandmother said to her daughter, "O my daughter, you have departed and made the first path to the world from which I came bringing your life. When you reach that homeland make ready to receive many beings from this place below, for I think the path will be trodden by many."

Good Mind watched at the grave of his mother and watered the earth above it until the grass grew. He continued to watch until he saw strange buds coming out of the ground. Where the feet were the earth sprouted with a plant that became the stringed-potato; where her fingers lay sprang the beans; where her abdomen lay sprang the squash; where her breasts lay sprang the corn plant; and from the spot above her forehead sprang the tobacco plant.

Now the warty one was named Evil Mind, and he neglected his mother's grave and spent his time tearing up the land and seeking to do evil.

When the grandmother saw the plants springing from the grave of her daughter and cared for by Good Mind she was thankful and said, "By these things we shall hereafter live, and they shall be cooked in pots with fire, and the corn shall be your milk and sustain you. You shall make the corn grow in hills like breasts, for from the corn shall flow our living."

Then the grandmother, Mature Flowers, took Good Mind about the island and instructed him how to produce plants and trees. So he spoke to the earth and said, "Let a willow here come forth," and it came. In a like manner he made the oak, the chestnut, the beech, the hemlock, the spruce, the pine, the maple, the buttonball, the tulip, the elm, and many other trees that should become useful.

With a jealous stomach the Evil Mind followed behind and sought to destroy the good things but could not, so he spoke to the earth and said, "Briars come forth," and they came forth. Likewise he created poisonous plants and thorns upon bushes.

Upon a certain occasion Good Mind made inquiries of his grandmother, asking where his father dwelt. Then she said, "You shall now seek your father. He lives to the uttermost east and you shall go to the far eastern end of the island and go over the water until you behold a mountain rising from the sea. You shall walk up the mountain and there you will find your father seated upon the top."

Good Mind made the pilgrimage and came to the mountain. At the foot of the mountain he looked upward and called, "My father, where are you?" And a great voice sounded the words, "A son of mine shall cast the cliff from the mountain's edge to the summit of this peak." Good Mind grasped the cliff and with a mighty effort flung it to the mountain top. Again he cried, "My father, where are you?" The answer came, "A son of mine shall swim the cataract from the pool below to the top." Good Mind leaped into the falls and swam upward to the top where the water poured over. He stood there and cried again, "My father, where are you?" The voice answered, "A son of mine shall wrestle with the wind." So, there at the edge of a terrifying precipice, Good Mind grappled with Wind and the two wrestled, each endeavoring to throw the other over. It was a terrible battle and Wind tore great rocks from the mountain side and lashed the water below, but Good Mind overcame Wind, and he departed moaning in defeat. Once more Good Mind called, "My father, where are you?" In awesome tones the voice replied, "A son of mine shall endure the flame," and immediately a flame sprang out of the mountain side and enveloped Good Mind. It blinded him and tortured him with its cruel heat, but he threw aside its entwining arms and ran to the mountain top where he beheld a being sitting in the midst of a blaze of light.

"I am your father," said the voice. "You are my son."

"I have come to receive power," said the son. "I wish to rule all things on the earth."

"You have power," answered the father. "You have conquered. I give to you the bags of life, the containers of living creatures that will bless the earth."

Thus did the father and son counsel together and the son learned many things that he should do.

Now the father said, "How did you come to find me, seeing I am secluded by many elements?"

Good Mind answered, "When I was about to start my journey, my grandmother gave me a flute and I blew upon it, making music. Now, when the music ceased the flute spoke to me, saying, 'This way shall you go,' and I continued to make music and the voice of the flute spoke to me."

Then did the father say, "Make music by the flute and listen, then shall you continue to know the right direction."

In course of time Good Mind went down the mountain and he waded the sea, taking with him the bags with which he had been presented. As he drew near the shore he became curious to know what was within, and he pinched one bag hoping to feel its contents. He felt a movement inside which

41

increased until it became violent. The bag began to roll about on his back until he could scarcely hold it and a portion of the mouth of the bag slipped from his hand. Immediately the things inside began to jump out and fall into the water with a great splash, and they were water animals of different kinds. The other bag began to roll around on his back but he held on tightly until he could do so no more, when a portion of the mouth slipped and out flew many kinds of birds, some flying seaward and others inland toward the trees. Then as before the third bag began to roll about but he held on very tight, but it slipped and fell into the water and many kinds of swimming creatures rushed forth, fishes, crabs, and eels. The fourth bag then began to roll about, but he held on until he reached the land when he threw it down, and out rushed all the good land animals, of kinds he did not know. From the bird bag had come good insects, and from the fish bag had also come little turtles and clams.

When Good Mind came to his grandmother beneath the tree, she asked what he had brought, for she heard music in the trees and saw creatures scampering about. Thereupon Good Mind related what had happened, and the grandmother said, "We must now call all the animals and discover their names, and moreover we must so treat them that they will have fat."

So then she spoke, "Cavity be in the ground and be filled with oil." The pool of oil came, for Mature Flowers had the power of creating what she desired.

Good Mind then caught the animals one by one and brought them to his grandmother. She took a large furry animal and cast it into the pool and it swam very slowly across, licking up much oil. "This animal shall hereafter be known as bear and you shall be very fat." Next came another animal with much fur and it swam across and licked up the oil, and it was named buffalo. So in turn were named the elk, the moose, the badger, the woodchuck, and the raccoon, and all received much fat. Then came the beaver, the porcupine, and the skunk. Now Good Mind wished the deer to enter, but it was shy and bounded away, whereupon he took a small arrow and pierced its front leg, his aim being good. Then the deer came and swam

42

across the pool and oil entered the wound and healed it. This oil of the deer's leg is a medicine for wounds to this day and if the eyes are anointed with it one may shoot straight.

Again other animals came and one by one they were named weasel, mink, otter, fisher, panther, lynx, wild cat, fox, wolf, big wolf, squirrel, chipmunk, mole, and many others.

And many animals that were not desired plunged into the pool of oil, and these Good Mind seized as they came out and he stripped them of their fat and pulled out their bodies long. So he did to the otter, fisher, weasel, and mink. So he did to the panther, wolf, big wolf, and fox, the lynx and the wildcat. Of these the fat to this day is not good tasting. But after a time Evil Mind secured a bag of creatures from the road to the cave and unloosed it, and evil things crawled into the pool and grew fat. So did the rattlesnake and great bugs and loathly worms.

Thus did Evil Mind secure many evil monsters and insects, and he enticed good animals into his traps and perverted them and gave them appetites for men-beings. He was delighted to see how fierce he could make the animals, and set them to quarreling.

He roamed about visiting the streams of pure water made by Good Mind and filling them with mud and slime, and he kicked rocks in the rivers and creeks to make passage difficult, and he planted nettles and thorns in the paths. Thus did he do to cause annoyance.

Now Good Mind sat with his grandmother beneath the tree of light and he spoke to her of the world and how he might improve it. "Alas," said she, "I believe that only one more task awaits me and then I shall go upon my path and follow your mother back to the world beyond the sky. It remains for me to call into being certain lights in the blackness above where Heavy Night presides."

So saying she threw the contents of a bag into the sky and it quickly became sprinkled with stars. And thus there came into being constellations, and of these we see the bear chase, the dancing brothers, the seated woman, the beaver skin, the belt, and many others.

Now it seems that Good Mind knew that there should be a

luminous orb and, so it is said, he took his mother's face and flung it skyward and made the sun, and took his mother's breast and flinging it into the sky made the moon. So it is said, but there are other accounts of the creation of these lights. It is said that the first beings made them by going into the sky.

Shortly after the creation of the stars, the grandmother said to Good Mind, "I believe that the time has come when I should depart, for nearly all is finished here. There is a road from my feet and I have a song that I shall sing by which I shall know the path. There is one more matter that troubles me, for I see that your brother is jealous and will seek to kill you. Use great care that you overcome him and when you have done so confine him in the cave and send with him the evil spirit beasts, lest they injure men."

When morning came she had departed and her journey was toward the sky world.

Good Mind felt lonely and believed that his own mission was about at end. He had been in conflict with his brother, Evil Mind, and had sought, moreover, to overcome and to teach the Whirlwind and Wind, and the Fire Beast.

Soon Evil Mind came proposing a hunting trip and Good Mind went with him on the journey. When they had gone a certain distance Evil Mind said, "My elder brother, I perceive that you are about to call forth men-beings who shall live on the island that we here have inhabited. I propose to afflict them with disease and to make life difficult, for this is not their world but mine, and I shall do as I please to spoil it."

Then did Good Mind answer and say, "Truly I am about to make men-beings who shall live here when I depart, for I am going to follow the road skyward made first by my mother."

"This is good news," answered Evil Mind. "I propose that you then reveal unto me the word that has power over your life, that I may possess it and have power when you are gone."

Good Mind now saw that his brother wished to destroy him, and so he said, "It may happen that you will employ the cattail flag, whose sharp leaves will pierce me."

Good Mind then lay down and slumbered, but soon was awakened by Evil Mind who was lashing him with cattail flags, and yelling loudly, "You shall die." Good Mind arose and asked his brother what he meant by lashing him and he answered, "I was seeking to awaken you from a dream, for you were speaking."

So, soon again the brother, Evil Mind, asked, "My brother, I wish to know the word that has power over you." And Good Mind perceiving his intention answered, "It may be that deerhorns will have power over me; they are sharp and hard."

Soon Good Mind slept again and was awakened by Evil Mind beating him with deerhorns, seeking to destroy him. They rushed inland to the foot of the tree and fought each other about it. Evil Mind was very fierce and rushed at his brother, thrusting the horns at him and trying to pierce his chest and his face or tear his abdomen. Finally, Good Mind disarmed him, saying, "Look what you have done to the tree where our grandmother used to care for us, and whose branches have supplied us with food. See how you have torn this tree and stripped it of its valuable products. This tree was designed to support the life of men-beings and now you have injured it. I must banish you to the region of the great cave and you shall have the name of Destroyer."

So saying he used his good power to overcome Evil Mind's evil power and thrust him into the mouth of the cave, and with him all manner of enchanted beasts. There he placed the white buffalo, the poison beaver, the poison otter, snakes, and many bewitched things that were evil. So there to this day abides Evil Mind seeking to emerge, and his voice is heard giving orders.

Then Good Mind went back to the tree and soon saw a being walking about. He walked over to the place where the being was pacing to and fro. He saw that it was Great Defender,[6] who was a giant with a grotesque face. "I am master of the earth," roared this being, for he was the whirlwind. "If you are master," said Good Mind, "prove your power."

Defender said, "What shall be our test?"

---

6. The leader of the False Faces. The False Face Society is one of the Iroquois medicine societies, so called because those who have been cured by the society's ritual's having been performed for them are members of it. It is called the False Face Society because wooden masks are used in the rituals of the society.

45

"Let this be the test," said Good Mind, "that the mountain yonder shall approach us at your bidding."

So Defender spoke saying, "Mountain, come hither." And they turned their backs that they might not see it coming until it stood at their backs. Soon they turned about again and the mountain had not moved.

"So now, I shall command," said Good Mind, and he spoke saying, "Mountain, come hither," and they turned their backs. There was a rushing of air and Defender turned to see what was behind him and fell against the onrushing mountain, and it bent his nose and twisted his mouth, and from this he never recovered.

Then did Defender say, "I do now acknowledge you to be master. Command me and I will obey."

"Since you love to wander," said Good Mind, "it shall be your duty to move about over the earth and stir up things. You shall abandon your evil intentions and seek to overcome your evil nature, changing it to be of benefit to men-beings, whom I am about to create."

"Then," said Defender, "shall men-beings offer incense tobacco to me[7] and make a song that is pleasing to me, and they shall carve my likeness from the substance of trees, and my orenda[8] will enter the likeness of my face and it shall be a help to men-beings and they shall use the face as I shall direct. Then shall all the diseases that I may cause them depart and I shall be satisfied."

Again Good Mind wandered, being melancholy. Looking up he saw another being approaching.

"I am Thunder," said the being.

"What can you do to be a help to me?" asked Good Mind.

"I can wash the earth and make drink for the trees and grass," said Thunder.

"What can you do to be a benefit to the men-beings I am about to create?" asked Good Mind.

"I shall slay evil monsters when they escape from the

---

7. For a discussion of burning tobacco to such beings as the False Faces see chapter two.

8. See Introduction for a discussion of "orenda."

underworld," said Thunder. "I shall have scouts who will notify me and I shall shoot all evil beings."

Then was Good Mind satisfied, and he pulled up a tree and saw the water fill the cavity where the roots had been. Long he gazed into the water until he saw a reflection of his own image. "Like that will I make men-beings," he thought. So then he took clay and molded it into small images of men and women. These he placed on the ground and when they were dry he spoke to them and they sprang up and lived.

When he saw them he said unto them, "All this world I give unto you. It is from me that you shall say you are descended and you are the children of the firstborn of earth, and you shall say that you are the flesh of Mature Flowers, she the Ancient-Bodied One."

When he had acquainted them with the other first beings, and shown them how to hunt and fish and to eat of the fruits of the land, he told them that they should seek to live together as friends and brothers and that they should treat each other well.

He told them how to give incense of tobacco, for Mature Flowers, Ancient-Bodied One, had stripped the heaven world of tobacco when she fell, and thus its incense should be a pleasing one into which men-beings might speak their words when addressing him hereafter. These and many other things did he tell them.

Soon he vanished from the sight of created men-beings, and he took all the first beings with him upon the sky road.

Soon men-beings began to increase and they covered the earth, and from them we are descended. Many things have happened since those days, so much that all can never be told.

An Onondaga Cosmological Myth[9]

[The beginning of this version is a long description of events in the sky world, the world above, leading up to the marriage of Mature Flowers to the chief of this world, whose

---

9. J.N.B. Hewitt, *Iroquoian Cosmology—Second Part*, Annual Report of the Bureau of American Ethnology 43 (1928), pp. 479–487. Onondaga text by John Arthur Gibson, a leading Iroquois ritualist of the time, recorded in 1900 on the Grand River (Six

name may be translated "Earth Grasper." The following is an account of what happened after their marriage.]

It was the custom that when they lay back down to sleep, they placed their feet sole to sole, that when they sat up their breathing met and commingled.

Then her body gave evidence that she would become a mother. When the time was near when she would become possessed of a child, the owner of the lodge[10] said, "I have dreamed a dream. So then I desire that the people should seek my word. And the reason for this is that the kind of thing of which my soul has visions should be fulfilled. For, as is well known, it is a recognized dream."

He then gave a feast to the inhabitants. They began to seek his word. They did so for a long time, and perhaps all, men and women and game animals, made the attempt. Due to evil influences it was not possible to give satisfaction to his mind. Then the Fire Dragon (Meteor), whose body was white, arrived there and said, "Let me in my turn make the attempt to find your word. Is it not a certain matter that your life may have seen the need that we should uproot your standing tree, Tooth (Tiger Lily)?" Then he who was giving the feast said, "I am thankful. Now my dream has been fulfilled. Now then I will tell you. I thought that I saw it come to pass that they did uproot my standing tree; that then an opening was made through the ground. I thought that I saw my wife and I sitting together at the edge of the broken ground, her feet hanging down into the chasm. Then we two ate food at the edge of the chasm of the broken earth. This is the character of my dream. I saw all the things that shall come to pass."

Then a large body of men assembled there, and said,

Nations Reserve) in Canada. This extract has been much edited, principally to eliminate those Biblical constructions introduced by Hewitt, apparently to indicate the importance of the narrative to the Iroquois and to eliminate certain awkwardnesses introduced into the translation by Hewitt's very literal translation. (Although this translation by its faithfulness to the Onondaga text conveys a flavor of the original to those familiar with Iroquoian grammatical constructions, unfortunately this aspect of the translation is largely meaningless to those unfamiliar with the structure of these languages, and hence more distracting than illuminating.) I am indebted to Marianne Mithun for advice in the editing of this selection.

10. I.e., the chief of the world above, Earth Grasper.

"Come, let the suggestions of the dream of our chief be under-taken." The men grasped and then uprooted the tree. It left an opening through the ground; a chasm was made through the earth. Then the men said, "Now we have fulfilled the require-ments of what caused our chief to dream." Then the owner of the lodge said, "Now all that which is of fate has come to pass. The flowers of the tree that stood for me have withered. All that the earth at present contains shall change; all shall become new. All things shall be metamorphosed." Then he said, "Now we two, my wife and I, will eat together at the edge of the chasm."

Then Mature Flowers brought and set the food beside the place of the broken earth. She seated herself there and said, "Now all that your dream suggests has been fulfilled."

Then he seated himself there and said, "Now all kinds of things that are ordered are fulfilled. You and I shall eat to-gether, and this too is ordained. And, it will come to pass that those things which will become low will think of this place."

Then he stood up and said, "Now you will depart from the earth here." And he shoved her and her body fell through the place where the earth was broken. She disappeared in the chasm. Then the men set up the tree of light again.

Now as her body was floating down she saw the Fire Dragon, whose body was white, who seized her in flight and said, "Where do you travel? Are you departing from home? I will aid you as much as possible. That will be in accordance with the measure of the power I possess, so that you may continue to live when you arrive below. And the reason is that your former husband accused me of the things for which he cast you down. I am bringing with me that upon which you shall live when you arrive below."

Then she saw that he held corn and meat, both dried. She received both. Then he said, "I will accompany you half the distance to the place where you go."

Not very long after and not much farther did she go when he said, "This far only am I able to be of assistance to you. You bear with you power. It will be possible that you will safely pass through this ordeal. The time will not be long when it will

become again as it was in the place from which you departed."
Then the woman thanked him (by nodding her head) and then
he went back.

There were there below many Ducks[11] of all kinds. So
then one of these Ducks there present, who was at all times
looking upward, suddenly cried out, "It would seem that a
human being is falling down from above." Then Leon cried
out, "Come, now, rise up, go to meet her, so that her body will
land gently."

Then the Ducks of all kinds flew up and there, high above,
they met her; and the Ducks joined their bodies together and
she seated herself on them. Slowly downward they returned.
When they arrived below they continued floating about, their
bodies joined together, and there the woman sat, going about.

Then Loon shouted, saying, "Now all come here." After
all had assembled, Loon spoke, saying, "Now we are assembled, we who were the first to arrive here. It becomes necessary
that we should assist her who is next to come. The extent of the
power of each one of us will become apparent in order that the
woman should continue to live. Bittern was the first to see her
as her body floated down. Let someone perhaps plan what we
should do that this woman should continue to live. In what
place shall she live?"

Then the various kinds of Ducks made the attempt, but
they were not able to devise a suitable plan. Then Loon said,
"You who are able to travel about in the depths of the water
will make an attempt. It may be that one of you will discover
what could keep her body from sinking." All made attempts.
Then Muskrat said, "I will fetch earth from the bottom of the
water. If I am able to bring back earth with me, then we shall
be fortunate. For is it not well known that she bears with her
power?"

Then Muskrat dove down into the water. The time was
long. Then his body came to the surface. He was already long

---

11. Although both Parker (see above) and Hewitt use the word "duck" for these
beings, it is apparent that the reference is to various kinds of water birds, not just to
kinds referred to in English as ducks.

dead, and Loon said, "Now seek out how it is that he is not alive."

Then Beaver said, "Let me volunteer." He searched Muskrat and found that he held earth in both paws, and in his mouth the earth was packed full. Then Beaver said, "What shall we do? This one whose body has come to the surface brings earth."

Then Loon said, "Let someone volunteer to hold up this earth so that it will be possible to place this woman on it."

Then Beaver said, "I will be the first to make the attempt." They took all the earth that Muskrat brought back, and they placed it on the back of Beaver. After a very short while he cried out, "It seems, perhaps, that I am not able to do it, because it is excessively heavy." Then they took off the earth. Then Great Turtle spoke, saying, "Then I will now make the attempt." Then they placed the earth on his back. Then Great Turtle said, "It is all right, I will be able to uphold it. If the earth will grow in size, I also will continue to increase in size."

Then Loon said, "Now, we who came on ahead have done all that is possible." They placed the woman thereon. Then Loon said, "Now, we have arranged your affairs, you whose body has stopped here." Then the large group of helpers who had arranged her affairs went away.

Then this thing on which the woman lived now began to grow. Just as the earth had reached a suitable size, she gave birth to a child. The child was a woman child. She cared for her, and the child grew rapidly.

Before long her daughter became a maiden. She went about from place to place; she went about examining carefully the size of the earth where the two women lived. She was surprised then at seeing a man there watching her. He said, "Will you not consent that we should marry? It seems you are seeking somebody."

Then she looked him over carefully. She saw that his raiment was yellow in color. Then she said, "Not of my own will should I answer you. I will tell my mother first. It is she who shall will it." Then she turned about and they went home. When she reached the place where her mother lived she said, "I saw a man standing yonder. He asked that he and I should marry." The Elder Woman asked, "What did you answer?" She replied, "I said that my mother will decide what I will reply to you." Then the Elder Woman said, "You did right. What did he look like and what kind of raiment did the man have?" She answered, "He was handsome and his raiment was yellow."

The Elder Woman said, "I will not consent to it. Go back there and say, 'My mother does not consent to the matter which you ask.'" The girl went back. When she arrived at the place where the man was standing she said, "My mother did not consent." Then he said, "I am not offended." And he turned around and left. The girl looked and saw him transform himself. He was no longer a human being; he had become again a fox. Then the maiden returned to her home.

A few days later she again went to travel about. She went along examining things on the shore of the water. While she was moving along she was surprised to see a man sitting there on a rock. He said, "It seems that you are looking for a companion. Would you consent that you and I should marry?" Then the girl said, "My mother must decide. I will go back to tell her what you are asking of me." Then she looked at him. She saw then that his raiment was of gray color and that his face was striped with black. Then she returned home. When she reached home, she immediately said, "I saw a man sitting far yonder. He asks that we should marry." Then the woman said, "What did you say?" The girl replied, "I said, 'My mother will decide that.'" Then the Elder Woman said, "In that also you are right in what you did. What kind of raiment did the man wear?" The girl replied, "His raiment was gray in color, and his face was striped with black." Then the Elder Woman said, "I will not consent to that. Go back there and say 'She will not consent to the thing you asked.'" Then the girl returned to the place where the man sat. When she arrived, she said, "My mother did not consent that you and I should marry." Then the man said, "Nothing has gone amiss in what has taken place." Then he turned around and transformed himself. She looked and saw he became again a raccoon. Then the maiden returned home.

A few days later the girl went out to fetch wood. She

obtained the wood and made a bundle of it. Just as she had finished her bundle, there arrived a man who said, "Would you consent that we marry?" She looked at him and saw that his body was dirty and that his cape had long scallops all around it. Then said she, "I will not decide. I will go to tell my mother first; she will decide that." Then she took up the bundle of wood and departed for home. After she arrived, she said, "I saw a man standing far yonder. His body was dirty and the flaps were broad on his leggings, and his cape had deep scallops all around, and he said, 'Let you and I marry.'"

Then the Elder Woman said, "What did you say?" The girl said, "I said, 'My mother will decide the matter of which you speak.'" Then the Elder Woman said, "My daughter, I am thankful that you did. That man, as is well known, is immune [invulnerable]. I confirm the matter that you two shall marry. Invite him to come." The girl returned to the place where the man was standing. When she arrived there she said, "My mother confirmed the matter about which you are asking. I invite you to come. You will go to the place where my mother and I live." Then the man said, "Not immediately will I accompany you home. I will first return to the place where I started (my home). After I have completed my preparations there, I will go to visit the lodge of you two. I will tell you then that I shall not settle down there where the lodge of you two stands. I will only go there and return." Then the girl returned. When she returned the Elder Woman asked, "Why does he not accompany you?" Then the girl said, "He returned home. He will first pay a visit to the place where he started. As soon as he has completed his preparations, he will come here. He will not settle down here. He will only pay a visit here."

Then the Elder Woman said, "As I have said, it is well known that he is immune [invulnerable to witchcraft]." Then they awaited the time when he should come. When it grew dark, they lay down to sleep. After they had laid down, he came in and said "I have arrived. I will tell you what will happen. I will leave my arrows here during the night. Tomorrow early in the morning, I shall come for them." She saw that he held two arrows, one having a flint point and the other having no point. He straightened the arrow that had no attached point. Then he laid the two arrows side by side on her body. Then he said, "Thus let them be during the night. Do not undo them until I come again and I myself will undo them." Then he left the lodge and returned home.

Early in the morning he returned, removed the two arrows and returned home. The girl was happy. After the lapse of time she became aware that her life was different. Now the Elder Woman said, "We have good fortune. You will have a child in the near future."

The time was not long when it became very evident from her appearance that she was about to be a mother. Then she was surprised that she heard two male persons conversing within her body. One kept saying, "What things will you do after you and I are born?" The other replied, "I will cause human beings to dwell as peoples. Game animals also I will cause to dwell as groups of beings, and I will create that by which human beings shall live and that by which game animals shall live here on this earth, and as many things as grow shall bear fruit, and those things shall make glad the minds of human beings who will dwell as people here on the earth."

Then she heard him ask, "What things will you do when you and I are born?" He replied, "I will make the attempt too, also to do thus as even you are about to do. If I should not be able to do so, I will make the attempt in some other way. I too will have something to say on this earth."

When she heard them talking together, one of the male persons kept saying, "What shall happen now the time has come that you and I will go forth? Who shall take the lead?" She heard the other male person say, "You take the lead. As for me, I will go straight through here where there are light spots showing through. I will go out that way." Then she heard the other say, "It will not result in good that you do as you intend. You will kill our mother that way. Now I will go forth." Now then that one was born. It was not a long time after that the other came forth through her armpit. As she gave birth to the children she died. The Elder Woman took up the two children and attended to them. She placed them under the couch and she gave attention to the body of her daughter. She laid the body of her daughter in the entrance of the house of the two women and said, "At the end of ten days she will arise again." Her children were all right and they were large in size.

These two children continued to grow very rapidly. In a few days it was possible for them to converse with the Elder Woman, their grandmother. Then this Elder Woman said, "Do you two know from where you have come and where you will go when you leave this place?"

One of them replied, "I myself know the place from which we have come. It is from the sky, from the earth situated on the upper side of it. I will not forget that. I will continue to grasp with both hands the place from which I came. When the time comes when I shall depart from this place I shall go back to the place where we started."

His grandmother said, "It is true that you know the entire matter. I will name you He who Grasps the Sky. And the reason is that your mind is certain about this matter."

Then the other in his turn was asked, in that she said, "What is your opinion on this?" He replied, "I am not thinking about the place along which I came. Neither am I thinking of the place from which I started nor where I should go when I depart from here. It is sufficient that I have arrived in this place. By and by it will become exceedingly delightful here. As to myself, I trust in the thing my father gave me." Then the Elder Woman said, "What kind of thing is it in which you trust and which thing your father gave you?" Then he said, "That is the arrow that has a point attached to it. He intended that I should use it for defending myself. And that is the reason that I am not thinking of any other place." Then the Elder Woman said, "Then I call you Flint."

The Iroquois Thanksgiving Address

Another Iroquois cosmological statement is contained in the Thanksgiving Speech, or Address—so called because it gives thanks or, more accurately, returns thanks to the various beings on this earth and above. This account is more familiar to the Iroquois themselves than the cosmological myth, for few Iroquois now know the long myth; recreational attractions of Western civilization, including most recently television, have tended to reduce interest in hearing the myths, tales, and legends retold and knowledge of them has become more limited among most North American Indians than it once was. However, those Iroquois who attend the ceremonies that are still "kept up," as the Iroquois say, and who understand the language can scarcely not know the content of the Thanksgiving Speech—for this speech begins and concludes virtually every ceremony except those honoring the dead (it would be inappropriate to be thankful for death). As Foster has noted, "the speeches serve constantly to remind speakers and the assembly of the principal features of the cosmology and the uses and duties of the items to mankind."[12]

In delivery, the Thanksgiving Speech exhibits much the same variation as do the various tellings of the cosmological myth. Depending on the occasion and the speaker, it may be short (less than a minute) or long (over three-quarters of an hour). Different speakers use slightly different versions and the same speaker does not use exactly the same words on each occasion he gives the address. Nonetheless, each repetition of the speech is similiar. And the intent of all versions is to return thanks—that which Chafe has noted is also translated as "thank, be thankful or grateful to or for, rejoice in, bless, greet"—for, as he also notes, "the Seneca concept is broader than that expressed by any simple English term, and covers not only the conventionalized amenities of both thanking and greeting, but also a more general feeling of happiness over the existence of something or someone."[13]

In all but the brief recitations, each section of the speech is devoted to an item (being, beings, or what we would classify as "things") on this earth or above. Mention is first made that the

---

12. Michael K. Foster, *From the Earth to Beyond the Sky: An Ethnographic Approach to Four Longhouse Iroquois Speech Events*, National Museum of Man Mercury Series, Canadian Ethnology Service Paper no. 20 (1974), p. 131.

13. Wallace L. Chafe, *Seneca Thanksgiving Rituals*, Bureau of American Ethnology Bulletin 183 (1961), p. 1.

COSMOLOGY

Creator decided on, ordained, planned, determined, willed it, and its purpose is explained—how it benefits mankind—that is, its assignment is described. Mention is next made that it is still being seen, it is still carrying out its assignment. Finally, thanks are returned to it, with the statement that it will continue in our minds.[14]

Although different speakers may list these items in a slightly different sequence and expand or contract the number of sections slightly, the general sequence is the same: from the earth upward to the things above, ending with the Creator. The first part is devoted to things below, on this earth. Mention is first made of the people, then the earth. Next or at virtually any point in this part of the speech, mention is made of the water—springs, streams, rivers, and lakes. Then the plants on the earth—grasses, berries, weeds, and medicinal herbs, and bushes and saplings are noted, followed by the larger trees and forests. Then the animals who live in the forests and the birds are mentioned. Also included are cultivated foods—corn, beans, and squash. The second part of the speech usually begins with mention of the wind and of the Thunderers. Next come the sun, moon, and stars. Then the Four Beings, the four messengers from the Creator to the prophet Handsome Lake are mentioned; then Handsome Lake himself, and finally the Creator.

It is evident that the inclusion of Handsome Lake is a recent one. Handsome Lake, a Seneca chief as well as prophet who died in 1815, had had in the later years of his life visions in which the Four Beings gave him a number of messages from the Creator concerning what the Iroquois generally and Handsome Lake specifically should do.[15] In fact, neither Handsome Lake nor the Four Beings are mentioned in a version of the Thanksgiving Speech recorded in the late 1840s.[16]

---

14. Ibid., p. 7; Foster, *From the Earth*, pp. 136–137.

15. For Handsome Lake's teachings, see Arthur C. Parker, *The Code of Handsome Lake, the Seneca Prophet*, New York State Museum Bulletin 163 (1913), and Lewis H. Morgan, *League of the Ho-de-no-sau-nee, or Iroquois* (Rochester: Sage and Brother, 1851), pp. 233–259.

16. Morgan, *League of the Ho-de-no-sau-nee*, pp. 219–221.

It is also apparent that the name "Creator" is used in the Thanksgiving Address rather than that of the older Twin Brother (Tharonhiawagon, "He who Grasps the Sky" or Sky-Holder) used in the cosmological myth. The personage would, however, seem to be the same.

The various cosmological items listed in the Thanksgiving Address are also listed in other speeches, notably the Tobacco Invocation to the Creator that forms one of the rites of the Midwinter ceremonial and the speeches that form part of the dance called the Thanksgiving Dance or Drum Dance. But it is the Thanksgiving Address that is best known to the Iroquois themselves, and it is one example of such a speech that is given here.

A Seneca Thanksgiving Address[17]

And now, we are gathered in a group. And this is what the Sky Dwellers[18] did: They told us that we should always have love, we who move about on the earth. And this will always be first when people come to gather, the people who move about on the earth. It is the way it begins when two people meet: They first have the obligation to be grateful that they are happy.[19] They greet[20] each other, and after that they take up the matter with which just they two are concerned. And this is what Our Creator[21] did: He decided, "The people moving about on the earth will simply[22] come to express their gratitude." And that is the obligation of those of us who are gathered: that we continue to be grateful. This, too, is the way

---

17. From Chafe, *Seneca Thanksgiving Rituals*, pp. 17–45. Seneca text recorded in 1959 by Corbett Sundown, leading ritualist on the Tonawanda Reservation in New York State. The translation was made by Chafe, a linguist with special interest in and familiarity with the grammar of the Seneca language, with the aid of Sundown and other Seneca speakers. The notes are from Chafe's translation with the exception of notes 26, 28, 30, 32, 35, 42 and 43 which are mine.

18. The Four Beings, i.e., the messengers from the Creator to Handsome Lake.

19. Literally, "that they are thinking well," with reference to both mental and physical health.

20. Or "are thankful"; see above.

21. Literally, "he fashioned our lives."

22. I.e., it is all that will be required of them.

things are: We have not heard of any unfortunate occurrence that there might be[23] in the community. And the way things are, there are people lying here and there, held down by illness; and even that, certainly, is the responsibility of the Creator.[24] And therefore let there be gratitude; we are always going to be grateful, we who remain, we who can claim to be happy. And give it your thought: The first thing for us to do is to be thankful for each other. And our minds will continue to be so.

And now this is what Our Creator did: He decided, "I shall establish the earth, on which the people will move about. The new people, too, will be taking their places on the earth. And there will be a relationship when they want to refer to the earth: They will always say 'Our mother, who supports our feet.'" And it is true: We are using it every day and every night; we are moving about on the earth. And we are also obtaining from the earth the things that bring us happiness. And therefore let there be gratitude, for we believe that she has indeed done all that she was obligated to do, the responsibility that he assigned her, our mother, who supports our feet. And give it your thought, that we may do it properly: We now give thanks for that which supports our feet. And our minds will continue to be so.

And now this is what the Creator did. He decided, "There will be plants growing on the earth. Indeed, all of them will have names, as many plants as will be growing on the earth. At a certain time they will emerge from the earth and mature of their own accord. They will be available in abundance as medicines to the people moving about on the earth." That is what he intended. And it is true: We have been using them up to the present time, the medicines the Creator made. He decided that it would be thus: that people would be obtaining them from the earth, where the medicines would be distributed. And this is what the Creator did: He decided, "Illness will overtake the people moving about on the earth, and these

---

23. More literally, "that a difficult thing might accidentally occur"—a euphemism for death.

24. I.e., it is for him to decide whether or not they will recover.

will always be there for their assistance." And he left on the earth all the different medicines to assist us in the future. And this too, the Creator did. With regard to the plants growing on the earth he decided, "There will be a certain plant on which berries will always hang at a certain time. I shall then cause them to remember me, the people moving about on the earth. They will always express their gratitude when they see the berries hanging above the earth." And it is true: We see them when the wind becomes warm again on the earth; the straw-berries are indeed hanging there. And it is also true that we use them, that we drink the berry water.[25] For this is what he did: He decided, "They will always bring them to their meeting place and give thanks, all the people, as many as remain. They will be thankful when they see the berries hanging." That is what he did. And it is true: It comes to pass. When in the course of things it becomes warm again on the earth, we are thankful for everything. And give it your thought, that with one mind we may give thanks for all the plants, our medicines. And our minds will continue to be so.

And this is what the Creator did: He decided, "There will be springs on the earth. And there will be brooks on the earth as well; rivers will flow, and will pass by under the earth. And there will also be ponds and lakes. They will work hand in hand, the way I fashion them on the earth. And moisture will continue to fall." And it is true: Fresh water is available in abundance to us who move about on the earth. And, in fact, to all those things that he provided for our contentment, fresh water is abundantly available too. And it is true: We have been using it up to the present time. It is the first thing we use when we arise each new time. When the new day dawns again, the first thing we use is water. And let there indeed be gratitude. It is coming to pass as Our Creator intended. And give it your thought, that we may do it properly: We now give thanks for the springs, the brooks, the flowing rivers, and the ponds and lakes. And our minds will continue to be so.

And now this is what the Creator did. He decided, "There

---

25. The mixture of strawberries and water used in the Strawberry ceremony.

will be forests growing on the earth. Indeed, the growing forests will be of assistance to the people moving about on the earth." He decided, "There will always be a certain period when the wind will become warm, and a certain length of time, also, when it will become cold. And the forests growing on the earth will provide heat for them." That is what the Creator intended. And it is true: It continues unchanged up to the present time. We are using them for heat, the forests growing on the earth. And this also he did: He made them medicines as well, the trees growing on the earth. He decided, "They can also be available as medicines to the people moving about on the earth." And he even did this as well: He decided, "Again, there will be a certain tree that I shall cause to remind the people moving about to think of me. The maples will stand on the earth, and the sweet liquid will drip from them. Each time when the earth becomes warm, then the sap will flow and they will be grateful for their happiness. When the time arrives again, they will attend to the maples standing there." And for those people who take notice of it, it continues unchanged: They do indeed tap them and store the sugar. For he decided that it would be available in abundance to the people moving about on the earth. And it is true: It continues unchanged up to the present time; we are still using it. And therefore again let there be gratitude that it all still continues as the Creator planned it. And give it your thought, that we may do it properly: We now give thanks for the forests growing on the earth. And our minds will continue to be so.

And now this is what Our Creator did: He decided, "I shall now establish various animals to run about on the earth. Indeed, they will always be a source of amusement for those who are called warriors,[26] whose bodies are strong." He decided to provide the warriors, whose bodies are strong, with the animals running about, to be a source of amusement for them. "And they will be available as food to the people moving about on the earth." And up to the present time we have indeed seen the small animals running about along the edges of

---

26. "Warriors" is a virtual synomyn for "adult men."

the forests, and within the forests as well. And at the present
time we even catch glimpses of the large animals again. There
were in fact a number of years during which we no longer saw
the large animals. But now at the present time they are actually
available to us again as food. And we are using them as Our
Creator intended. And therefore let there be gratitude that it
all does still continue as he intended. And give it your thought,
that we may do it properly: We now give thanks for the
animals running about. And our minds will continue to be so.

And this is what Our Creator did. He decided, "I shall
establish various creatures that will spread their wings from
just above the earth to as far upward as they can go. And they
too will be called animals. They will begin just above the earth,
and will go all the way into the clouds. And they too all have
names, the birds with outspread wings." And with respect to
the small birds he decided, "There will be a certain period
when they will stir, and they will turn back, going back to
where it is warm. And it will become warm again on the earth,
and they will return. With all their voices they will sing once
more their beautiful songs. And it will lift the minds of all who
remain when the small birds return." And he arranged as well
that they are available to us as food, the birds with outspread
wings. It is true: We are using them too, the birds with outspread wings. They are available to us as food. And we believe
that they too are all carrying out their responsibility. They all,
as I said, have names, according to their type. And give it your
thought, that we may do it properly: We now give thanks for
the birds with outspread wings. And our minds will continue
to be so.

And now this is what Our Creator did. It was indeed at
this time that he thought, "I shall leave them on the earth, and
the people moving about will then take care of themselves.
People will put them in the earth, they will mature of their
own accord, people will harvest them and be happy." And up
to the present time we have indeed seen them. When they
emerge from the earth we see them. They bring us contentment. They come again with the change of the wind.[27] And

27. I.e., not a change in direction, but from cold to warm.

they strengthen our breath. And when the Good Message[28] came we were advised that they too should always be included in the ceremonies, in the Four Rituals.[29] Those who take care of them every day asked, too, that they be sisters. And at that time there arose a relationship between them: We shall say "the Sisters, our sustenance,"[30] when we want to refer to them. And it is true: We are content up to the present time, for we see them growing. And give it your thought, that we may do it properly: We now give thanks for the Sisters, our sustenance. And our minds will continue to be so.

And now this is what Our Creator did: He decided, "Now it can't always be just this way."[31] And this, in fact, is what he decided. "There must be wind, and it will strengthen the people moving about whom I left on the earth. And in the west he made the thing that is covered by a veil; slowly it moves and revolves. There the wind is formed, and we are happy. It indeed strengthens our breath, for us who move about on the earth. And the wind is just the strength for us to be content with it and be happy. But the Sky Dwellers[32] told us: They said, "We believe that your kinsmen[33] will see that in future days it may happen that it will be beyond our control. It is the most important thing for us to watch. It may become strong in its revolving, and we believe that it will scrape off everything on the earth. The wind may become strong, we believe, and bring harm to the people moving about." That is what they said. And indeed up to the present time we can attest to it: The way it occurs, it destroys their homes.[34] From time to time it is destructive, for the wind can become strong. But as for us, we are content, for no matter how strong the wind has been we have been happy.[35] And give it your thought, that we may do it

---

28. I.e., the teachings of Handsome Lake.

29. I.e., this should be one of the items for which thanks is expressed. The Four Rituals (i.e., Feather Dance, Thanksgiving Dance, Rite of Personal Chant, and Bowl Game) are here synonymous with public ceremonialism.

30. I.e., corn, beans, and squash—the three cultivated foods of the Iroquois.

31. I.e., there is something missing.

32. The Four Beings.

33. Meaning here "your descendants."

34. Literally, "where they are content"—referring to the homes of white men in the surrounding area.

35. See Chafe, *Seneca Thanksgiving Rituals*, p. 9: "The Four Beings predicted that

properly: We give thanks for the thing that is covered by a veil, where the wind is formed. And our minds will continue to be so.

And now this is what Our Creator did: He decided, "I shall have helpers who will live in the west. They will come from that direction and will move about among the clouds, carrying fresh water." They will sprinkle all the gardens that he provided, that grow of their own accord on the earth. And he decided, "There will be a relationship when people want to refer to them: They will say 'Our grandparents, the Thunderers.' That is what they will do." And he left them in the west; they will always come from that direction. And truly they will always be of such a strength that the people, their grandchildren, who move about, will be content with them. And they are performing their obligation, moving about all through the summer among the clouds, making fresh water, rivers, ponds, and lakes. And give it your thought, that we may do it properly: We now give thanks for them, our grandparents, the Thunderers. And our minds will continue to be so.

And now this is what Our Creator did: He decided, "There will be a sky above the heads of the people moving about. I must have a helper in the sky as well." And indeed he assigned him to be attached to the sky. There he will move about, and will cross the earth. He will always come from a certain direction, and will always go in a certain direction. And he also prescribed a relationship when we want to refer to it: We shall say "Our elder brother, the sun." And it is true: He is carrying out his responsibility, attached there to the sky; there is beautiful daylight, and we are happy. And we believe that he too has done all that he was obligated to do; everything that he[36] left to grow of its own accord is flourishing. He gave him the added responsibility of making it warm on the earth, so that everything he left to grow of its own accord would flourish. And we believe that he is performing his obligation up to the present

---

one day [a revolving object that is the source of the wind] would revolve too fast and cause great destruction, but to date destructive winds have always bypassed the reservations, another cause for thanksgiving."

36. The Creator.

time, the assignment he was given. And give it your thought, that we may do it properly: We give thanks for him, our elder brother, the sun. And our minds will continue to be so.

And now this is what Our Creator did: He decided, "There will be a certain period when the earth will be in shadow, as well as a certain period when it will be day." And indeed he saw well that the people moving about were taking care of themselves. And he decided, "They will rest. They will lay down their bodies and rest while it is in shadow." That is what he intended. "And perhaps it will happen that somewhere at a distance[37] they will run into darkness. And I shall have another helper, another orb in the sky. People will say 'Our grandmother, the moon.' That is how they will do it. It can be a sort of guide for their steps, providing them with light." And indeed it is a measure for us as we go along, we who move about on the earth. He decided, "The moon will change its form as it goes." They have called it "phases." And it is true: It is still a measure for us up to the present time, the way it is as we go along, we who move about on the earth. And we believe that they come from there too, that it continues unchanged: the little ones taking their places on the earth.[38] They are here and they come from our mothers. And therefore we believe that she has done all that she was obligated to do, the assignment she was given. And now give it your thought, that we may do it properly: We now give thanks for her, our grandmother, the moon. And our minds will continue to be so.

And now this is what Our Creator did. He decided, "There will also be stars arrayed in the sky while it is dark." And he assigned to them certain things as well, the way it would continue to be. He decided, "They too will all have names, all the stars in the sky. And they too, in fact, will be indicators, to be used for measuring by the people moving about. If it happens that they run into darkness on their journey, they will use them, the people moving about. And indeed they will lift their faces to the stars and will be set straight.

---

37. I.e., from home.
38. I.e., the cycle of reproduction is determined by the moon.

They will head back directly toward their home." And up to the present time they have had an added responsibility. While it is dark they will cause moisture to fall on everything that he left to grow of its own accord on the earth. And truly they enjoy water throughout the night, everything that he left to grow of its own accord. It comes from the stars arrayed in the sky. And we believe that they are performing their obligation, the responsibility that they too have. And give it your thought, that we may do it properly: We now give thanks for them, the stars arrayed in the sky. And our minds will continue to be so.

And now Our Creator decided, "I shall have the Four Beings as helpers to protect the people moving about on the earth." Indeed, he saw well that it was not possible for them alone, that they could not continue to move about alone. It was true: All sorts of things were going on on the earth where they would move about. It was inevitable that the people moving about on the earth would have accidents. The people moving about on the earth would have accidental things happen to them that would be beyond their control. And indeed we too can attest to it, we who move about on the earth: It will happen that people are involved in accidents that are beyond their control. It is the way with us who move about on the earth. And indeed they also have the added responsibility of keeping watch over those of his helpers called the Four Groups.[39] They will continue to look after us whom he left on the earth, and will bring us contentment. And we believe that they too are performing their obligation, the assignment they were given, those who are called the Four Beings, our protectors. And therefore let there be gratitude, for we believe that we are happy. Give it your thought, that with one mind we may now give thanks for his helpers, the Four Beings, our protectors. And our minds will continue to be so.

And now this is what Our Creator did. He did indeed decide it, and it must happen according to his will. Indeed he[40] was among us who moved about on the earth. Illness took hold

---

39. I.e., the wind, the Thunderers, the sun, and the moon.
40. Handsome Lake, who is not regarded as an incarnation of the Creator as the translation might be taken to imply.

of him, and he was confined to bed. For a number of years he lay helpless. And the way things were, he had to be thankful during the nights and the days, and he thought that there must be someone there who made all the things that he was seeing. And thereupon he repented everything, all the things he thought he had done wrong when he moved about on the earth. And indeed he was thankful each day for each new thing that he saw. And now it happened that the Creator saw well how the people on the earth were acting. It seemed that nowhere was there any longer any guidance for the minds of those who moved about. And now it happened that he sent his helpers to speak to our great one, whom we used to call Handsome Lake, when he moved about. They gave him the responsibility to tell us what we should do in the future. And for a number of years he told about the words of the Creator. And the way things went, he labored until he collapsed. And let there indeed be gratitude that from time to time now we again hear the words of the Creator. And therefore let there be gratitude that it is still continuing as he planned it. And give it your thought, that we may do it properly: We give thanks for him, whom we called Handsome Lake. And our minds will continue to be so.

And now this is what Our Creator did. He decided, "I myself shall continue to dwell above the sky, and that is where those on the earth will end their thanksgiving. They will simply continue to have gratitude for everything they see that I created on the earth, and for everything they see that is growing." That is what he intended. "The people moving about on the earth will have love; they will simply be thankful. They will begin on the earth, giving thanks for all they see. They will carry it upward, ending where I dwell. I shall always be listening carefully to what they are saying, the people who move about. And indeed I shall always be watching carefully what they do, the people on the earth." And up to the present time, indeed, we people believe that we are happy. And therefore let there also be gratitude that we can claim to be happy. And give it your thought, that with one mind we may now give thanks for him, Our Creator. And our minds will continue to be so.

And that is all that I myself am able to do. What they[41] did was to decide that a ritual of gratitude, as they called it, would always be observed in the future, when in the future people would gather. And that is all that I myself am able to do; that is all that I learned of the ritual that begins the ceremony.[42] That is it.[43]

---

41. The Four Beings.
42. Such a statement regarding inadequacy is customary in Iroquois speeches of this sort.
43. This phrase customarily concludes Iroquois speeches.

II. Dreams and Visions

As the preceding account of Iroquois cosmology illustrates, the great sacred traditions of North American Indians are little concerned with enjoining on the people a set of moral precepts. This is not to say that they have no such standards, only that morality is not equated with religiosity to the degree it is in the Western world. Violation of moral standards is apt not to be punished by the supernatural nor are rewards given by these beings for good behavior. Rather, the sanctions involved are apt to be informal social ones—ridicule and gossip, being made fun of for bad behavior or esteem in the eyes of others for good behavior. Admonitions are apt to be justified not by reference to what the supernatural will do or think, but by reference to "what people will say."

For these reasons, the most explicit statements of Indian moral standards are to be found in the admonitions of the people to one another, particularly the admonitions of parents to children—as children might not be expected to know how they should behave. Parents and grandparents were apt to instruct children by discoursing to them often and at some length while they were growing up—a procedure that is often reported in the literature as being a rather formal one, perhaps leaving the impression that it was more formal than it actually was. By Indian etiquette, a person speaks until he has finished saying what he wants to. It is not polite to interrupt, and consequently to a westerner, Indian conversations are apt to have the character of a series of short speeches. To Indians, western practice often is impolite—as a missionary noted over a century and a half ago:

> They are very much disgusted with the manner they say some white people have of asking questions on questions, without allowing them time to give a proper answer to any one of them. They, on the contrary, never ask a second question until they have received a full answer to the first. They say of those who do otherwise, that they seem as if they wished to know a thing, yet cared not whether they knew it correctly or properly.[1]

*　　*　　*

The following is a summary of what one Winnebago was told as a child by his father. It will serve as illustration of moral standards Indian men were expected to uphold.

A Winnebago Father's Teachings to His Son[2]

You ought to be of some help to your fellowmen and for that reason I counsel you to fast. Our grandfather who stands in our midst[3] sends forth all kinds of blessings. Try then and

---

1. John Heckewelder, *An Account of the History, Manners, and Customs of the Indian Natives Who Once Inhabited Pennsylvania and the Neighbouring States*, Transactions of the Historical and Literary Committee of the American Philosophical Society 1, pp. 1–348, (1819), p. 319.

2. Originally written in the Winnebago syllabary. Radin published the account several times in slightly different translations: in *The Autobiography of a Winnebago Indian*, Univ. of California Publications in American Archaeology and Ethnology 16, no. 7 (1920), pp. 450–466; in *The Winnebago Tribe*, Annual Report of the Bureau of American Ethnology 37 (1923), pp. 166–177; and in *Crashing Thunder: The Autobiography of an American Indian* (New York: D. Appleton, 1926), pp. 56–68. The version used here is that in *The Autobiography of a Winnebago Indian*, with a few minor changes. Almost all the notes are extracts from the footnotes in this version.

3. I.e., the fire.

obtain one of these. Try to have one of our grandfathers, one of the war chiefs,[4] pity you.[5] Then some day as you travel along the road of life you will know what to do and encounter no obstacles. Without any trouble you will then be able to seek the prize you desire. Then the honor will be yours to glory in, for without any exertion[6] have you obtained it.[7] All the war power that exists has been donated to our grandfathers who are in control of warfare, and, if, reverently, you thirst yourself to death,[8] then they will bestow blessings upon you. Now if you do not wear out your feet,[9] if you do not blacken your face,[10] it will be for naught that you inflict sufferings upon yourself. These blessings are not obtainable without effort. Try to have one of all the spirits created by Earthmaker[11] take pity upon you. Whatever he says will come about. If you do not possess a spirit to strengthen you, and therefore are of no consequence to the people around you, they will show you little respect. They will make fun of you.[12]

It is not good to die in the village. This we tell all those who are growing up. Do not permit women to journey ahead of you in your village,[13] for it is not proper. For these reasons do people encourage one another to fast. Some day you will be traveling on a road filled with obstacles and then you will wish that you had fasted. So that you will not find it necessary to blame yourself I counsel you to fast. If you have not obtained any knowledge[14] then some day when the warriors return from the warpath and the women are dividing the prizes, your

---

4. I.e., any of the spirits who are in control of the powers for victory on the warpath.

5. I.e., bless you.

6. I.e., by virtue of the spirits' blessings.

7. I.e., you will have no difficulty in finding where the enemy is located and obtaining war honors.

8. I.e., fast.

9. I.e., fast repeatedly (a reference to repeated journeys to the fasting lodge).

10. With charcoal. To obtain blessings, a Winnebago should blacken his face with charcoal. Blessings are not obtained by mere desire alone.

11. The Creator.

12. I.e., ridicule you.

13. I.e., do not let women die before you; do not die of old age, but die on the warpath.

14. Been blessed.

sisters will stand there empty-handed envying the others. If you obtain blessings from those in control of warfare, then if you are one of the victorious men, your sisters will be very happy; and how proud they will be to receive the prizes, to wear them, and to dance the victory dance! Your sisters thereby will also be strengthened.[15] You will be well and happy.

Now all this it would be well for you to obtain. However, the older people say that it is difficult to be a leader of men. If you are not such a one and are, instead, merely what we call a warrior, and you do what we call throwing away a human life,[16] you will have committed the greatest of all shameful acts. Why, a mourner might hurt you and burn you with embers,[17] and then all your relatives would feel sad on your account. Not with the blessing of one spirit, not even with the blessings of twenty spirits, can you go on the warpath. You should be blessed by all the spirits, those on the earth, those who are pinned through the earth,[18] and those underneath the earth, by all of these; and by all those in the waters, and all those on the sides of the earth,[19] all four of them; and by Disease-Giver,[20] the sun; by the moon, the day, the earth; indeed by all those whom Earthmaker put in charge of war blessings and whom he put into the world for that purpose, should you be blessed before you lead a war party.

If you cast off your dress for many people,[21] they will be benefited by your deeds. You will likewise have helped your people. It is good to be honored by all the people and they will then certainly like you if you obtain a limb.[22] Far more will

---

15. Gain strength to overcome life crises.

16. I.e., cause someone to lose his life needlessly.

17. I.e., a relative of the deceased, as he prepares to go into mourning by blackening his face with charcoal (embers), might suddenly in his anger and sorrow actually apply a burning ember to you.

18. I.e., those four spirits, one in each of the four directions, that Earthmaker created to pin down the earth and stop it from spinning around in space.

19. I.e., the winds.

20. An approximate translation. He is an important spirit, a being who dispenses life from one side and death from the other.

21. I.e., give away things to the needy.

22. I.e., war honors (coups).

they honor you if you obtain two or three or four limbs.[23]
Then, whenever people boil an animal, head and body, you
will always eat it.[24] However, when you are recounting your
war deeds in behalf of departed souls,[25] do not try to add to
your honor by claiming more than you actually accomplished.
You will thereby merely make the souls of the departed stumble on their journey to spirit-land.[26] If you tell a falsehood
there and exaggerate your account, you, in consequence, will
die soon after. Those spirits who are in control of war blessings
will hear you. Tell less than you did. The old men claim that it
is wiser.

It is good to die on the warpath. If you die in war, your
soul will not become unconscious.[27] You will then be able to do
what you please with your soul.[28] Your soul will always remain in a happy condition.[29] If you choose to go back to earth
as a human being and live again you can do so. You can live a
second life on earth or live in the form of those who walk on
the light,[30] or in the form of an animal, if you choose. All of
these benefits will you obtain if you die in battle.

If you have not obtained war blessings, fast for your position in life. If you fast in this way, after you get married you
will get along well. You will then not have to worry about
having children nor about your happiness. If you dream of
your home,[31] throughout life you shall be in want of nothing.
Fast for food you are to receive. If you fast often enough for
these things, then some day when your children ask for food,
they will be able to obtain without difficulty a piece of deer

---

23. I.e., can count coup four times.

24. I.e., you will have the right to eat the choicest parts of the animal, an honor
accorded to great warriors.

25. During the Four Nights' Wake.

26. I.e., stumble as they cross the bridge over the abyss of fire, fall in, and thus
not reach their destination.

27. I.e., your soul will pass directly from one existence to the other without any
loss of consciousness.

28. I.e., you can decide for yourself whether you prefer to remain among the
ghosts or to become reincarnated.

29. I.e., will not suffer in death or after.

30. I.e., in the form of a bird.

31. I.e., fast and have the spirits bless you with all that concerns happiness in a
home—a good wife, children, wealth, and long life.

meat, or perhaps even a piece of moose meat. You have it within you to see to it that your children shall never be hungry.

Do not abuse your wife. If you make your wife suffer, you will die in a short time. Our grandmother, the earth, is a woman, and in mistreating your wife, you are abusing her. Most certainly will you be abusing our grandmother if you act thus. Since it is she who takes care of us, by your action you will be practically killing yourself.[32]

When you have your own home, see to it that whoever enters your house obtains something to eat, however little you may have. Such food will be a source of death to you if you withhold it. If you are stingy about giving food someone might kill you on that account; someone might poison you. If you hear of a person traveling through your country and you want to see him, prepare your table and send for him. In this manner you will do good and it is always good to do good, it has been said.

If you see a helpless old person, help him if you have anything at all. If you happen to possess a home, take him there and feed him, for he may suddenly make uncomplimentary remarks about you. You will be strengthened thereby. Or it may be that he happens to carry a bundle of medicines, which he cherishes very much, under his arms, and offers it to you. If it is a medicine without a stem,[33] keep it to protect your house with. Your home will then never be entered by anything evil, and nothing[34] will enter your house unexpectedly.[35] Such will be your life if you do what I tell you. Witches will keep away from you. Thus, if you fast, your fellowmen will be benefited thereby. Earthmaker created the spirits who live above the earth, those who live on the earth, those who live under the earth, and those who live in the water; all these he created and

---

32. I.e., she may withhold from you the produce of her body and you will starve to death.

33. I.e., a plant consisting entirely of roots, no part of which appears above ground.

34. I.e., evil spirits, ghosts, disease, or unhappiness in any form.

35. I.e., without giving you warning and a chance to take precautionary measures.

placed in charge of some powers. Even the minor spirits who move around, Earthmaker caused to have rule over some blessing. In this fashion he created them and only afterwards did he create us. For that reason we were not put in control of any of these blessings.[36] However, Earthmaker did create a weed[37] and put in in our charge, and he told us that none of the spirits he had created would have the power to take this away from us without giving us something in exchange. Thus said Earthmaker. Even he, Earthmaker, would not have the power of taking this from us without giving up something in return. He told us that if we offered him a pipeful of tobacco, if this we poured out[38] for him, he would grant us whatever we asked of him. Now all the spirits came to long for this tobacco as intensely as they longed for anything in creation, and for that reason, if at any time we make our cry to the spirits with tobacco, they will take pity on us and bestow on us the blessings of which Earthmaker placed them in charge. Indeed so it shall be, for thus Earthmaker created it.

You are to fast. If you are blessed by the spirits and breathe upon people[39] you will bring them back to life.[40] You will help your fellowmen by doing this. If you will be able to do this, you will be of even more than ordinary help to your fellowmen. If you can draw out pain[41] from inside the body you will be of aid to all your fellowmen and they will greatly respect you. If you are not working at anything, what you need for sustenance they will give you as long as you live. After your death people will speak about your deeds forever. In life they will say, "Really, he has power."

Although you are not able to fast now, do try to obtain

---

36. Radin, *Winnebago Tribe*, p. 170—as he had exhausted all the powers to be disposed of.

37. Tobacco.

38. I.e., offered. Tobacco is "poured" from the pipe bowl into the fire.

39. I.e., blow upon them to cure them—part of a common Winnebago curing method.

40. I.e., restore them to health.

41. I.e., can suck out the object causing the illness—another part of a common Winnebago curing method. Curing by sucking out such objects is a common medical technique among North American Indians.

this: There are individuals who know of certain plants.[42] It is sad enough that you could not obtain blessings during fasting, but at least ask those who possess these plants to take pity on you.[43] If they take pity on you, they will give you one of the good plants[44] that give life to man and thus you can use them to encourage you in life.[45] However, one plant will not be enough for you to possess. All that are to be found on grandmother's hair,[46] all those that give life, you should try to find out about, until you have a medicine bundle full. Then you will indeed have great reason for being encouraged.

Some of the medicine men[47] were blessed with life by water-spirits.[48] If you wish to obtain real[49] blessings, so that you can cure even more people, you will have to fast a long time and sincerely for these blessings. If four or perhaps ten of the powerful spirits bless you, then someday when you have children and anything happens to one of them,[50] you will not have to go and look for a medicine man, but all you will have to do will be to look into your own medicine bundle. Look therein and you will be able, with the medicine you find, to cure your children of whatever ailments they have. Not only that, but after a while you will be called to treat your fellowmen. Then you can open your medicine bundle and you will not be embarrassed,[51] for you will know how to treat an individual who is ill and needs medicines since you will possess those that are good for him. You will know where the seat of his trouble exists, and since you will have obtained these blessings only after the greatest effort on your part, whatever you say and do will be efficacious. If you declare that he will live,

---

42. I.e., know the medicinal qualities of plants.
43. I.e., help you.
44. Both medicinal and nonmedicinal plants.
45. I.e., to spur you on and prevent you from despairing when calamities befall you.
46. I.e., all the plants that grow upon the earth.
47. Variously termed in the anthropological literature medicine men, doctors, and shamans.
48. Radin's translation. A type of mythical animal spirits, hereditary enemies of the Thunderbirds.
49. I.e., powerful.
50. I.e., one of them becomes sick.
51. I.e., at a loss.

then he will live. If you make proper offerings to your medicine, and if you speak of your medicine in the way you are accustomed to do, and if then you ask your medicine to put forth its strength in your patient's behalf, the medicine will do it for you. If, in truth, you make good offerings of tobacco to your plants, if you give many feasts in their honor, and if you then ask your medicines to put forth their strength, and if, in addition, you talk to them like human beings,[52] then most certainly will these plants do for you what you ask. You can then accept the offerings[53] patients make to you without any embarrassment and your children will wear these offerings and will gain strength from them. They will be well and happy. So be extremely diligent in the care you take of your medicines. Medicines are good for all purposes. That is why they were given to us. We are to use them to cure ourselves. Earthmaker gave them to us for that purpose.

If anyone tries to obtain these life sustainers,[54] and inflicts suffering upon himself,[55] then our grandmother[56] will certainly learn of it. So whatever you spend, she will have cognizance of. She knows all that you have lost in obtaining the medicines, and in the long run you will receive back all that you have lost.[57] You gave your offerings for the future. However, even if you obtain more knowledge than this, it will be a blessing to you. It is good for people to look forward to their future. For all ailments, for everything, people have medicines. Surely you will not want to be without those things that all the people possess.

If, for instance, you should want to obtain the paint medicine,[58] you would indeed have to make yourself pitiable. If

---

52. I.e., as though they were capable of understanding you as another human being would.

53. Gifts.

54. I.e., the medicines.

55. I.e., fasts.

56. I.e., the earth.

57. I.e., the cost of your feasts and the suffering in your fasts will be repaid in kind and degree by the food you will obtain and the happiness you will enjoy.

58. A powerful medicine.

your paint medicine overcomes your enemy[59] and you keep it in your home, you will never be in want of wealth. This most valued possession people will give you. You will be beloved by all and all this will be caused by the paint medicine. This paint medicine is made out of the blood of the water-spirits and is consequently holy. Some thirsted themselves to death, and were then blessed by the water-spirits, and thus obtained it. Indeed the water-spirits blessed them. Earthmaker put the water-spirits in charge of these blessings so that the water-spirits might bestow these upon the people. Indeed, so it is.

Some people who wished to find good medicines discovered the race medicine.[60] Some know[61] it, and it might be well if you tried to learn something about it. Others have gambling medicines, and still others, hunting medicine. There are medicines for every purpose.

Some have a medicine for courting and some possess one to prevent married people from separating; others have one for marriage. Some have a medicine for getting rich. There are others who possess a medicine that will cause people to become crazy. If, for instance, one person has made another one sad at heart, then the latter can poison him with the medicine he possesses and make him crazy. A man can likewise cause a woman, whom he wishes to marry who refuses him, to become love-crazed by giving her some of this medicine. That is what she would become. This medicine that they know will make her fall in love with all men. Similarly if they wanted a man to be constantly following women, they would give him a medicine that would have that effect. Indeed, any kind of medicine you desire you can obtain from the keepers of these medicines, if you ask them. Some of them have knowledge of plants that put people to sleep, while others know medicines that keep you awake all the time. Such medicines they are acquainted with.

---

59. A person who had smeared his body with the paint medicine would be able to attract to himself any enemy he met, so overpowering is its force. It not only attracts everything to one's person, but can paralyze an enemy and utterly deprive him of the power of movement.

60. I.e., medicine used to outdistance others in running.

61. I.e., possess.

Some know how to overcome the viciousness of dogs who are put to watch over women[62] by the use of a certain medicine they possess. Some are acquainted with medicines that they use when in a crowd. If they use these when they are in a crowd, people will only notice this one person who is using the medicine and they will consider him a great man. Another medicine possessed by some is for the purpose of preventing people who are traveling from getting tired. They can even cause a dog fight to take place by the use of a certain medicine. They use medicine in connection with everything they do. They would put medicine on the fields they planted. If you protect your fields by having medicine attached to a stick placed in them, no one will pass through them.[63] They would certainly pass through your field if you possessed no medicines. They would molest your fields and do as they pleased with them.

People must look out for themselves and try to obtain knowledge of everything so that they can live in comfort and happiness. Do you also try to learn of all those things you will need. If you find out about these matters, then, as you go along in life, you will not have to buy those things you need, but you will be able to take your own medicines and use them. If you act in this manner, and if in addition you fast in the proper way, you will never be caught in life off your guard.[64] If you have a home of your own, your home will appear beautiful and you will never be in want. That is why I know you will never afterwards regret these things that I am telling you. If it so happens that you have to journey in the good[65] road taken also by your fellowmen,[66] your actions or fortune in life will never become the butt of other people's jokes.[67]

If you are not able to obtain anything through fasting, try to have one of the good plants take pity upon you. This I am

---

62. When they have retired to their menstrual lodges (houses in which women stay during their menses to prevent contact that might be harmful to hunters, religious objects, etc.).

63. I.e., because he would be poisoned if he did.

64. I.e., no unexpected crisis will arise.

65. I.e., proper, virtuous.

66. I.e., a normal life.

67. Or sarcasm.

telling you and if you do not do it, you will certainly suffer thereby. If you do all the things I am telling you, you will benefit by them. If you have not been able to obtain anything in fasting, at least make use of medicines. If you ever go on the warpath you should also use medicine so as not to be hit. Of that medicine you should also have knowledge. There is also a medicine to prevent you from getting tired, to enable you to run as long as you wish, and that you should also become acquainted with. If it is good, you will never get hungry,[68] and it is this medicine that has accomplished this.

Help yourself as you travel along in life. The earth has many narrow passages scattered over it. If you have something with which to strengthen yourself, then when you get to these narrow passages, you will be able to pass through them safely and your fellowmen will respect you. See to it that people like you. Be on friendly terms with everyone, and then everybody will like you. You will be happy and prosperous.

Never do anything wrong to your children. Whatever your children ask you to do, do it for them. If you act in this manner people will say that you are good-natured.

If anyone in the village loses a friend through death, if you are worth anything,[69] cover the expenses of the funeral of the deceased if you can. Help the mourners likewise, if you can, in defraying the expenses of feeding the departed.[70] If thus you act, you will do well. All the people you have helped will then know you; everyone will know you.[71] For the good you do, all will love you.

It is not good to be a winner in gambling. You might become rich thereby, but that is no life for anyone to lead. If you are blessed with the luck of a gambler, you might indeed win and have plenty of wealth, but none of the children you have will live.

Now if you do all that I have told you, you will lead a

---

68. While running.
69. I.e., are wealthy.
70. I.e., for food brought to the grave for the first four nights after burial when the spirit of the deceased is still hovering around.
71. I.e., know what a fine man you are and you will stand high in their esteem.

happy and prosperous life. It is for that reason that when the Indians have a child whom they love they preach to him, so that he would never become acquainted with the things that are not right and never do anything wrong. Then if in later life a person did anything wrong, he would do it with a clear knowledge of the consequences of his action. This is all.

Now this is what they also used to say to the men. When you get married, do not make an idol of the woman you marry; do not worship her. If you worship a woman, she will insist upon greater and greater worship as time goes on. Thus the old people used to say. They always preached against those men who hearken too strongly to the words of women, who are the slaves of women. Sometimes they used to say the following. Now your brother has had many warnings,[72] yet it may so happen that he pays no attention to any of them. Perhaps when you are called upon to take part in a war bundle feast, you will refuse to go. It may also be that if you are married, you will listen to the voice of your wife, and you will refuse to go on the warpath. You will appear as if you had been brought up like a girl.[73] All who are men perform the deeds of men; you, on the other hand, will never perform a real man's deed. When you are invited to a war bundle feast, they will only give you a lean piece of meat.[74] That is what they will place before you. Why should you run the risk of thus subjecting yourself to the risk of being made fun of? A real brave man when he attends a war bundle feast will be given a deer's head and you will receive only a lean piece of meat in a dish. And that is all you will get to eat. It will dry up your throat.[75] After a while you will not even be allowed to go to a feast at all; your wife will not let you go. If you keep on listening to a woman in this way, all your relatives will scold you. In time even your sisters will not think anything of you. They will speak of you and say, "Do not ever

72. I.e., has been told about his attitude by his relatives and in the teachings.

73. And not like a man.

74. I.e., the worst part of the meat, given only to people who do not amount to much and have never led a warrior's life.

75. Meant in a double sense. It is so dry it will dry up your throat and you will feel so humiliated and disgraced that your saliva will stop flowing.

go there." Why, they will not be of any help to you. Finally, when you have become a real slave to your wife, if your wife tells you to hit your own relatives, you will do it. It is for these reasons that it is not good to listen to women. Guard yourself against it. Do not listen to women. You will be regarded as different from other people. It is not good.

Remember also that women cannot be watched. If you try to watch them and show that you are jealous about them, your female relatives in turn will be jealous of them. Finally, after your jealousy has developed to its highest pitch, your wife will leave you and run away with someone else. You have let her know by your actions that you worship a woman and one alone, and in addition you are watching her all the time. As a result she will run away. On account of this incessant annoyance she will run away. She will be taken away from you. If you think that a woman[76] is the only one to love, you have humbled yourself,[77] and, in consequence, after a while this woman will be taken away from you. You have made the woman suffer; you have made her feel unhappy. Everyone will hear about it. No woman will want to marry you. You will be known as a very bad man. Now this is all.

Perhaps you will even act in the following way. When, for instance, people leave the village and go on the warpath, then you will join them knowing that there it is good to die. Thus you will say because you will feel unhappy about your wife's having left you. However, you should not act in that way. You are simply throwing away a life; you cause the leader to throw away a life.[78] If you want to go on the warpath, do not go because your wife has been taken away from you, but if you want to go, go because you feel courageous enough to do it.

On the warpath is the place where you will have fun! However, do not go on the warpath unless you have fasted. You must fast for that particular warpath, for if you do not and

---

76. Your wife.
77. I.e., humiliated yourself.
78. Because you have had no authority from the spirits to go on the warpath and because your attitude of mind is not the proper one.

you nevertheless try to join such a war party, then when you are present at a fight, when you are in the very midst of it, a bullet will come your way and kill you. That will be due to the fact that you did not fast. People know this and if, therefore, you depend upon yourself, you will certainly do a man's deed. If you have performed any deeds of valor recount them to your sisters and your sisters' children and your aunts. Those who are in charge of war bundles[79] are good to listen to in these matters. Then those whom they counsel will eat an excellent dish,[80] and if they do not succeed in that, then they will be able to eat in the middle of the lodge. Of such things it was that the older people spoke and I want you to do the things about which they are speaking. That is the advice I give you; that is what I wish to say to you—whatever was to be done in life that they spoke about to one another clearly.

I myself never asked for these things, but my father did. He asked for them, he told me. And your grandfather did the same; he asked for the information relating to the manner in which human beings are to behave. Never when you are older should you allow yourself to get in the predicament of not knowing what is the right thing to do, if you are asked. Ask for this instruction, my children, for it is not an ordinary affair.[81] You must learn these teachings.

*   *   *

Among a number of Eastern Indians, and particularly among those living south of the Upper Great Lakes, boys beginning at the age of puberty were encouraged to seek visions and by so doing obtain a guardian spirit, or helper. The following is a Menominee description that will supplement the preceding Winnebago account.

---

79. I.e., the custodians of the war bundles.
80. I.e., will eat the choice part of the deer served to the distinguished warriors at the war bundle feast.
81. I.e., is not anything you can think out in a minute or two; it is something that must be learned and thoroughly known.

The Menominee Puberty Fast[82]

Long ago in the ancient time our ancestors, the Indians of old, used to have supernatural power, for the spirits took pity on them and blessed them, giving them their help. This was the rite they always performed: They fasted, afflicting their own souls. They ate nothing and drank nothing. Parents made their children fast so that they might therefrom gain a continuance of mortal life. This was what the faster was to get as a blessing from the spirits; this was the thing: He was to see an evil vision or else to see a good vision; this was what the faster gained, if he was really helped by the spirits. And it was through this that a person succeeded in prolonging and assuring his life.

At the beginning of the fast the father of the family handed him a bowl filled with food, and some charcoal. And then the one who was performing the puberty fast chose what he wanted to do for himself. Well, then, if he had a good foreboding, he took the charcoal and painted his face, that he might be favorably observed by all the spirits that dwell above, as well as those underneath, inside the earth. And this alone was what he desired, whoever performed the puberty fast, that he might see a good vision, that he might be given a supernatural blessing, having earned it for himself. And as a matter of fact, those who properly performed this rite lived quite a while, as did also their descendants down to their great-grandchildren.

If this person in his fast was deceived by an evil underground spirit, that was when he saw an evil vision, and if he accepted it, that was then the reason why he would turn bad, be of evil character, and not lead a good life. This was what he had by mischance gained for himself.

When a young person began to fast, his body was really clean, as was symbolized by his painting his face with charcoal. And this was why he was able to see a vision, because there was nothing in his stomach. The father, when he arranged his child's fast, would ask him from time to time what sort of

82. Leonard Bloomfield, *Menomini Texts*, American Ethnological Society Publication 12 (1928), pp. 5–7.

vision he had seen. If the faster related an evil vision, then the father would needs tell his son to eat. He did this so that the latter should reject that bad dream.

Now, on the other hand, if this puberty faster saw a proper vision, because a good spirit was disposed to bless him, then the father would tell his son to keep on fasting, so that he might reach a greater number of days. In this way he was able to bring it about that that good thing was firmly placed, that blessing which he was seeing in dreams.

This puberty faster would do this; this was the way he was made to do: Somewhere on clean ground a little hut was built for him. There that faster would stay, lying there and desiring as he fasted to see a good vision. In that way he would endure a large number of days. Then finally he would burn with hunger and be parched with thirst. After a while, when he became too thirsty, he was helped by being made to put a piece of lead into his mouth, so that his tongue and throat would not be too dry. This was, along with other things, a reason why he was able to endure many days; some fasters ten days and some fifteen days. A person like this was one who properly and in all form succeeded in making the fast.

If, however, a faster by mishap set foot on something dirty or on the ground where it had been defiled, then he was not for a long time able to be blessed by the spirits.

*   *   *

Boys were instructed as to what to expect while seeking such a vision. The following is an account of what one Winnebago was told.

How the Spirits Might Bless a Winnebago[83]

"The first night spent there[84] one imagined himself surrounded by spirits whose whisperings were heard outside of

---

83. Radin, *Winnebago Tribe*, pp. 308–309.

84. A particular place where, it was said, anyone who fasted there for four nights would be blessed with war power and power to cure the sick.

the lodge," they said. The spirits would even whistle. I would be frightened and nervous, and if I remained there I would be molested by large monsters, fearful to look upon. Even the bravest might be frightened, I was told. Should I, however, get through that night, I would on the following night be molested by ghosts whom I would hear speaking outside. They would say things that might cause me to run away. Toward morning they would even take my blanket away from me. They would grab hold of me and drive me out of the lodge, and they would not stop until the sun rose. If I was able to endure the third night, on the fourth night I would really be addressed by spirits, it was said, who would bless me saying, "I bless you. We had turned you over to the monsters and the like and that is why they approached you, but you overcame them and now they will not be able to take you away. Now you may go home, for with victory and long life we bless you and also with the power of healing the sick. Nor shall you lack wealth. So go home and eat, for a large war party is soon to fall upon you and as soon as the sun rises in the morning they will give the war whoop, and if you do not go home now they will kill you."

Thus the spirits would speak to me. However, if I did not do the bidding of this particular spirit, then another one would address me and say very much the same thing. So the spirits would speak until the break of day, and just before sunrise a man in warrior's regalia would come and peep in. He would be a scout. Then I would surely think a war party had come upon me, I was told.

Then another spirit would come and say, "Well, grandson, I have taken pity upon you and I bless you with all the good things that the earth holds. Go home now, for the war party is about to rush upon you." And if I then went home, as soon as the sun rose the war whoop would be given. The members of the war party would give the war whoop all at the same time. They would rush upon me and capture me and after the fourth one had counted coup, then they would say, "Now then, grandson, this we did to teach you. Thus you shall act. You have completed your fasting." Thus they would talk to me, I was told. This war party was composed entirely of spirits, I was told, spirits from the heavens and from the earth; indeed, all the spirits that exist would be there. These would all bless me. They also told me that it would be a very difficult thing to accomplish this particular fasting.

*   *   *

Typically, in the vision experience, a being or beings appeared to the faster and not only gave him power to do something but also directions for how to exercise that power. The following are two Winnebago examples.

A Winnebago Vision Experience for War Power[85]

There was a village near Big Lake, and at this village the upper people and the earth people played lacrosse. The Bear was the chief clan of the lower people, and those representing that side in the game defeated the representatives of the other side by sheer strength. Then one of the upper people said, "What effeminate fellows those Bear people are. They are very strong, but it would be much better if instead of being so strong in playing lacrosse they were strong when on the warpath." Thus he spoke. Then one of the Bear people (the one whose fasting is about to be described) felt very much grieved and went out into the wilderness to fast. His desire was to be blessed by those spirits who are in control of war, and in his longing to be blessed by them he cried bitterly. Soon he heard someone saying, "Do not cry any more, we have come after you from above. The spirits have blessed you. You are going to be taken to the lodge of your friends." When the young man got there he saw four men. They were called cannibals, and they were brothers. "Our friends have blessed you and we also bless you," said the four spirits. These four spirits were catfish. Then some white crane spirits said, "Our friends have blessed you. With spears, they have blessed you. Indeed, for good

---

85. Radin, *Winnebago Tribe*, p. 296.

reason was your heart sad.[86] With victory on the warpath do we bless you. Here is your bundle. Here also are your spears and your bow and arrows. This bundle you must use when you go on the warpath. Here also are some songs to use when you start out and when you return. With these songs I bless you. Here they are:

Where they gathered, there did you go?

Well, my friend, shout at it for him.

"When the enemy is close upon you and aim their guns at you, if you sing these songs they will not be able to hit you. If you sing these songs then, those who gave you a name will honor you. Thus we bless you. With life also we bless you."

A Winnebago Vision Experience for Curing Power[87]

In the wilderness I went, and there near an oval hill I sat down and wept. Below the hill lay a round lake and there I saw the rising dew coming in a fog. This first spread itself out over us, and then, in turn, shrank and became small. All this time I sat there weeping. There was something moving in the lake, but although I was looking in that direction I did not see anything. They were sneaking up on me. Two flames of fire suddenly burst forth extending from above to the lake. Then a report like that of a gun sounded. The two spirits were causing it. Suddenly a great noise was heard. I kept right on crying, for I was trying to be blessed. I sat there with staring eyes looking at the spirits. "I must be receiving a blessing," I thought. I continued crying and after a short time it began to rain very much. "How is this," I thought to myself, "only a little time before it was so nice and now it is raining." Yet in spite of the rain no water seemed to fall upon me. "How is it," I thought, "here it is raining and yet no rain is falling upon me." Then I

---

86. I.e., did you make yourself suffer while fasting.
87. Radin, *Winnebago Tribe*, pp. 297–298. The notes are Radin's.

looked above and I saw that it was very cloudy, yet straight above me in a direct line the sky was blue. This blue spot was like a round object covering me as though it were an umbrella. The Thunderbirds were blessing me. With the blue sky, they were blessing me. Soon the noise stopped, and when I looked above I saw four men standing with packs upon their backs. These the spirits killed. Then they blessed me with the power of killing. They spoke to me and said, "Stop your crying. What you have longed for and fasted for, with that we have blessed you. Just as these four men have been killed, so you will be able to kill people. But you will also be able to restore them to life again. Upon your body now we will make a mark and those whom you wish to bless will be given an opportunity of selecting life for themselves,[88] so that, even when a person be practically dead, he will be restored to health. What is above you, the blue sky, that we place on one of your fingers,[89] and with that we bless you. If the patient picks the finger with the mark upon it, he will live."

The Thunderbirds were the spirits speaking to me. They had spears and little war clubs in their hands and wreathes made of flat cedar leaves upon their heads. Thus did four Thunderbirds bless me.

*   *   *

Among some Indian peoples, particularly the more northerly ones such as the various Northern Algonquian ones and to a lesser extent the Northern Iroquoians, the dream assumed more importance than the vision, and it was the dream that provided a guide for action, prophecy as to what might be expected to occur and hence what should be done. The dream could provide such information in any area of human concern, including where animals could be found and how they might be taken, the cause of illness and how the sick might be cured,

---

88. I.e., a sick person will have to guess at the part of the body that has been blessed by the Thunderbirds, and if he guesses correctly he will become well.

89. I.e., we will place a mark made with blue clay upon your finger.

and where enemies (including witches) were and what they were doing.

Although the distinction between the vision and the dream is not a sharp one, a vision is usually regarded as a special experience that occurs while awake and a dream as one that occurs while asleep. However, not all dreams are regarded as equally important, but only those that have an uncommon quality about them. And, as in the case of visions, not all dreams are true; the dream may mislead as well as the vision.

Not expectedly, among those peoples such as the Northern Algonquians who rely heavily on the dream there is also a concern with cultivation of the dream. Mothers ask their children in the morning if they have dreamed that night—for by so doing they encourage the children to pay attention to their dreams. In turn, this practice is part of a more general one. All feel that they should pay attention to their dreams, and thus to what the "soul"—as it is usually translated in English—says. By so doing, the soul will favor the individual with more accurate information and on more occasions than otherwise, rather as a friend if listened to will provide helpful guidance.

Among these northern peoples, who of necessity rely heavily on hunting for their subsistence, the dream often concerns the location of game. The following is an example of such a dream.

A Montagnais-Naskapi Dream[90]

Dreaming about the beaver is called "great dreaming." An Indian was sleeping and he dreamt that he saw a man coming toward him. He dreamt, "It was as though he was coming close to me and as though he was giving me a beaver!" He dreamt that he was going to burn the hair off this beaver. But he dreamt that the man commanded, "Cut out *only* the backbone, and then you boil it whole. And after it is cooked you will put

---

90. From Frank G. Speck, *Naskapi: The Savage Hunters of the Labrador Peninsula* (Norman, Okla.: University of Oklahoma Press, 1935, 1963; New Edition, 1977). Quoted material appears on page 113; notes are from Speck's text.

it into your dish.[91] Do not use a knife when you are eating. For you know how he, Short Tail,[92] does when eating. And so you do the same when you are eating. So eat then. And do not leave it until the next morning. You know over there is a mountain." He then pointed out a distant mountain. "Over there you will go." I thought he told me all this. "You will look for a birch tree standing and bending directly toward the north. There beneath the root, in there you try to get your food for your children."[93]

In the morning when he arose, the hunter said, "I dreamed last night!" "Wonder what he dreamed!" his wife thought, and asked him. Then I went to look at my beaver traps. And there was caught one big beaver. That indeed was what I saw last night in my dream. Then I took it back to camp and arriving there I singed it, and afterwards I ate the beaver. The next day I started off, and went there to the place that the man of my dreams indicated. I arrived over the mountain and found little else than birch trees standing about and leaning in different directions. Which way should I dig to search for it (the one bent as indicated in my dream)? Never mind! At last I walked straight ahead, and while going saw the birch tree leaning over toward the north. "Well sure enough, this is the one," I thought. And there standing close by, I first of all smoked. And then having smoked, I shoveled away the snow. And there, behold, I found my children's food.[94] I obtained a big supply of it from him who was feeding me.[95]

*　　*　　*

As has been noted, the dream might in some way involve curing, often by indicating what should be done to cure a sick individual. And, as illness might be caused by another person, the dream might so indicate. The following is a Penobscot

---

91. A special form of birchbark dish used for beaver meat.
92. I.e., the bear.
93. I.e., more beaver.
94. I.e., the beaver promised in the dream.
95. I.e., his soul.

example, in this case one in which the person causing the illness appears in the dream as a bird.

A Penobscot Dream[96]

Once when my wife was sick, I sat up with her and soon fell asleep. While sleeping I dreamed that the ground suddenly began to heave like a wave, rising and falling round and round near where the sick one, my wife, lay. Then I saw the movement of a bird flying about under the ground and I said, "Don't hide yourself, I have seen you." The bird emerged. "I have seen you already. You were doing this while my wife was sick." As I said this the bird came out, fluttering, and died. Then I woke up. When I awoke my wife felt better and fell asleep right away. She got completely well.

*   *   *

Dreams could also provide information as to the location and condition of people as well as animals. The following is one Penobscot example.

A Penobscot Dreamer[97]

An old man and his son went hunting. His wife and daughter-in-law did not like to stay at home so they went with him. They built their camp out of boughs and made a fire in the midst of a shelter. The father and son went out hunting and left the women at the camp alone. They were to be back in three days, but at the end of three days they did not return. The son's wife got weary and did not know what kept them so long, since it was four or five days since they had gone. That night the mother-in-law, who was very fond of smoking, lay down near the fire to smoke. Her daughter-in-law was lying in one corner of the camp on the boughs. The old woman told the

---

96. Frank G. Speck, *Penobscot Shamanism*, American Anthropological Association Memoir 6 (1919), pp. 237-288, 286-287, with one editorial change.
97. Ibid., p. 288.

younger that she was going to sleep and dream about where the
men were, and what they were doing. When she finished
smoking she lay on her back. Finally the young woman saw a
ball of fire come out of her mouth. She became very frightened.
She jumped up and tried to arouse the old woman, she turned
her on her side and shook her. Then she believed the old
woman to be dead. The ball of fire that came from the old
woman's mouth went round and round the camp and around
the old woman. The young woman turned her over again and
when she did so the ball of fire went back into the old woman's
mouth. Then she began to move about. She said that she had
had a long sleep. She said, "Don't worry, they will be back
tomorrow. They have had good luck and are bringing lots of
game. I just saw them sitting by their fire eating supper." The
next day the hunters appeared with an abundance of game of
all sorts.

*   *   *

As has been noted in the Introduction human persons as
well as persons-other-than-human might transform themselves,
and the ability to do so is one measure of power granted by a
vision or dream. The following are two Penobscot examples of
such power.

A Penobscot Account of Transformation[98]

Long ago there were two young men who acted as spies.
Both were indeed great magicians. They went to spy about an
Iroquois stockade so that they could overcome the Iroquois.
After having done what they intended they went to sleep upon
a pile of corn husks, and they overslept. When the sun arose,
suddenly the Iroquois began whooping and the young men
awoke, jumped up and rolled themselves down the other side
out of sight. Being thereupon out of sight of the enemy they
transformed themselves, one into a bear, the other into a pan-

---

98. Ibid., pp. 281–282.

ther. The Iroquois then rushed upon them but they had run away. To be sure they left the place but they had looked it all over and they knew what could best be done when it was time to attack the stockade.

Another Penobscot Account of Transformation[99]

A hunter and his partner were once away up the river trapping. They set their traps everywhere but had bad luck. When they looked after the traps they always found them sprung but could not find the cause. So one night they were sitting around their camp talking about their bad luck when they heard a noise outside and, lo, there was a porcupine looking right in at them with a face like a man's. When he saw them staring at him the porcupine made off. Pretty soon the hunters heard another noise on the outside of their wigwam and looking up through the smoke-hole beheld there the same porcupine peering down. Now they could see its place and it was the face of a man in their village. The older hunter took a big stick and threw it at the porcupine. It hit him in the face and he tumbled off and made away into the woods. "Now," said the hunter, "we will have good luck after this." That was a shaman. When they next visited their traps they found a good catch, and their luck continued good. When they got home they told their story and discovered that a certain man in the village had, as he claimed, met with an accident. He had his face disfigured. The hunters went up to see him and found that his face was broken just where he had been hit with the big stick.

*   *   *

Individuals who have had contact with supernatural beings, persons of the other-than-human class, through a vision or dream and who thus have acquired special knowledge are often called "shamans"—a term that contrasts with "priests," those religious leaders who gain their knowledge of religious practice

99. Ibid., pp. 287–288.

and belief by learning it from other human beings. But such a distinction is often of little utility when the belief and practice of a particular people is being considered in any depth. As is evident in the above description, the difference between individuals is not that a few have such knowledge and such experience while others have not, but that some have had more and that it is these individuals who are often referred to as shamans or priests. Nor is the source of knowledge that characteristic: Shamans may well learn from other human persons as well as persons-other-than-human.

Somewhat similarly, the distinction between beings with whom the shamans have special contact and those known to the people generally is not a sharp one, and all these beings are apt to be treated in the same manner. Among the Indians here considered, these acts importantly are apt to include singing, feasting, and the giving of tobacco, frequently by burning it in a fire. These beings after all are like friends, and, like other friends, are offered food and tobacco.

Little can be said here about feasting, other than to note that a feast, the giving of food to all in attendance, usually accompanies any public ritual and that this is not a token gift. Little also can be said about the songs, both those accompanied by dancing and those not. Here the difficulties involve the fact that not only are the verses apt to be short—a line or two—and to contain illusions of the sort we associate with poetry and hence difficult to translate, but also the songs not infrequently contain a number of syllables, bearing some resemblance to "burden syllables," that are not translated as they do not have meaning in the sense words do.

Of greater interest here is the practice of offering tobacco (a custom also referred to above in "A Winnebago Father's Teachings to His Son"), for in a number of instances the offering is accompanied by a speech, and from this speech some understanding of the character of the persons involved can be gained. Such is evident, for example, in the following account of a tobacco invocation that formed part of one Winnebago shaman's curing ritual.

A Winnebago Shaman's Curing Ritual[100]

Here is the tobacco, Fire. You promised me that if I offered you tobacco you would grant me whatever request I made. Now I am placing tobacco on your head as you told me to, when I fasted for four days and you blessed me. I am sending you the plea of a human being who is ill. He wishes to live. This tobacco is for you and I pray that the one who is ill be restored to health within four days.

To you too, Buffalo, I offer tobacco. A person who is ill is offering tobacco to you and asking you to restore him to health. So add that power which I obtained from you at the time I fasted for six days and you sent your spirits after me who took me to your lodge, which lies in the center of this earth and which is absolutely white. There you blessed me, you Buffaloes, of four different colors. Those blessings that you bestowed upon me then, I ask of you now. The power of breathing with which you blessed me, I am in need of now. Add your power to mine, as you promised. The people have given me plenty of tobacco for you.

To you, Grizzly Bear, I also offered tobacco. At a place called Pointed Hill lives a spirit who is in charge of ceremonial lodge and to this all the other grizzly bears belong. You all blessed me and you said that I would be able to kill whomsoever I wished, and that at the same time I would be able to restore any person to life. Now, I have a chance to enable a person to live and I wish to aid him. So here is some tobacco for you. You took my spirit to your home after I had fasted for ten days and you blessed me there. The powers with which you blessed me there I ask of you now. Here is some tobacco, Grandfathers, that the people are offering to you.

To you, the Chief of the Eels, you who live in the center of the ocean, I offer tobacco. You blessed me after I had fasted for eight days. With your power of breathing and with your inexhaustible supply of water, you blessed me. You told me that I could use my blessing whenever I tried to cure a patient. You

---

100. Radin, *Winnebago Tribe*, pp. 273–275.

told me that I could use all the water in the ocean, and you blessed me with all the things that are in the water. A person has come to me and asked me for life; and as I wish him to live, I am addressing you. When I spit upon the patient may the power of my saliva be the same as yours. Therefore I offer you tobacco; here it is.

To you, the Turtle, you who are in charge of a shaman lodge, you who blessed me after I had fasted seven days and carried my spirit to your home, where I found many birds of prey. There you blessed me and you told me that should, at any time, any human being have a pain I would be able to drive it out of him. For that reason you called me One-Who-Drives-Out-Pains. Now before me is a person with a bad pain and I wish to take it out of him. That is what the spirits told me when they blessed me, before I came down to earth. Therefore I am going to heal him. Here is the tobacco.

To you, who are in charge of the snake lodge, you who are perfectly white, Rattlesnake, I pray. You blessed me with your rattles to wrap around my gourd and you told me after I had fasted for four days that you could help me. You said that I would never fail in anything that I attempted. So now, when I offer you tobacco and shake my gourd, may my patient live and may life[101] be opened to him. That is what you promised me, Grandfather.

I greet you, too, Night Spirits. You blessed me after I had fasted for nine days, and you took my spirit to your village, which lies in the east, where you gave me your flutes, which you told me were holy. You made my flute holy likewise. For these I ask you now, for you know that I am speaking the truth. A sick person has come to me and has asked me to cure him; and because I want him to live I am speaking to you. You promised to accept my tobacco at all times; here it is.

To you, Disease-Giver, I offer tobacco. After I had fasted two days you let me know that you were the one who gives diseases and that if I desired to heal anyone it would be easy for me to do so were I blessed by you. So, Disease-Giver, I am

---

101. I.e., an additional number of years.

offering you tobacco, and I ask that this sick person who has come to me be restored to health again as you promised when you bestowed your blessing upon me.

To you, Thunderbirds, I offer tobacco too. When you blessed me you said that you would help me whenever I needed you. A person has come to me and asked me to cure him, and as I want him to live, I wish to remind you of your promise. Grandfathers, here is some tobacco.

To you, the Sun, I offer tobacco too; here it is. You blessed me after I had fasted for five days and you told me that you would come to my aid whenever I had something difficult to do. Now, someone has come to me and pleaded for life, and he has brought good offerings of tobacco to me because he knows that you have blessed me.

To you, grandmother, the Moon, I also offer tobacco. You blessed me and said that whenever I needed your power you would aid me. A person has come to me and asked for life, and I therefore call upon you to help me with your power as you promised. Grandmother, here is some tobacco.

To you, grandmother, the Earth, I too offer tobacco. You blessed me and promised to help me whenever I needed you. You said that I could use all the best herbs that grow upon you, and that I would always be able to effect cures with them. Those herbs I ask of you now, and I ask you to help me cure this sick person. Make my medicine powerful, grandmother.

To you, Chief of the Spirits, I offer tobacco. You who blessed me and said that you would help me. I offer you tobacco and ask you to let this sick person live, and if his spirit is about to depart, I ask you to prevent it.

I offer tobacco to all of you who have blessed me.

*   *   *

As has been noted, such a tobacco invocation is not limited to those beings who have appeared in a vision or dream, but is part of the more general custom of a number of these peoples. This is illustrated in the following four Menominee texts.

Menominee Tobacco Offerings to Medicinal Herbs[102]

Now this earth is the grandmother of us all; and it is from her that these roots spring forth that this Indian is to use. This is the way the Indian curer does: He goes and digs up roots and herbs. And this: He first makes an offering of tobacco to them; he sings to them as he picks them, that they may act effectively when he uses them in doctoring. His prayer is heard; he cures those whom he treats. Thus did the great fathers above prepare and plan it. And in all truth it did work with success when this Indian made correct use of it.

Menominee Tobacco Offering to the Thunderbirds[103]

The way the Indian is given to making offerings of tobacco: Whenever the Thunderers are approaching with noise, he makes an offering to them, pleasing them with a gift of tobacco, and begging them to pass by in peace. And this is what the sacrificer does: He goes out of doors and lays down his tobacco; and sometimes he places it on the fire. When he makes the offering, then this is the way he sometimes chants, that they may take pity on him, even as they have in the past taken pity on him and blessed him, that things may go well with him: "Now, I make you an offering of tobacco, my grandfathers. With gentleness go by, my grandfathers!"

A Longer Menominee Speech to the Thunderbirds[104]

You Thunderers are our eldest brothers! Now we have asked you to come with your rain to water our gardens, freshen

---

102. Bloomfield, *Menomini Texts*, p. 9.
103. Ibid., p. 61.
104. Alanson Skinner, *Associations and Ceremonies of the Menomini Indians*, Anthropological Papers of the American Museum of Natural History 13, no. 2 (1915) p. 207.

our lives, and ward off disease. We beg you not to bring with you your terrible hail and wind. You have four degrees of tempest, come with a moderate rain and not a deluge. Do not bring too much lightning. Grant this, that we may be happy till the next time of offering. This tobacco we offer you, you can see it before us. It is all for you.

A Menominee Account of a Tobacco Offering to the Spring Being[105]

Now, once in my life this is what happened to me; I shall tell the story; I shall tell it to my friend here, that on this day he may know it. That is the reason I am going to tell it.

I was twenty years old at the time; I was married. I had a wife. At that time when I was twenty years old, I had one child; it was a girl.

Now at one time I had gone off to hunt; I had my gun with me. To some place, perhaps thirty miles it was that I had gone on my hunt. I had not taken along anything to eat. As I walked about, off there on my hunt, at noon somewhere by the road I saw some water. It was a hillside; halfway down the slope was where I saw the water. There from the hillside the water was welling forth. It was a little brook; its water came from the high ground there. There I seated myself and watched the water come forth.

Now this was my thought: "My grandfather told me when I was little: 'Grandchild, I shall tell you: A spirit dwells where this water comes forth,' said my Grandfather."

Now this was what I thought: "Probably there is no spirit here, whence comes this water. Suppose I lay some tobacco into this water; suppose I give it to the spirit. If he accepts this tobacco, it will spin about here in the water; it will go down under the water. If he accepts it, I shall believe that the thing is really so. But if it goes that way, downstream, there will be no spirit there."

That was my thought. Then I took my tobacco; I took my

---

105. Bloomfield, *Menomini Texts*, pp. 37–43.

knife and cut off a piece of tobacco. Then I placed it into the water. There it lay in the water.

"Oh, my grandfather, I give you this tobacco that you may smoke!"

That is what I said. Then at one time it began to move; here in the water, here the tobacco began to swim. Four times it went in a circle round the water; and then in the very center of the water the tobacco went under, as the spirit accepted it.

"Now do I believe it; truly a spirit dwells here whence this water comes forth."

Such was my thought. That was what happened in this place.

Thereupon I went from there, continuing my hunt, and walking about. All day I had eaten nothing. Toward dark, as I walked on, I came to a house; a white man was he who dwelt there.

"Well, let me go there!" I thought.

Then I saw the white man in his house.

"Hello! Where are you going?" said the man to me.

"I am going around trying to hunt," I answered him.

"Oh, so that's it!" said he.

"Please, friend," I said to him, "I want to sleep here in the stable."

"Very well," said my friend.

"I have had nothing to eat, walking all day," I said to him.

"Why, then," said he to me, "you must take some food; come inside!" said he.

Then he told his wife: "Come, give this man something to eat; he has not had anything to eat, walking all day," said he to his wife.

"Yes," said the woman, "I shall give him food."

So then I ate. When I had eaten, I left; I went to the stable to sleep. The next morning the white man came.

"Now, friend, eat," he said.

So I went and ate, as my friend gave me food.

When I had eaten I started out. All day long I walked about without any food. When I got back to where I was camping, I had no food. In the morning I set out and hunted;

all day long I did not come across a thing—deer, partridge, rabbit, or squirrel. When night came I lay down and rested. For two days now I had had no food. The next morning I set out again.

"Yes, if I come across a deer, I shall shoot it and have a meal!" was my thought.

I did not see any game, walking about all day; at nightfall I came to where I was staying. Now for three days I had had no food.

Then, as I sat there, I reflected: "My grandfather told me that sometime I should suffer hunger; this he said to me."

That was my thought, as I rested there. I cut off a piece of tobacco: Into the fire I placed my tobacco, fixing my thought upon the spirit, in my hunger.

"Pray, help me! I wish to eat in the morning," I said, telling it to the spirit.

Then I slept. When I awoke it was near dawn; I took up my gun and set out to hunt. Perhaps half a mile, and I saw a big bear; it was eating acorns up a tree. I shot it; it fell to the ground. I went up to it: There lay the big bear.

"Well, now at last I shall eat!"

I took my knife; I cut a piece from it. When I had built a fire, I put in the meat to cook it. When I had cooked it done, I ate.

"At last I am saved!" I thought.

The sun had not yet risen. Then I skinned and dressed the bear. While I was busy at this, suddenly I heard something make a noise. I laid down my knife. When I looked about, why, there was a bear walking straight up to where I was. I took up my gun; good, a hit! and it fell. So then I had killed two bears before sunrise.

"Thanks be given," thought I, "to the spirit for helping me in my hunting."

Thereupon I arranged my pack and set out. I had gone perhaps two miles, when I came to where the white man lived. I went there; I saw the woman; the man was not there.

"Where is the man?" I asked her.

"Why, he has gone to town to work," said she.

"I have killed some bears," I told her.

"Why, then," she said, "bring it here," she told me.

I went and brought it to the house.

"Very well," said she, "I shall cook; we shall have a meal."

I was glad indeed, as the woman cooked. When she finished her cooking, she set the table.

"Come, eat," she said; "I shall eat, too; I am very fond of this kind of meat," she said.

When we had made a hearty meal, I went off and brought the other bear to the house there.

"Please," I said to her, "I want to leave my store here in your house."

"All right," answered the woman.

"I am going home to my people; I am going to get a horse," I told her.

"Very well," said the woman.

I set out, and when I reached our house, I told my wife of it.

"I have killed two bears," I told her; "I have come to get the horse. My father-in-law will go with me."

"Very well," said she.

In the morning we set out. When we got there, the horses carried the packs, with the bears, as we brought them home. So now I was saved; two bears; there was plenty of meat.

This was the way I fared once upon a time, my friend.

That is all.

III. Delaware Big House Ceremonial

On occasion, dreams and visions may be incorporated into or form the basis of community rituals. The manner in which they do so varies and the Delaware Big House ceremony in which the recital of visions has a prominent place is only one such way.

The ceremony takes its name from the building in which it is held: a house made of logs, rectangular in plan, with one door on the west and the other on the east end, and with faces, twelve in all, carved on the central post of the house and the wall posts. There are two fires, one to the east and one to the west of the central post. Its form, the Delawares say, was dictated at the time the ceremony originated:

The Origin of the Big House Ceremony[1]

The first beginning of this Big House was the beginning long ago of that worship that the Delawares now call *ngamwin*,

---

1. Retranslated by Ives Goddard from Frank G. Speck, *A Study of the Delaware Indian Big House Ceremony*, Publications of the Pennsylvania Historical Commission,

when there was a quaking of the earth throughout where the Delawares lived. And even all the animals were frightened; people could do nothing because the earth was shaking greatly. And from great distances came crevices in the earth. Everyone was greatly disturbed of mind when they saw how huge the gaps were, of unknown depth, extending here from the world below; there was utmost great disturbance of mind. Even the animals were terrifed; they say even the animals prayed. And accordingly, everyone came into council to consider a possible way to proceed so that we might please that Pure Manitou, Our Creator.

Now at the time the earth quaked, a great cracking, rumbling noise arose here from down below the ground, and there came issuing out dust and smoke, while here and there came issuing out something looking like tar. It was a black fluid, that substance which flowed from under the earth, where great gaps opened in the ground, in our mother's body here where we dwell.

To this day it is not known what was the purpose of the black fluid substance that issued forth from below, where the earth split open and dust and smoke were seen. They say that was the breath of the Evil Manitou.

And then when the men were called together, it was said: "The Delawares ought to pray, for it would seem that we have very seriously angered the Great Manitou. That is why he frightened us." One after another, people arose and said, "This is my dream, and I can explain and sing everything for sure the way I saw it.

"Now, it was said, first of all we are to build a house. And also it was specified how that house should look, and how big inside and how high, and also it was said, 'This is the size of that door.' It will have doors here in the direction of the setting sun and in the direction of our sunrise. And at the sides the logs will join end to end three times and three posts will be

vol. 2 (1931), pp. 80–85. Text narrated in 1928 by J. C. Webber, who was born about 1880 in Indian territory. Original translation by Speck and Weber. Goddard's translation here and below is based on an analysis of the original Delaware text in consultation with Ollie Anderson, a native speaker of Delaware.

used. Two posts will be at each door, opposite each other, reaching to the height of the top of the roof. In the middle shall be the big post, and it shall reach as high as the height of the house. All the posts shall be notched on top, and those at the sides where the logs join shall stand as stud-posts opposite each other[2] and held together at the top with short cross-ties.[3] And up at the top of the posts [rafter] poles run across. And that ridge pole is in two pieces that join in the center. At a little more than a person's height, the roof shall be begun. Everything used shall be wood, including the rafters and flat boards. Also, bark shall be used for roofing.

"And on opposite sides of the center post is where the fires shall be made. Directly above each the roof shall have an uncovered hole, where the smoke will go out. And on every post at about a person's height there shall be carved a *mesingw*,[4] and half the face shall be painted red and the other half black.

"And around the sides where the people sit, hay shall be used. And three men and three women shall be selected—one each from the Turkey group, the Turtle, and the Wolf[5] to be appointed to labor as long as the *ngamwin*. For ten and two days people pray. All this time they furnish sufficient well-dried wood. But it is those women who are appointed to grind up corn and cook meat."

*   *   *

The principal ritual of each night of the Big House Ceremony is the recital by older adult men of their visions, and on the last night, the twelfth night of the ceremony, the recital of their visions by those women and young men who wish to do so. Two other special rites are held during the ceremony. One is the departure of the hunters on the fourth morning to obtain meat and their return on the seventh night; both are accompa-

---

2. I.e., paired posts on the inside and the outside of the house wall.
3. I.e., the notched binders fitted into notches of the posts to lock them.
4. Sacred carved face.
5. The three divisions of the Delaware. They have been termed "clans" (see chap. 6), but are perhaps more accurately characterized as "phratries."

nied by speeches.[6] The other occurs on the ninth night and includes the kindling of new fires.

The Big House Ceremony begins with a speech by the sponsor's phratry[7] chief:

Opening Speech on the First Night[8]

We are thankful that so many of us are alive to meet together here once more, and that we are ready to hold our ceremonies in good faith. Now we shall meet here twelve nights in succession to pray to Our Creator, who has directed us to worship in this way. And these twelve *mesingw*[9] are here to watch and to carry our prayers to Our Creator in the highest heaven. The reason why we dance at this time is to raise our prayers to him. Our attendants here, three women and three men, have the task of keeping everything about our House in good order, and of trying to keep peace, if there is trouble. They must haul wood and build fires, cook and sweep out the Big House.

When they sweep, they must sweep both sides of the fire twelve times, which sweeps a road to Heaven, just as they say that it takes twelve years to reach it. Women in their menses must not enter this house.

When we come into this house of ours we are glad, and thankful that we are well, and for everything that makes us feel good that the Creator has placed here for our use. We come here to pray him to have mercy on us for the year to come and to give us everything to make us happy; may we have good crops, and no dangerous storms, floods, or earthquakes. We all realize what he has put before us all through life, and that he has given us a way to pray to him and thank him. We are thankful to the East because everyone feels good in the morning when they awake, and sees the bright light coming from the

---

6. These speeches are not reproduced below.
7. See note 5.
8. From M. R. Harrington, *Religion and Ceremonies of the Lenape*, Indian Notes and Monographs, Museum of the American Indian, Heye Foundation, vol. 19 (1921), pp. 87–92, with minor editorial change. This is the speech as given by Charley Elkhair.
9. I.e., the faces carved on the posts of the Big House.

East, and when the Sun goes down in the West we feel good and glad we are well; then we are thankful to the West. And we are thankful to the North, because when the cold winds come we are glad to have lived to see the leaves fall again; and to the South, for when the south wind blows and everything is coming up in the spring, we are glad to live to see the grass growing and everything green again. We thank the Thunders, for they are the manitous that bring the rain, which the Creator has given them power to rule over. And we thank our mother, the Earth, whom we claim as mother because the Earth carries us and everything we need. When we eat and drink and look around, we know it is Our Creator that makes us feel good that way. He gives us the purest thoughts that can be had. We should pray to him every morning.

Man has a spirit, and the body seems to be a coat for that spirit. That is why people should take care of their spirits, so as to reach Heaven and be admitted to the Creator's dwelling. We are given some length of time to live on earth, and then our spirits must go. When anyone's time comes to leave this earth, he should go to the Creator, feeling good on the way. We all ought to pray to him, to prepare ourselves for days to come so that we can be with him after leaving the earth.

We must all put our thoughts to this meeting, so that Our Creator will look upon us and grant what we ask. You all come here to pray; you have a way to reach him all through life. Do not think of evil; strive always to think of the good that he has given us.

When we reach that place, we shall not have to do anything or worry about anything, only live a happy life. We know that there are many of our fathers who have left this earth and are now in this happy place in the Land of Spirits. When we arrive we shall see our fathers, mothers, children, and sisters there. And when we have prepared ourselves so that we can go to where our parents and children are, we feel happy.

Everything looks more beautiful there than here, everything looks new, and the waters and fruits and everything are lovely.

No sun shines there, but a light much brighter than the sun—the Creator makes it brighter by his power. All people who die here, young or old, will be of the same age there; and those who are injured, crippled, or made blind will look as good as the rest of them. It is nothing but the flesh that is injured: The spirit is as good as ever. That is the reason that people are told to help always the cripples or the blind. Whatever you do for them will surely bring its reward. Whatever you do for anybody will bring you credit hereafter. Whenever we think the thoughts that Our Creator has given us, it will do us good.

This is all I can think of to say along this line. Now we will pass the turtle[10] around, and all that feel like worshiping may take it and perform their ceremonies.

*   *   *

Following the conclusion of the speech, various men recite their visions, starting with the sponsor. Each alternately recounts his vision and dances along the dance path in the Big House while singing the song received from his guardian manitou. Drummers beating on a special hide drum provide an accompaniment to the recital. Two examples of such vision recitations follow.

A Vision Recitation[11]

I must now come to the point of relating my narrative about Kansas River when I was a child, when my now-deceased father told me, "Now, indeed, for your younger brother life is ended." He caused me great sorrow, since I really grieved for my younger brother. For I used to think that later on I would play with him. Truly indeed it bothered me very much. I did not know what to do. That is why I began to wander away, and walked along there toward the edge of the timber. I was un-

---

10. I.e., turtle shell rattle.

11. Retranslated by Ives Goddard from Speck, *A Study of the Delaware Indian Big House Ceremony*, pp. 116–127. This is J. C. Webber's narration of Charley Elkhair's vision recital.

aware that night was beginning to overtake me, and more and more my thoughts bothered me. I really did not know what to do. Then, suddenly, I made up my mind to let whatever might become of me happen. Then under a tree I doubled up to the ground. In a short time I began to feel that my grief had begun to flow out. It seemed as though I were not asleep, for I thought: "I don't care if I die right here; I don't have a younger brother now anyway." It was not long before I heard something land on the ground nearby. I did not realize that I had apparently gotten up halfway while looking over toward the north.

Pitiful me, I saw nothing although I could hear the being well. From right over the ridge I heard him say, "Do not think that you are not cared for; I do, my friend!" Then he was walking about! Indeed the being really startled me when I looked over. Then I saw him stretched out; he seemed to me to extend from the north. He was kind of red looking. And he said, "My friend, pay close attention! Look at me! This is what I do when I walk about in this place!" Every little while he would start running. When he started running, the sound he made was tammmmm, tammmmm![12] That being looked as odd as could be.

When I thought about him when I looked at him, it was over at the edge of the southern land where he apparently came to the ground. And every time that being started running, he sounded like ooooo ooooo![13] And he said when he landed there, "This is what I do when I pass by here bestowing my blessings." For he spoke, and that being sounded like he said, when he came to the ground:

> It goes off,
> The worship
> Of the Delaware,
> All over the world.[14]

---

12. Here the drummers beat the drum in response.

13. At this point, the drummers strike the drum rapidly.

14. This is the song the reciter received from his guardian manitou. While singing it, the reciter dances in a shuffling manner along the path around the fires. The words are sung with extensive distortion that gives Delaware vision recital songs an esoteric quality that reflects their spiritual effectiveness.

There in the direction of the north I heard him. That being every so often started running. More and more I was concerned by what that being said. And he said when he started running:

> It goes off,
> The worship
> Of the Delaware,
> All over the world.

Truly thank you, my kindred. I am glad that we have so far had good health and that I can bestow on you all kinds of spiritual blessings, even including all of those grandfathers of ours. And before long we shall shake hands with these drummers,[15] who are lifting up the worship of the Delawares with song. And he, what he kept saying, every time that he started running, was:

> It goes off,
> The worship
> Of the Delaware,
> All over the world.

More and more clearly could I see that being. I took him to be over there in the north where he originated, and he seemed, as I saw him going by, to be of red appearance. And what that being kept saying was:

> It goes off,
> The worship
> Of the Delaware,
> All over the world.

Truly I am utterly inadequate to it, my kindred, but I shall nevertheless do as well as I can and with all my heart, pitiful

---

15. Literally, "cranes." The reciter in his circuit of the Big House is approaching the drummers. When he is almost in front of them, he stops and shakes hands with them. All those dancing behind him do likewise.

me! For that is what I thought when I heard that being saying, "My friend look at me carefully. I too bring blessings when I come here!" So it sounded when he started running:

> It goes off,
> The worship
> Of the Delaware,
> All over the world.

My kindred, I am glad that I have reached this Fine White Path, our Father's Road.[16] And now we have come here to where our grandfather[17] stands. And also we used to hear our now-deceased ancestors worship in the proper manner. They said, "This is how many times we dance around the place where our grandfather stands." So let us, too, state it: It will be four times. And then for a while we shall cease talking about that being. But if only I have good health a little longer, we shall never cease for good talking about that being, who spoke, as he said:

> It goes off,
> The worship
> Of the Delaware,
> All over the world.

Truly indeed my kindred we are enjoying very good fortune when we are given an abundance of pure game animals[18] as our prayer meal, as a result of which all of us shall become glad when he our Father, the Great Manitou, comes to our aid. But still, we pitiful people, that is why our pitiful utterances are heard here in our Father's House. And he, this is what he kept saying:

> It goes off,
> The worship

---

16. The oval dancing path in the Big House. It symbolizes the path of life.
17. A reference to the center post on which two faces are carved.
18. I.e., wild animals.

> Of the Delaware,
> All over the world.

Now, my kindred, we have gone once around our Grand-father, the *mesingw*. Truly thank you for taking care of us until now and for our being in good health, including these our children. Now greet our grandfather. Twice we shall lift up our appeal, hooooo hooooo!

> It goes off,
> The worship
> Of the Delaware,
> All over the world.

And again, my brothers and sisters and also my children, we have danced up to where stands this grandfather of ours. All together there are twelve of our grandfathers, by whom every manitou alike is represented: Here is our grandfather Fire, and here is our mother Water, and all the food that supports our life. It is enough, my kindred, to make us happy when we are given all the things that are growing. All of that is what our Father, the Great Manitou, has provided, which is why it is possible for us to see it.

And that being appeared to me right there in the south; he appeared to me and he seemed to possess power in all things. And it sounded so when he started running:

> It goes off,
> The worship
> Of the Delaware,
> All over the world.

Truly, my kindred, one more time we dance around where our grandfather stands. And this will be the last time we shall go around. And then also will everyone lift the prayer twelve times up to where this worship of the Delaware belongs, to the twelfth level of the sky, where dwells our Father, the Great Manitou.

And this is what that being said:

It goes off,
The worship
Of the Delaware,
All over the world.

Truly thank you, my kindred. Now we have come here to where our grandfather stands. Now the time has come for us to offer up our adoration, to lift up our prayer ten and two times to where dwells he who owns us, the Great Manitou, Our Creator.

Truly thank you that I shake hands with you, my brothers, my sisters, and these our children. I give thanks that I bless you with all and every kind of spiritual blessings. Truly it greatly oppresses my heart when I see how we are orphans now. Many times we have heard how pitiful our now-deceased ancestors sounded when they recounted how pitiful were the conditions then. I make myself grieve very much, my kindred, when I see what happened in the past. But, nevertheless, still try your utmost, let us every one be helpful. Maybe if our pitiful plea is heard by the Great Manitou, we would sometime earn something good that he might do for us.

Truly, my kindred, I feel utterly unable to give blessings from here where our grandfather stands. And I am truly thankful to greet all those manitous, all of them sitting round about and above. And when we remember how our now-deceased ancestors so thoroughly took care of the obligations of this worship, it is very good that we can still perform the ceremony as we used to see our now-deceased ancestors do it. This is sufficient for this occasion. Thank you!

Another Vision Recitation[19]

All of you, my kindred, are acquainted with where I spent my childhood, at Raccoon Creek, where lived my now-deceased

---

19. Retranslated by Ives Goddard from Speck, *A Study of the Delaware Indian Big House Ceremony*, pp. 128–135. This is J. C. Webber's narration of his own vision recital.

parents. Once my now-deceased mother really scolded me. She drove me away because I was continually looking at books. That is why she scolded me. She told me, "Go away somewhere into the wilderness, since all you seem to do is look at books." And she said, "For all the days to come you will be pitiful because the book blocks your path. Never will anything be revealed to you in a vision, for you live like a white man."

Truly, my kindred, great sorrow did my late parent cause me. Then and there I began walking aimlessly toward the direction of our sunset here,[20] toward the timber. My grief was heavy when I thought about myself: "Truly that is really so; my parent spoke the truth in saying that never would anything be revealed to me in a vision." And I though it very likely that I would never be blessed the way that the Delaware is blessed. Indeed, my kindred, I was humble in spirit for many years.

When I became a grown man, far away in the country of the Creeks when I was camping with a group, one time after dark, in the course of the night, I heard some beings coming toward me in the midst of the clear sky. It was here from the direction of our sunrise that they were coming.

And when they came and stopped right here above where I had collapsed in sleep, I well remembered what my now-deceased mother had said to me, and I thought, "There it is. It must be that those are the manitous my parent had talked about." I do not know just how my mind acted, when I looked toward them. I saw nothing, pitiful me, although I well heard those beings. I thought there must be four of them, and I thought they must look terrible, for they greatly upset me when they said to me, "Do not think that you will never be blessed the way that the Delaware is blessed!"

I am truly thankful, my kindred, and happy that I have attained this our Father's Road, the Fine White Path of the Great Manitou.[21] I am utterly inadequate, pitiful as I am,

---

Actually, at the time he dictated this text, Webber had not recited his vision during the first nights of the ceremony, but only on the last night. He is here anticipating how he would recite it on the first nights of the next Big House ceremony.

20. Typically a gesture accompanies mention of direction.

21. See note 16.

because never did I think that I would be able all of a sudden to perform in this our ceremonial House, where I heard our now-deceased old people, who worshiped properly. But still I will do my utmost. Take heed, my brethren. Help me, because now we know that we are growing weaker and weaker. So perhaps if we help each other earnestly, we might quite unexpectedly earn blessings, if the Creator hears us with pity.

That is what those beings kept saying over and over:

> Your blessing is the same
> As the blessing
> Of the Delaware,
> All over the world.[22]

Truly thank you that I address you, you men, you young men, you women, and also you our children; I address you with every form of this blessing. I am very glad that so far we have enjoyed good health while we are gathered here in this House of ours. Truly, I make myself grieve when I recount how my parent used to instruct me, and I well remember how pitiful the old men sounded long ago, when they described their life in the past and what happened then. When I listened to them it was really that way, but now it is worse. At this time it looks hopeless, considering how few we are. Even a few years ago, my kindred, there were quite a few people sitting all around. But nevertheless I shall try my utmost.

Truly I am quite inadequate. I never even thought that I would survive long enough to suddenly be instructing from this spot, where long ago our now-deceased ancestors who performed the worship so well have instructed. And thank you, my kindred, when you help me in my recitation, for that has been the strict rule since the beginning of the world, that people should help each other. For even a little child may suddenly remind people of something. That is why it is a great

---

22. This is the song received by the reciter from his guardian manitou; see note 14. The identity of the last two lines of this song to the last two lines of the song in the previously given vision recital is typical of the highly conventionalized nature of vision recital songs.

help when anyone is assisted in his recitation. There might very well be something more I should say, but thank you that you and I are addressing prayers to all our grandfathers, around here, and all over the earth, and up above where they dwell. All of that our Father, the Great Manitou, has arranged, and it is why we are happy when he does something good for us.

This is all I have to say for a while now.

*　　　*　　　*

The recital of visions is repeated on succeeding nights. On the ninth night, new fires are kindled and other special rites performed as the following speeches indicate.

Sponsor's Opening Remarks on the Ninth Night[23]

Now, attendants, you know the rules of this teaching, that you keep in mind, all of you, that a person must act in purity. All of us have heard the instructions of our now-deceased ancestors. They said that a pure person shall make fire. Because when those fire-making manitous are used, if someone cannot make fire, it would clearly be seen to be a fact that the one trying to make fire is not pure. Nevertheless, my brothers, everything is easy when done right. Now you know to purify these two places where fire always is. All the ashes shall be carried out there through the west door. That is what it is used for. Such is the rule for our prayer-worship.

Thank you, my kindred, that I greet you. I am really happy when I address you with every form of blessing. Now, my kindred, we have lived on to the point where we are purifying this fire here in our ceremonial House. Indeed thank you that we have come in good health to this very evening. For tonight we know how we used to see our now-deceased aged

23. Retranslated by Ives Goddard from Speck, *A Study of the Delaware Indian Big House Ceremony*, pp. 146–151.

people properly carry out the instructions and the regulations.

And, my kindred, everyone who owns a turtle rattle should bring it with him when coming into the Big House. And right here in front of where the Bringer-in[24] sits all those turtle rattles should be put in a straight line. And, attendants, you know that you are to prepare and make ready everything, for those drum sticks,[25] and the cedar,[26] and also the red ochre, the blood root,[27] and the prayer sticks,[28] everything that is used now on this night, has to be all ready. Now, the first thing, the leading attendant takes one yard[29] of wampum.[30] Carefully measure those turtle rattles. Everyone will be given a string of wampum beads as long as the back of his turtle rattle. And, my kindred, now we have lived to the Calling-of-Names. Attendants, summon those people whom I send for. [Here the names of the men selected are called by the attendants, and those summoned gather before the sponsor.]

My brothers, here is one yard of wampum. My kindred, go give the prayer-call outdoors. When twelve times you shall have lifted up the supplication then you shall divide the wampum equally among you. [The men whose names have been called now file outside by the east door and facing east raise their right hands giving the prayer call hooooo six times and haaaaa six times.]

Attendants, build up a bright fire. Now is the time when everyone who owns a turtle rattle goes and takes it and the turtle rattle is shaken. It is just a little while before everything is ready, including those forked drumsticks,[31] and all those

---

24. The sponsor.

25. Referring to both the plain drumsticks and those with carved faces on them. The latter are used on the ninth and following nights.

26. For the use of cedar, see below.

27. Used for paint.

28. These are peeled wands about 18 inches long. There are twelve, six decorated with spirals burnt on their surfaces and six undecorated.

29. Literally, "one back length." It is the distance from the point of the shoulder to the fingertips of the extended arm, the standard unit of measurement for strung wampum.

30. A particular kind of shell beads. Because wampum was regarded as particularly valuable by Eastern Indians, it was frequently used in ceremonial contexts.

31. The carved drumsticks used on the ninth and following nights have a forked end.

prayer sticks are scattered in an even number on each side of the Big House. Now, my kindred, again these manitous are beginning to touch us, those who carry our prayer-ceremony.

*   *   *

Visions are next recited as on the preceding nights. When this is completed, the attendants build up the two fires, one east of the center post and one west of it, on which cedar is burned. While the cedar is burning, the sponsor gives the following prayer, dividing his time before each of the two fires, and immediately after gives instructions for the concluding ritual.

Speech before the Fires[32]

Thank you, O Great Manitou, that we have lived until now to purify with (cedar) smoke this our House. For that has been the firm rule from ancient times since the beginning, when anyone recalls how fortunate his children are, and when he sees them enjoying good health. And it is the cause of a feeling of happiness when we consider how greatly we are benefited by the benevolence of our Father, the Great Manitou. And also we can feel the strength of our grandfather Fire, which is why we please him when we purify him and take good care of him, and when we feed him this cedar. All of this we offer in prayer to our grandfather, because he has compassion with us when he sees how pitifully we behave while we are pleading with every manitou above, where they were created, and with all those all over the earth. Do everything for us, our Father, that we ask of you, Great Manitou, Our Creator.

Sponsor's Concluding Remarks[33]

Now the leading attendant carries around a wooden bowl of wampum beads. Every person shall be given equally three

---

32. Retranslated by Ives Goddard from Speck, *A Study of the Delaware Indian Big House Ceremony*, pp. 150–151.
33. *Ibid.*, pp. 150–153.

wampum beads. But the woman attendant who follows shall carry around a bark bowl in which she has ochre and bloodroot; everyone shall be painted.

When all is ready then shall either one of these attendants paint every *mesingw* in the House. That, my kindred, since long ago has been the rule and conduct of the Delaware when they intended to please our Father, the Great Manitou.

Attendants, bring into the House your cooking and your dishes. Each one who brings a dish is to be given some hominy and meat. When the eating is finished, then shall everybody who desires to sleep in the House bring something, whatever he uses, it is up to him what kind of blankets. Now it is nine evenings since we camped.

*   *   *

On the two succeeding nights, the tenth and eleventh nights of the ceremony, the vision recitations of the older men are repeated. But on the twelfth night, women and young men give their recitations and songs. The rituals of this night are begun with the following speech by the sponsor:

Opening Speech on the Twelfth Night[34]

I am thankful, my kindred, that we have come to the point where we bring to a close our worship, which is so greatly esteemed. I am indeed thankful that so far we have enjoyed good health from way back when we started camping, for, my kindred, there are many things that we have to do tonight. I am glad, my brothers and my sisters and also our children, for the extent of our good fortune, including how much good weather we have had day after day. For in addition, our grandfather Fire and our grandfathers[35] sitting around here make us joyful this evening.

And, my kindred, this night it is permitted for someone to "Sing-the-Fires-out." For that has been the firm rule since

34. *Ibid.*, pp. 154–157.
35. A reference to the *mesingw*.

ancient times when the Delawares first began the *ngamwin*. It is and is known to be that the twelfth evening is the time that our women and any other person who feels competent among our young people take part and help. If his mind is made up, anyone truly is permitted to "Sing-the-Fires-out." For there are those older men who have been assigned the duty to help this our prayer-worship. For truly indeed this performance is a heavy burden, because it is a very great thing. That is why our elder brother, the white man, considers it a wonderful thing. Because they see us earnestly perform pitifully in this our house of worship, on account of it the government has great wonder. And that is how we obtain help and also are furnished with a police officer to look after us. And, my kindred, it is evident that we have help, this Delaware tribe, and it has been known since ancient times everywhere the Delawares successively migrated from. Because truly indeed, in the ancient world since the beginning of the earth, the Great Manitou used to arrange it, back in the direction of our sunrise on the coast[36] where our now-deceased ancestors lived. All of this should make us joyful, because tomorrow when it is morning, before we reach noontime, we must conclude the ceremony.

* * *

The Big House ceremony concludes the following morning with this speech by the sponsor:

Final Speech on the Thirteenth Morning[37]

Thank you, my kindred, that again I greet you all, my brothers, men, young men, and my sisters and also all those our children. It is truly fine that we have good weather this morning, that we are so well treated by our elder brother, the sun, when he sheds illumination down here on all the earth. For

---

36. A reference to the Atlantic coast region where the Delawares lived at the time of first contact with whites. The Big House ceremony here described took place in Oklahoma.

37. Retranslated by Ives Goddard from Speck, *A Study of the Delaware Indian Big House Ceremony*, pp. 158–163.

now it is ten and two days that we have been doing this here when pleading earnestly with our Father, the Great Manitou. We all know it. It is truly fine and I am glad when we are helping each other. And really great things are said about this prayer-worship of ours. And marvelous is the service of our attendants, which they will soon finish. And here is one yard of wampum for each one that we pay them, although their services are worth much more, because exceedingly heavy is this that we are doing.

Hardly, for example, can I tell how precious it is. But still we have heard what our now-deceased ancestors spoke about. They said, "The labor of the attendant, when he makes fire, when he feeds us, when he provides plenty of firewood, and when he sweeps—all these are acts of purity with which we bring joy to the One who owns us." For now our work has come to where we conclude the ceremony. Let us consider, my kindred, if only we have good health, that we do this next year right here again.

Oh, and my kindred, there is one more thing I want to say. Bear it well in mind. It is said that when any one meditates on good, the thought is formed in his heart, and when he thinks of good it is easy to behave well. But when he does wrong, it is evil, since when a person seriously thinks about his life, it is exceedingly hard. For we want to prepare the soul-spirit, so that we shall be able to take it back home again to where it belongs, to our Father, when it is no longer used here where we live. But here the body shall remain always, because here below is where it belongs.

Indeed, my kindred, that is why I beg you that someone help me or tell me, since sometimes I forget something. That is how I have always seen it since long ago. Yet at times I feel I have not studied it enough. That is why I am pleased when anyone calls my attention to something.

The attendants must prepare wampum in a wooden bowl. Every person shall be given three beads, and anyone, if he wants, when all are now leaving, there is a hominy mortar outside, and he may deposit there those wampum beads that he was given.

And now, my kindred, when for the last time we are touched by those our grandfathers, the turtle rattles, now is the beginning of our concluding the ceremony. Now at last we are ready to end this our Father's service. And, my kindred, from now hence as we are going home, you must keep it firmly in mind. For you are carrying with you the worship of the Delaware, whereby for one year we shall be happy. For all the manitous given us on top of the earth, and those up above where they were created, come to our aid, as well as our Father, the Great Manitou, Our Creator. This is all for this time.

Now, my kindred, for the last time we go out to pray, everybody with all his heart. And we know that we shall all go out to the east and carry with us the wampum that is left unused (for that is our heart) when we address our prayer to our Father, up to where the soul belongs. And let us study it. Everyone earnestly addresses his prayer up above, and we express our prayer with this wampum, our heart. Through ten and two levels of the sky we lift our prayer to where dwells our Father, the Great Maritou, Our Creator.

*   *   *

Although the Big House ceremony is no longer held, its importance and the consequences of its demise were recounted by one of its prominent leaders before it ceased to be performed. His reflections follow.

The Purpose of the Big House Ceremony[38]

The Delaware meeting helps everybody in the world, for they pray for good crops and everything good, even wild fruits. About ten years ago the people thought they would give up holding these meetings, and the following year they had high winds and big rains, and everyone was frightened. Then grasshoppers came in swarms, but they came in the fall a little too

---

38. From Harrington, *Religion and Ceremonies*, pp. 113–115 with minor editorial change. The speaker is Charley Elkhair.

late to get all the crops. So the people held a council and talked about the Big House again. They finally decided to resume it, before any more bad luck came; so they began the ceremonies again in the fall.

Then it seemed as if all the trouble stopped. Of late there has been talk of again giving up the meeting, but if we do give it up we are likely to have a tornado or maybe dry weather to ruin the crops.

Once the Delawares owned a great deal of land, but that is nearly all gone now, and the people seem to have no power to do anything. When the Creator looks down from Heaven, he sees but very few Delaware people, and the reason for this is that they cannot follow the Big House ceremonies now. When I was a little boy, I heard my people say that this thing would happen just as it is happening now. You see, the young people raised during the last thirty years do not believe in the old ways. We are having good times yet, but we do not know when we shall catch it. If anything happens to us, and once really begins, we cannot stop it—it will be too late. Even if they take up the meeting again—they cannot do right, even when the ceremonies are going on.

They cannot accomplish anything in the Big House; they cannot raise it up, because there are a lot of young folks who do not even try to do what the speaker tells them, for they do not believe in it.

The people could get along fine, if they followed the rules of the meeting—not only the Delawares, but the other people round about. For when the Delaware prays, he prays for things that will benefit everybody; he prays for the children as well as for himself; he prays for future time. But if anything comes to destroy the world, it will be too late to think of starting the Big House then.

IV. Winnebago Night Spirits Society Ceremonial

Among the Winnebago those who had been blessed in a vision by the same spirit might belong to the same society. There were at least four such societies in which membership was dependent on the blessings from one and the same being: a society of those blessed by the Night Spirits, a society of those blessed by the Buffaloes, a society of those blessed by ghosts, and a society of those blessed by Grizzly Bears. The following is a description of the ceremony held by the society of those blessed by the Night Spirits.

As is evident in this description, the ceremony begins with an opening speech by the host, offering of tobacco by all present, and the singing of songs by the host. The four principal invited guests then enter in turn. Each speaks, sings his songs, and briefly speaks again before taking his assigned seat. After all have so entered, the host greets the guests, mentioning how the ceremony originated in a vision and also its benefits.

After a dance, the first guest to enter speaks and pipes are smoked. Then the first guest speaks again, songs are sung, and after another speech by him, more songs—a general procedure repeated by each of the other principal guests. This finished, the host speaks again and each of the four principal guests very briefly replies in turn saying that they and those with them will sing. After the songs, a feast concludes the ceremony.

Ceremony of Those Who Have Received Blessings from the Night Spirits[1]

Once a man went hunting so that he might be able to get the game with which to give a feast. All of those who were to participate in the feast went along with him. After they had killed some deer they built a lodge. Then all the other feast givers came into the lodge, bringing something toward the feast, as well as the tobacco they were to offer. Some brought other things, even dogs, as their contributions to the feast. The dogs would be killed, singed, then boiled, and prepared in the same way as the deer. The meat would then be mixed with dry corn. The attendants, who were generally the nephews of the feast givers, would look after the boiling of the food. Every time they gave a feast they selected these nephews to do the cooking and the general work connected with this ceremony.

The nephew who acts as attendant accompanies a feast giver on the warpath, where likewise he has to endure a great deal. Should his uncle be killed, it is his duty to be killed likewise and not to return home.

He acted in this way because of his love for his uncle. The attendants do all the work whenever their uncles give a feast. They also arrange for the place where the feast is to be held, make the four invitation sticks, blacken them with charcoal, and decorate them at the ends with fine and fluffy white eagle feathers. Then they prepare a bundle of tobacco containing

---

1. Radin, *Winnebago Tribe*, pp. 329–342. Notes are from Radin's account. Radin's methods of obtaining and translating Winnebago texts is discussed in his *Culture of the Winnebago: As Described by Themselves* (in the International Journal of American Linguistics Memoir 2, 1949), pp. 1–10.

about a pipeful. After these preparations have been made one of the nephews goes around the village and presents the invitation sticks to every individual who had been blessed by the Night Spirits. These are called the night-blessed children. The night-blessed children thank the messengers and assure them that they now feel they are obtaining life. Then those to whom the invitation stick has been presented go around asking their relatives to accompany them to the feast. There the guest and his relatives would meet at the appointed time. All those who receive invitation sticks do the same.

The host at the same time puts himself in readiness to receive the guests.

The two drums to be used are placed in the proper position with tobacco on top as an offering. The two gourds to be used are arranged in the same way, with offerings of tobacco on top. These four articles are placed in a row in front of the host, who pours tobacco on them again and asks them for life.

The host now rises and speaks as follows: "Grandfathers, when you blessed my grandfather with life you promised that as often as we would boil food for you and offer you a pipeful of tobacco, you would smoke it. So it has been said. Boiled water from an animal whom you considered the same as our own body, and spirit food he extended to you, as well as a pipeful of tobacco. This we also are sending you. And what could we ask of you in return but war? That it may be directed toward us, we pray you. Grandfathers, you who are called Happy Nights, when you blessed our grandfather you blessed him with endless war. So it has been said. That is what we ask for, that as you blessed our grandfather, so you bless us. We ask for the same things. You likewise, grandfather, you who are called The One-with-Rounded-Wood, when you blessed my grandfather you blessed him with life. That is what he said, and you asked him in return to make offerings of tobacco. Here is the tobacco. This night we are going to ask life of you. We desire that you give us, and all who will be here tonight, life. As many people as will be seated here, we ask life for all of them."

Then all who are present rise and, holding tobacco in each hand, walk around the lodge, pouring tobacco on the drums and the gourds, and some of it into the fire. They pour tobacco into the fire for the Night Spirits. For the Beings-with-Rounded-Wood they offer tobacco by pouring it upon the drums. The offering is made both to the drums and to the gourds directly. The tobacco bundles tied to the invitation sticks are offered to the four cardinal points and the four specially invited guests smoke this tobacco, because they are supposed to represent the four cardinal points. Behind the respective invited guests are placed two women, next to the wall, so that they might lead in the dance. When the invited guests come to the feast these women remain outside until the starting songs have begun.

The host sings these songs first and when he has finished the first invited guest enters the lodge, ejaculating peculiar sounds.[2] Continuing these sounds, he walks around the lodge until he comes to the place from which he has started. There he stops and speaks: "You who obtain life, you that council, relatives, all who are seated here, I greet you. It is good that you have taken pity on me. All those that I have along with me, my relatives you have caused them to think that they were to obtain life; that a great life was to come to us through you. And all this you have done when we were leading worthless lives. It is good. If such an invitation were to be extended to people when they are sick and weakly, it would heal them; it would overcome their illness, it is said. It is good. When I think that our sick people will get well by reason of this feast, I am thankful. Up to the present our children have all been sickly, but from now on we will have no cause to worry. I am thankful. The principal tree of the night-soldiers, standing in front of their doorway and in full bloom, has not a dead leaf upon it, not one that is dried. It is beautiful to look upon. They obtained it for us and caused it to come down to us, and we feel grateful. It will strengthen our families. This lodge that we have entered is like the first lodge,[3] and just as we were strengthened by it so will we surely be strengthened by enter-

---

2. That are probably meant as greetings.
3. The night-soldiers' lodge.

ing this lodge today. In the night-soldier's lodge fine white feathers are scattered all over the ground, ankle deep, it is said. As we are about to go over the past, we certainly will be strengthened thereby. The lodge of the night-soldier was fair to behold from the inside, we are told. We will consider ourselves blessed with life today, even though we are not children of the night-blessed ones, and even though we will not be able to conduct ourselves as it is meet. We will, however, do what we can in order to obtain life. You children of the night-blessed ones, who are seated around here, I greet you."

Then he sings the entrance songs and walks around the lodge. His singing is generally finished at about the same time that he has made the complete circuit of the lodge. Then he starts around the lodge again uttering the peculiar sounds mentioned before, until he comes to the seat of the host. There he stops and makes a circle in the air with his hand and addresses him as follows: "I greet you. A great day has come to me and all my relatives have tasted thereof in the hope that they might thereby be strengthened. I have also brought along with me a pipeful of tobacco to be given to you, that we may all be strengthened. So it is said. It is for that reason that I am acting thus and am greeting you."

With these words he concludes and walks to the place that has been assigned him in the lodge, opposite the host and, still standing, he says the following: "Children of the night-blessed spirits who are seated here around me, I greet you all. The councilor, I mean the host, has seen fit to give me and my relatives a seat. We will sit in it so that we may be strengthened thereby. We will now take our seats, but before that let me send forth my greetings to all."

Then the second invited guest enters. He utters the same sounds as his predecessors and makes the circuit of the lodge. When he reaches the place from which he started he stops and addresses the host as follows: "Councilor, you who obtain life, relatives who are seated here I greet you all, and your seats do I greet likewise. You that are seated in the first place, I greet you, too. All you children of the night-blessed spirits who are in this lodge, I greet you. It is good that you wish me to live; that I am here. I am not a child of a night-blessed one, that this invitation should have been extended to me, but you probably knew the nature of my life and that is why, I suppose, you extended this honor to me. My relatives are even greater weaklings in the properties and goods of life than I am. That happens to be our manner of life. It is good. Henceforth we shall be stronger as we journey through life. Our men, women, and children shall all live in peace. As many of us are living today, that many shall continue to live.[4] I am thankful. Of all the spirits that exist, these truly are in control of most life. So it is said of the Night Spirits. This is a great thing. These spirits have given us the occasion for a great counciling. Many of us are not able to take part in it, especially the one now speaking. The songs that have been used by our fathers we will not be able to sing, but whatever we say I know will be acceptable to you, children of the night-blessed spirits. I send forth greetings to you all."

Then he sings an entrance song, and after he has made the circuit of the lodge, he sings another one. Then he goes around the lodge again making his strange utterances, until he comes in front of the host. Here he makes a circle with his hand and stops. Then he greets the host as follows: "A great day has come upon us, both upon me and upon all of my relatives. We all have tasted thereof so that we might live thereby. We have all brought you a pipeful of tobacco, just as we were told. It is said that we would thus strengthen one another, and that is why we have done it. I greet you all."

Then he goes to his seat, the second one in the lodge, and sits down. Then all the members of his band sit down, each sending forth a greeting as they take their seats. When they are all seated, the third man invited prepares to enter.

The third one invited now enters, uttering strange sounds, and makes the circuit of the lodge, when he pauses and addresses the host as follows: "Councilors, life-obtainers, relatives who are seated in your respective seats, I greet you all. Here I have been blessed, although I am not worthy of it. My grandfa-

---

4. On account of my participation in this ceremony.

ther, and my father, too, once said to me, 'Some day when there is a dearth of people, some night-blessed one will take pity on you. Submit to it.' Thus he spoke to me and what he referred to was this feast. These feasts are all sacred, but this is the most sacred one. That is what he used to tell me. It is not to be trifled with, even in respect to the rituals within the lodge. Never should one cross the lodge directly. If you trifle with this rule you will bring sorrow to yourselves. The so-called night-soldiers are not to be trifled with. So he told me. The so-called night-soldiers, like soldiers on this earth, are stern. Truly they are stern, said my father. If we were to slight one of them we would most assuredly be punished for it, and punishment by them means death. So he spoke to me. But, said he, 'If, on the other hand, anyone attends to all that pertains to this ceremony it will be a means of obtaining life. It will be a good thing to do, and one would thereby obtain a good life. Therefore, I have always looked upon the night dance with awe, for it is a very holy thing.' So spoke my father. For that reason, consequently, whenever my father gave a night feast he would encourage us to pay careful attention to it, and that is why I have always tried to do so. Remember, however, that I am not a child of the night-blessed ones, and that, therefore, I have very little to say. However, I will start a song, which will be a greeting to this lodge, and I will sing it as I am passing around the lodge. Children of the night-blessed ones, who are seated here, I greet you."

Then he sings an entrance song, first at the west end of the lodge and then near the position occupied by the host. When he has finished the circuit of the lodge he goes around again, making the accustomed peculiar utterances, until he comes in front of the host. There he stops and addresses the host as follows: "I greet you. You have caused this day to come upon me and all my relatives. We have all tasted thereof and we have all felt ourselves in connection with life. We are thankful. We have thought of this blessing of life in connection with ourselves. I greet you."

Then he walks to the place assigned to him in the west end

of the lodge and sits down. The other members of his band do the same, one after the other, greeting the people in the lodge at the same time.

When they are all seated the fourth one come in. He repeats the utterances of the former guests and then starts around the lodge until he reaches the entrance. There he stops and addresses the host: "Councilors and life-obtainers, I greet your seats. I likewise greet you, host. You who are seated in the north and you who are seated in the west, your seats I greet. Children of the night-blessed spirits who are within this lodge, all of you I greet. It is good. As far as I understand this night ceremony is considered a life-giving one. The so-called happy Night Spirits alone are in control of most of life. So I was told, and that is why this ceremony is called a life-giving one. If I participated in this ceremony, I would be able to call it life, I was told. But I did not pay any attention to it. They told me it was good and that I would at the same time be making offerings to Those-with-the Rounded-Wood, and that thus I would be able to make use of all the plants that these spirits control, so that I would never be embarrassed when I wished to use them. I have caused people who were ill to become well by means of this ceremony. All of the plants that these spirits control are good ones, and it is easy to obtain life with them. In this ceremony we may also obtain life by dancing. But we must dance earnestly. The leaders of this ceremony have held council over everything, and yet they have selected us for a seat of honor, so that we might greet them in this lodge and that we might be able to use this song while greeting them. You children of the night-blessed ones, I greet you all."

Then he sings an entrance song, and when he finishes he repeats the utterances used in entering and gradually makes the circuit of the lodge singing. When he is through singing, he again continues the utterances until he comes to the place of the host, where he makes the circle with his hands and stops. Then he addresses the host as follows: "I greet you. You wish me to live, and therefore caused a great day to come upon me and upon all my relatives. We have all received a taste of it, and we have all thought of ourselves in connection with life. We are also bringing you a pipeful of tobacco, so that we may strengthen one another. That is what we thought and that is why we are doing it. I greet you."

Then he walks around the lodge until he comes to his seat. There he stops and addresses his seat as follows: "Seat that is reserved for me and for my relatives, we are about to sit in you; we will do it, and we will think that our lives have been helped thereby. I greet you." Thus he speaks and sits down. Then all the other members of his band sit down one by one.

When they are all seated the lodge is full. Then the host rises and speaks as follows: "You who are seated in the first position, I greet you; you who are seated in the north position, I greet you; you who are seated in the west position, I greet you; and you who are seated at the end of the road, I greet you. Children of the night-blessed ones who are here, I greet you. My father and my grandfather spoke to me of this ceremony, and they told me it was good. They told me that the one who first obtained it was named 'Little Red Turtle.' He fasted and was blessed by those whom he called the Beings-with-Round-Wood. By these was he blessed at the noon hour, and he was taught what to do. There they taught him all. At a place where the stars touched land they caused it to become night, and there they blessed him and taught him how to make four circles and also certain songs. Since then this ceremony has been performed. He was really blessed, and he was told exactly how everything should be performed. So it is said. As he was very fond of the night feast, he spoke in its behalf, and told of all the medicines that were associated with it and of the use to which they could be put. I myself know that these medicines are good to live on. If anyone uses them he will receive benefits therefrom and his children will receive life. I know that they are good. I would not have you think that I am one of those blessed by the Night Spirits because I say this. But I know that all the medicines of which I have personal charge and to which I make offerings of tobacco, for whom I boiled food, always make the individual to whom I offer them the better for it, provided that I do everything correctly. I was told to do this, and that is why I do it. I am now going to sing some songs audibly, and all these songs will be songs about medicines. I know that we will cause you to fan your faces,[5] but forgive us for it. Children of the night-blessed ones who are seated here, I greet you, and to take the place of their sister whom they always place ahead of them so we also will have our sisters lead the dance for us."

Two women now rise and stand side by side in front of the men and hold, one in each hand, the invitation sticks that had been returned. These two women lead in the dance. The men who shake the gourds stand with their backs to the women, facing the drummers. All sing together and all the dancers have partners at their sides. It is a very interesting dance. Then all get up and start around the lodge, making strange utterances. When they have made the complete circuit of the lodge they stop and sing. When they finish this song they start around the lodge again, repeating the utterances. They stop at the west end of the lodge, where they sing again. They thus sing at both ends of the lodge. They use all the songs they intend to. When the last song is over the individual who has sung it makes four circles and then takes the drum, gourd, tobacco, and so forth, and places them in front of the guest who occupies the first seat of honor. Then all sit down.

Then the east leader[6] rises and speaks as follows: "Councilors and life-obtainers, relatives who are seated here, I send you all greetings; and to you who are on the north side, and you who are on the west side, and you who are at the end of the road, your seats I greet. Our host has passed over to me the means of our meditation, the instruments through which we ask life. This instrument for asking life is the foremost thing we possess, so the old people said. We are thankful for it. We know that Earthmaker did not put us in charge of anything, and that for that reason the tobacco we received is our greatest and foremost thing. So the old people said. We were told that we should use it to ask for life. This must have been what they meant. This, the instrument with which to ask life, is, I feel

---

5. From perspiration brought on by making you work too hard.

6. From here on the terms east leader, north leader, west leader, and south leader are used to designate, respectively, the first, second, third, and fourth guests in the order of their invitation.

sure, sufficient to attract them and they will surely take notice of it. We may also follow him who is taking the place of the spirits, and we will consider all those who are in the lodge blessed. Those whom we call Nights have been offered tobacco, and the same has been offered to the four cardinal points, and to all the life-giving plants. To this many tobacco has been offered. It will strengthen us. This is what we call imitating the spirits, and that is why we are doing it. Children of the night-blessed ones who are seated here, I greet you all. The song we will now start is a pipe-lighting song."

When he finishes singing he greets all those in the lodge and then he lights his pipe. Then he takes a number of puffs. First he inhales some smoke and blows it toward the east, then toward the north, then toward the west, then toward the south. Then he passes it around and all smoke, except the host, who is not permitted to do so. Then the east leader speaks again as follows: "Night-blessed ones who are seated here, I greet you. The instrument with which to ask life I will now place here, and if any of you want to fill your pipes you may do so."

Then the leader of the north band rises and speaks as follows: "Councilors and life-obtainers, you who sit in the direction where the day comes from, you who sit on the other side, in the west, and you who sit at the end of the road, your seats I all greet. We, too, have been anxious to obtain the instrument whereby we ask life, and therefore we fill a pipe for ourselves. I greet you."

Then the leader of the south band rises and says as follows: "If the leader of the north band has finished his greeting, I also would very much like to have the instrument with which we ask life brought to me. We will immediately go and fill a pipe. I am speaking now because I wish to tell you what I intend to do. I greet you."

The leader of the north band does not pass the pipe that he had filled all around the lodge, but merely passes it to the members of his band. Only they smoke from it. In the same way the leaders of the other bands, with the exception of the host's band, pass the pipe only to members of their individual bands. Only the host passes his pipe all around the lodge. When the smoking is over the leader of the east band rises and greets everyone. Then he speaks as follows: "Our grandfathers used to carry on this ceremony, I have been told. They told me that if at any time the giver of this ceremony cannot find enough people to invite he would take pity on me. This is what I should say, my father told me. In the direction from which the day comes, there where the Nights are, live the night-soldiers, who blessed my grandfather and who made him try his powers in the middle of the ocean—there where it is deepest. They placed a round object of wood before him and the night-soldiers said that they would not take it away, and that every time my grandfather tried to seize it he would not miss. 'You have done well, human, you have won,' they said to him. For this reason it was considered an instrument of war, he told me. If you do your utmost in offering tobacco, it will be an instrument of war, he said."

And he also says the following: "All the plants with which I have been blessed are useful and a person can receive life through them if he takes good care of them. These plants can be very powerful and some of them can even be used in playing jokes, we are told. But we have never used any of them in such a manner, for if we did our plants would surely lose their strength. I have been told that should I frequently use any of my plants for the purpose of playing jokes and then for the purpose of curing a sick person, they would have no power at all. If, however, I never used them in jokes my medicine would always be powerful. Therefore I have never used them in that manner. Nor have I ever poisoned anyone with them. I never considered myself great or used a Night's trick-medicine or used fire, although I was told I could do so. This I never did. When I use one of the plants I like to have it do its work. I am saying this, although I am not a child of the night-blessed ones. It is now about time to permit our sisters to get hold of the 'chief sticks' and to permit them to sit here and sing together with us."

The women are then permitted to take two sticks apiece and sing wherever they are sitting. As soon as the men sing the women join in. They sing: "This is the way to do, I was told,

136

and that is why I am doing it. Children of the night-blessed ones, who are seated here in this lodge, I send you all greeting."

When he is through with his starting song he stands up and speaks to them again, as follows: "Night-blessed ones who are within this lodge, I greet you. I was not invited to take this seat because I was a wise man. I do not for a moment imagine that, but it was done in order to help me obtain life. We will now rise and go forth and we will brush against your faces, but you must take pity on us. Children of the night-blessed ones, I greet you. We will not remain seated here but we will rise and go forth in order to obtain the round stick. That is why I am making this announcement to you. I greet you."

Then they rise and make four circuits of the lodge, first stopping at the first seat, then at the second, then at the third, and last at the fourth. When they get back to their starting place they sing dancing songs, first stopping at the west end of the lodge and then at the entrance. This they repeat. By this time all the songs they had intended using have been sung, so they make four circuits of the lodge and then, taking the drum, gourd, and so forth, place them in front of the north band. When the dancers are all seated the leader of the north band rises, and greeting everyone speaks as follows: "I was not pitied because I was a child of the night-blessed ones, my father told me. Yet if I performed my duties aright I would be able to make the proper speeches when called upon, I was told. That I have been pitied now is due to the fact that these people here wished to have me obtain life. Certainly my invitation to this ceremony has made me think of life, as my father used to tell me. I do not for a moment imagine that they invited me because I was a great man. Nevertheless my father told me to say that it was good; and that if I really meant all that I said, my life would certainly be strengthened thereby. My father knew how to perform this ceremony correctly, but I am not able to do so. Although I was told it was a good thing, nevertheless, I was not able to pour tobacco. Those whom we call the Ones-with the Rounded-Wood are in charge of very much life and they are holy. This affair is not a thing to be trifled with, my father told me. Yet in spite of this we will sing some songs, even though we know that we will not be able to sing them as they have been sung heretofore. Perhaps, however, you will be kind enough to be satisfied with whatever we do. Children of the night-blessed ones, I greet you."

Then he sings the starting song, and when he is finished he rises again and, greeting all, speaks as follows: "When Those-with-the-Rounded-Wood start to walk, their sisters are placed in front of them. Our sisters we will now place in front of us, so that thereby they may be blessed with life and hold the principal sticks and staffs. We will use the toys so that we may be strengthened thereby, we think, and that is why I greet you."

Then they permit the women to lead the procession. These women walk in front, side by side, and are followed by the ones carrying the gourds, who dance with their backs toward them. Then come the drummers and the feast givers, and, after these, all those who desire to join. They walk around the lodge making strange utterances. Four times do they make the circuit of the lodge and then they come and stop at the east end, where they sing. When they are through here they start around the lodge again and stop at the west end and sing. Then they start again, making the same strange utterances as before, until they come to the east end of the lodge, where they sing once more. When they have in this manner sung all the songs that they wish to use the leader of the north band makes the four circles as before and brings the tobacco, gourds, and so forth, to the west band. Then they all take their seats.

Now the leader of the west band rises and speaks as follows: "Councilors, life-obtainers, relatives, to you all who are seated here, I send forth my greetings. You who occupy the first seat, you who occupy the north seat, and you who occupy the seat at the end of the road, I greet. I do not mean to say anything of consequence. I was taught this ceremony, but I do not know anything about it. However, I always honored it, for I was told that it was a good thing. Indeed, I knew it, but I could never perform it well. I was told that if I performed it well I would obtain life thereby, just as others have done. Well, some of you are able to do it. It is a very great council feast.

How, indeed, can the spirits ignore what you have done for them today? If they acknowledge it, we who are representing the directions will receive blessings through the host who is giving the feast. That is what I mean. When we hold our mediators[7] we will be strengthened thereby. So with this in our minds, let us take and hold them. Children of the night-blessed ones, I greet you."

Then he sings the starting song, and when he has finished he rises and speaks again. "Councilors, I send you greetings, as well as to you who sit in the first seat, to you who sit in the north, and to you who sit at the end of the road. It is said that when the night-soldiers come they walk over the entire extent of the earth. When they blessed my grandfather they blessed him with life. So he used to say of himself. We will now plead for these powers in our songs. We will place our sisters in front and follow them. That is what I wanted to announce to you. Children of the night-blessed ones who are seated here, I greet you."

Then they make the complete circuit of the lodge until they come to the place where they have been sitting. There they make a circle. Then they make another circuit of the lodge and stop in front of the south position and make a circle. Here they make another circuit of the lodge and stop at the east end and make a circle. Then they make the last circuit of the lodge and stop in front of the north band and make a circle. By this time all the songs that they were to use have been sung. The leader now makes four circuits and brings the gourds, drum, tobacco, and so forth, in front of the south band.

All now take their seats and when they are seated the leader of the south band rises and speaks as follows: "Councilors, life-obtainers, I greet you. You who sit in the first seat, you who sit in the north, and you who sit in the west, I greet. Children of the night-blessed ones who are seated within this lodge, I greet you all. It is good that tonight you have tried to imitate your grandfathers, that you have tried to take the place of the spirits. You have said enough with which to obtain life.

---

7. I.e., the drums, tobacco, etc.

But I am more unfortunate. I can never do what my ancestors did or say what they said, and for that reason I suppose my talk will be quite worthless. I was told that if at any time I should be pitied, not to talk foolishly about this ceremony. If I am a bad man I will act foolishly in this affair, I was told. My grandfather was blessed by those whom we call the night-soldiers, who blessed him with certain utterances. As many blackbirds as there are, that many appeared to him as Night Spirits. Our utterances will be an imitation of those he received when he was blessed. We can only guess at these. We were told that when we hold the mediators we will be strengthened by them. Night-blessed spirits who are seated here, I greet you."

Then he begins the starting songs, and when these are finished he rises and speaks again: "Councilors, life obtainers, I greet your seats. You who sit in the east, you who sit in the north, and you who sit in the west, I greet you all. Children of the night-blessed ones, I greet you. Those whom we call night-soldiers treated their sisters as holy and placed them in front. In imitation of these soldiers we will now put our sisters in front, so that we may be strengthened thereby. I wish to announce that we now place the women at the head of our procession. Let us all come together, so that we may be strengthened. That is our desire and that is what we are plead-ing for. I greet you."

When they are ready to begin the dancing songs all rise and form in line, having the women lead them. Then the men with the gourds, their backs turned to the women, follow, then the drummers. Then all those join who feel so inclined. When they have finished all the songs they intend to use they bring back the drum, gourd, and so forth, to the middle of the lodge and stop dancing. Then they return to their seats and the leader rises and says: "Councilors, relatives who are seated here, I greet you. You who are seated in the first seat, you who sit in the north, and you who sit in the west, night-blessed ones who are within this lodge, I greet you all. Whenever a night-blessed child holds council, when he is invited to a feast and is given the position at the end of the road, the intention of the feast giver is to enable him to obtain life. So they told me, and that is what they meant. Most assuredly have they caused me to think of life. When I hold the mediators in my hand I am holding life, and when I pass them on to the others, to my relatives and to my sisters, I am passing on life to all of them. In this way we were made to think of life. I will not detain you any longer. All that I wish to say is that I am thankful. Children of the night-blessed ones, I greet you."

Then he sits down and the host rises and speaks as follows: "You who sit in the east, you who sit in the north, you who sit in the west, and you who sit at the end of the road, I greet you all. It is good. This is what I wanted but have not been able to say. You, however, told it all in my place. It is good. Of all things this is the foremost, it is said. The instruments with which to ask life you have placed before me. That alone is enough to live on and that you have done for me. It is good. Your forefathers dreamed just as the spirits did, and how they obtained life, all of that you have told me tonight. It is good. You have said enough to obtain life. It is good. I say this because I am thankful. If you do anything, do it in the right way, I was told. I understand this ceremony, but nevertheless what I have done is the best I could do. I will now place the food before you. I am an old man, but I have always performed this affair just as I have performed it today, and, although I know that I have not done it in the right way, yet it was my turn to do it, and I did it. I am an old man, and for that reason I am not able to procure meat anywhere. My relatives helped me and that is why I have been able to do it. Here are four kettles of hot water. I will place them in the center of the lodge for you. The one in the east and the one in the north and the one in the west and the one at the end of the road; each one may have it. Children of the night-blessed ones, all who are seated here, to all do I send greetings."

Then the leader of the east band rises and says: "Councilors, I greet you. You who sit over there in the north, you who sit in the west, and you who sit at the end of the road, I greet you all. Children of the night-blessed ones who are in this lodge, I greet you. We are all to arise soon and that is why I announce this."

Then the leader of the north band rises and says: "We also will rise, as it is our turn. We greet you all."

Then the leader of the west band rises and says: "The time has come for us to rise. I and my relatives will now rise. We greet you all."

Then the leader of the south band rises and says: "Councilors, I greet you. I greet all who have been blessed by the Night Spirits, each one in turn. We are now going to rise."

Then the leader of the east band says again: "Councilors, I greet you. We will now greet the hot water and I will use a song."

Then the leader of the north band says: "I also will start a song. I greet you."

Then the leader of the west band says: "I also will start a song. I greet you."

Then the leader of the south band says: "I also will start a song. I greet you."

Then the leader of the east band sings a song, and the other leaders sing their songs. Each band sings its own songs, not paying any attention to the songs of the others. Each band sings different songs. This they do in order to drown out the voices of the others. Should one band overcome the other, it means that that particular band would be blessed with victory in war. What they are really saying is that their songs are more powerful than the others, and that their grandfathers' songs are the holiest. Then they all dance around the lodge, single file, and make their exit from the lodge. While they are dancing, the host sits still singing and beating his drum. They carry their kettles outside. Wherever they wish to eat, there they go and dance around the kettle of food first. Then they eat their meal. They dance in different bands.

The ceremony finishes with this feast. It is customary, however, for the one who has been given the seat of honor, that is, the east seat, to give a feast immediately afterwards. Then the one who has been invited first would do the same thing, so that all four would in this manner give dances in rotation. For this reason it generally took five nights before the ceremony was over. During those five nights no one could sleep. It is from this fact that the word "Sore-eye Dance," which is the general term used for this ceremony, originated. If a person does not sleep for five nights, his eyes generally get sore, and that is why they call this ceremony the "Sore-eye Dance."

V. Menominee Bundle Ceremonials

During the vision or dream, the tutelary being may inform the human person what objects he should obtain as a kind of token. Various objects—stones of some special shape or quality, animal and bird skins, tails, feathers, carved wooden objects, beads, and the like—may be so indicated, and, when obtained, are kept in a pouch—hence the term "medicine bundle." On the death of the owner, his bundle may be buried with him. But in some instances it is not, and it and the power it represents are inherited by another—usually a relative. Over time, a special ceremony may come to be regarded as appropriately performed for the bundle, and hence a ritual customarily performed.

Yet other bundles, although owned by individuals, had their origin in the distant past, and are regarded as having power of use to all, and hence have an associated ritual in which a number of people may participate. The following are examples from the Menominee—a people among whom medicine bundles of various types and with various uses have assumed some prominence, which is not always the case. The importance of bundles in religious belief and practice varies considerably among the Indians of North America.

The first illustration is an account of how Me'napus,[1] a culture hero similar to the Iroquois hero whose name may be translated Sky-Holder, obtained one of the great hunting medicine bundles for the Menominee; who may use it; and how it is used. The second illustration is an account of the origin of a bundle having war powers. This is followed by a description of how a war bundle is used.

Myth and Ritual of a Menominee Medicine Bundle[2]

In the beginning, Me'napus was troubled on behalf of his uncles and aunts, the men and women of the world, because they were subject to starvation. There were wicked medicine men who were befriended by the horned owl and who were ever abroad plaguing the people. These evil old men would circle about in the bushes in the guise of their guardian owls watching the Indians. If any man had good luck in hunting, one of these evil men would steal it away for himself. Just out of spite he would drive away the deer, bewitch the traps, and, drawing the leaden pellets from the hunter's rifles, he would substitute shadowy spirit bullets of his own so that no matter how truly they were aimed the hunter's shot had no more effect than if he had really missed. Me'napus was downcast in his heart, for he did not seem to have the power to destroy these men. And since he was so sorrowful in behalf of the people, the powers above, the grandfathers and grandmothers of the Indians, took council and decided to give him a mighty charm that he might pass on to the people to help and save them.

---

1. See Bloomfield, *Menomini Texts*, pp. 133–159 for Menominee accounts of the birth of Me'napus.

2. From Skinner, *Social Life and Ceremonial Bundles of the Menomini Indians*, Anthropological Papers of the American Museum of Natural History 13, no. 1 (1913), pp. 132–140. In the following, Skinner's spelling of the name of the culture hero has been changed to that used by Bloomfield, *Menomini Texts*. Most of the other changes here made have been to eliminate words in Menominee. The notes are taken from Skinner's account.

When the grandfathers prepared to give the bag to Me'napus, a little beaver, a young one, was at the far side of the great water and though he was so far away he knew by telepathy what was happening. Then he thought, "I too will help Me'napus and his uncles and aunts." So he swam quickly along the shore toward where the grandfathers were giving the bundle to Me'napus and he came so smoothly and so quietly that he left neither wave nor ripple. As he approached where Me'napus stood, he began to sing:

> Me too, nephew, now I am here,
> Me too, nephew, now I am here;
> If you obey me,
> If you obey me.

"Now," said he, "though I am not a hunting animal to have a right to be in the bundle, yet to show my good will to the people, your uncles and aunts, I will give my skin to be in the bundle to hold medicines."

"All right, my little brother, you can come in the bundle and help the people when they perform this ceremony," cried Me'napus. So he took in the little beaver to hold medicine.

The weasels, who are mighty hunters, who run softly like snakes through the grass in summer, and in winter under the snow, they who are always sure of game when they go hunting, they too came to show their good will toward the people, the aunts and uncles of Me'napus. The weasel came to Me'napus and said, "I shall enter by the deer's mouth and pass out of his rectum, I shall kill him as I pass through his vitals," and he sang a song.

"All right, my little brother, you too shall be in the medicine bundle to help my aunts and uncles, the people, to hunt." So Me'napus put the weasel in the bundle, and weasel's skin may still be found there.

The mink is a mighty hunter, he is always successful in getting game, he always returns quickly from the hunt with food. He asked to come in the bundle too that he might hold the tiny bow and arrows and their medicine, which the grandfathers and grandmothers had put there. He also sang a song to Me'napus.

"All right, my little brother," said Me'napus, "you too shall come in the bundle, even as you have asked, to hold the little bow and arrows and their medicine."

Then the bird begged to come in too, and Me'napus permitted him to enter that he might give the people the power to fly from place to place when they hunted as swiftly as he.

Now there were many medicines in the bag that the grandfathers gave Me'napus, and each one had its own song, and the chief of these medicines were: one for the deer, one for the wolf, one for the bear, and one for the skunk. And there was one to prevent the evil medicine man from harming whosoever was the possessor of the bundle, and there was one medicine to destroy the ordinary human enemies of the bundle owner.

So Me'napus took the bundle and learned its uses from the grandfathers. Then he passed it on to his uncles and aunts, the Indian people, that they might outwit those evil medicine men and have food to keep them alive. And it can only be possessed by a few; not any common man may have it, only such as receive it as a reward for their fasting and suffering or to whom it is given in a vision. Only men of great power may have it, and it may not be used or even opened without reason. Women must never use or touch the bag, it is only given to men. A woman who inherits one may learn its songs, but she must pass them on with the bundle to her husband or other male relative.

Now when one of those evil medicine men is plaguing the people, absorbing their luck, tampering with their guns and traps, and driving away the game so that the people starve; then they know it is time to call upon the owner of the bundle So a delegation of men approaches him with great gifts and tobacco. He accepts these gifts, and though he knows why the men have come he ask them their errand.

"Well, we have come because we are starving, one of those evil medicine men is tormenting us. Now we want you to open the bundle for us so that we may eat. That is why it was given you and you cannot refuse."

"Very well," says the bundle owner, "it shall be as you say! Tomorrow we will journey far off in the clean woods where we may not be disturbed, and there we will open it."

The time and place having been thus decided on, the party breaks up, to be on hand at the time appointed. Then the owner takes the bundle from the place where it is sacredly and carefully kept and brings it to the spot that they have decided upon, far away in the clean woods.

When they have all gathered in the evening, they make a feast of meat, if they have it, or of corn and bean soup, but if they have nothing, then tobacco must serve. They must eat all that is set before them and a cupful of maple sugar. Then the bundle is opened and before they feast, its contents are spread about. When they have feasted, the pipe is passed and the bundle owner makes a speech in which he explains how Me'napus got the bundle and its use to mankind. He explains that the feast is eaten in memory of the bundle. Then he opens the mink skin and takes out the little bow and the little arrows which are always fastened point foremost in a bag of red-colored medicine. He removes the arrows and strings the bow. His assistant, for he has chosen one to help him, draws the figure of a deer on the ground and the bundle owner shoots it with the little bow and arrow. This symbolizes the slaying of the game on the morrow, for which the young men have already built a scaffold as soon as they encamped, so fully do they believe that they will have game to hang there on the morrow.

Having shot the figure of the deer, the bundle owner takes two of the clappers and his assistant another pair, and they begin. The first song is called "a bag of leaves," and refers in an esoteric way to the bundle and its contents as they lie spread out before him. Then he sings:

> Leaves are applied to the animals as medicine,
> Leaves are applied to the animals as medicine;
> Yes, and I am the one who is unable to do it,
> Yes, and I am the one who is unable to do it.

The song is sung in this way for several reasons. One is to deceive the enemy who may be lurking about to hear, and make him believe that the shaman has only some old leaves. By denying, in a way, that the bundle can actually assist him, the owner is daring it to help, or, rather, trying to arouse its pride.

This song and the second song are not so important as the two following. The song runs:

> At that time when I was able to sit up,
> At that time when I was able to sit up;
> My parents' fire was in full blaze,
> My parents' fire was in full blaze.

That is, "When I was in my childhood, my parents were in the power and prime of life." It refers to Me'napus, who was as weak as a child, and unable to assist his aunts and uncles, until his parents, the great powers above and below, who were so much more powerful than he and full of mature vigor, lent their aid.

The next song, like all the others, is many times repeated:

> I will eat meat tomorrow,
> I will eat meat tomorrow;
> I will surely eat meat tomorrow,
> I will surely eat meat tomorrow.

After the third song comes the fourth and last of the chants:

> I will see him, Red Legs,[3] tomorrow,
> I will see him, Red Legs, tomorrow;
> The deer is killed,
> The deer is killed;
> A deer I am well pleased with,
> A deer I am well pleased with;
> I am dressing the carcass of a deer,

---

3. The deer.

I am dressing the carcass of a deer;
The man, the man;
The man, the man.[4]

During the singing of the last song all the company except the bundle owner and his assistant dance and during the dance they imitate the chase to take place the following day, that it may all fall about as they act it. One man will hold his two hands with fingers outspread close to his head to signify a big buck with horns. Another will hold up his two hands near his ears with the fingers closed to represent the big ears of a fat doe. Another will hold out both hands with the index and second fingers open and spread out and the rest clenched to signify the cloven hoofs of a buck. Another will go through the motions of shooting one of the animals, who falls, and another Indian pretends to draw, skin, and quarter him.

Then there are songs sung for each of the medicines. At the end of the ceremony a young man of clean life and who has not yet known woman is instructed by the bundle owner to carry the bundle a short distance from the camp to a clean spot, and hang it on the limb of a tree. Then all retire. Then the bundle owner throws a powder from the bundle in the fire so that an evil medicine man cannot approach, for should he attempt to do so he would be stricken blind. So he is unable to steal game from the bundle users and he has no power whatever over the owner.

During the night the bundle hunts, that is, the powers in the bundle go forth and pass about through the nearby forest, causing the deer and other game to become tame and sluggish. It attacks their heads and makes them stupid; it affects their lungs so that they have great difficulty in breathing; it gets into their legs so that they can neither run nor jump.

On the following morning, when the hunters arise, they eat a heavy breakfast. Ordinarily hunters never eat any breakfast for fear of ill luck, but the bundle party is protected from any such catastrophe. After breakfast, the bundle is opened

---

4. I.e., the buck deer, the male deer.

again and a smudge is made with one of the medicines contained in the bundle and the men hold their bows or their rifle
muzzles downward in the smoke to let the virtue of the medicine impregnate them and give them power. As they do this
they joke, laugh, and cry out, "seven deer," or "eight deer," or
whatever number they desire to kill for the entire party, and
individuals will cry, "I desire to shoot a doe with two fawns,"
"I want a big buck," "I want a fat doe," and so on. They imitate
at the same time the report of firearms, and all the things they
say and wish for will come to pass through the aid of the
medicine. They also paint small red spots on each cheek to
fascinate the deer.

The owner of the bundle now distributes its contents. He
puts on the wolfskin head band himself, and gives a medicine
to each of his men. The mink, weasel, and other skins are very
powerful medicines because they grant to the man carrying
them the ability to hunt like, and be as successful as, these
animals.

This entire ceremony is repeated every night and morning
for four nights. Each evening when the game is brought in and
butchered, the head, lungs, and legs may not be eaten without
ceremony at that time, because these parts are still filled with
the medicine that attacked them there, and he who is so
thoughtless as to partake of them will be punished, for the
medicine will pass into his body and turn his skin black, and he
will pine away and die. So tabooed parts are skinned and put
away until the four days are over. Should any of the party
desire to partake of them before the time is up, they are obliged
to make a little smudge of cedar leaves and a particular leaf
mixed together. By throwing some of this on some hot coals
held in a frying pan, they obtain a portable fumigant that they
carry beneath the infected parts and thus drive out the medicine and render them clean and fit to eat. This medicine is
called "the reviver back."

On the fourth and last day of the ceremony, the bundle
owner has the party bring all the carcasses together. The meat
is all held in common up to this time, but now the men agree
upon its division among themselves. The briskets, necks, and

breasts with part of the foreribs cut off all in one piece are given to the bundle owner as his share, for it is only right that he should get the choice bits since the success of the hunt was due to his goodness in using the bundle.

When the bundle owner arrives at his home he gets a large kettle and prepares a feast by boiling all the meat he has received. He invites all his family and relatives to partake of the bounty of the sack. Then, as a thanksgiving ceremony, he explains to the guests why the feast is made and tells them the origin and the success of the bundle, and offers it tobacco, begging that it may continue to assist them.

There is one medicine in the packet, the red medicine in which the heads of the tiny arrows are kept, that has one very important special use. Should an enemy pass the camp during the ceremony, or should the track of any enemy be seen, the bundle owner has merely to shoot it with his little bow and arrow and the man will die.

It is not always necessary to take the whole bundle out. Sometimes some of the contents only are taken. Even the smudge has had great effect when used alone. Men who have merely thought or dreamed of the bundle, either before or during a hunt, have been known to have had great success.

A Menominee War Bundle Myth[5]

In that early period in which all Menominee legends take their origin, the sun and the morning star looked down upon their grandchildren, the children of men, and found them constantly embroiled in wars, and, filled with pity for their suffering, they called a council to decide what could be done to bring about a better order of things. They sent for the swift-flying birds,[6] the buffalo, the weasel, and the pine snake, all of whom came to the council out of pity for their neighbors, the children of men.

The swift-flying birds promised to endow the warriors

---

5. From Skinner, *Social Life and Ceremonial Bundles*, pp. 97–101, with editorial changes as in the previous selection.
6. The hawks, the swallows, and the hummingbirds.

with the ability to travel as fast as they can fly, and, if the braves were defeated, they were empowered to put on bird skins and escape by flight. The buffalo gave them his strength and courage, and the weasel agreed to help them stalk their foes even as he pursued his game. He said that they should be as successful in taking scalps as he is in capturing his prey. The pine snake promised that they should have his skill to hide away in the undergrowth to spy upon the enemy, or to escape if they should be hard pressed.

When the animals had completed their donations, the sun and the morning star gathered the presents into a bundle, sent for their thunderbirds and gave it to them to transmit it to the children of men.

A young man named Club-in-his-Hand[7] sorrowed because of the reverses his people were suffering at the hands of their more powerful enemies. So sad was he that he blackened his face with charcoal and retired to an isolated spot to fast and pray. His entreaties reached the ears of the sun and his lieutenant, the morning star. According to their instructions, the Thunderers took pity on him, and sent him word to come to them. He was told to take a straight course westward across the ocean until he came to an island of rock projecting high above the surrounding waters. Here the vision told him he would find the Thunderers. When Club-in-his-Hand awoke from his vision he was overjoyed, but yet afraid. He made a sacrifice to the Powers Above and to the offering he invited seven pure young men who had never used tobacco or known women. When these youths were gathered in his medicine lodge Club-in-his-Hand offered tobacco to the Thunderers and then explained the purpose of the ceremony to his guests, relating his dream and his subsequent fears. The revelation made a profound impression on the young men, who believed his words, and after some discussion they resolved to accompany him on his westward journey to the home of the Thunderers.

Accordingly, the little party, headed by Club-in-his-Hand, set forth for the west. The journey was toilsome and the way

---

7. A "brave name," one of the type bestowed on valiant warriors.

beset with perils. Often the adventurers were tempted to turn back, but always, when it seemed as though human strength and courage could hold out no longer, spirits would appear to them and lure them on, until at length they reached the shore of the Western Ocean. Here they paused, unable to proceed, for they did not know how to go across the water. At this point the Thunderers appeared again to Club-in-his-Hand in a vision and instructed him to build an elm-bark canoe, the first one ever known to man, and the prototype from which all subsequent canoes were modeled.

When the boat was built by Club-in-his-Hand and his seven helpers, they launched it and paddled out to sea. They soon passed beyond sight of land, and for days they were frightened because they could see nothing. Yet invisible spirits accompanied and encouraged them until at last they reached their goal. Here were gathered a great number of Thunderbirds in human form, waiting for them. As soon as Club-in-his-Hand had landed, accompanied by his followers, the chief of the Thunderers, who was greater and handsomer than all others, came forward and addressed him as follows:

> Grandchild, you have come to me according to my command, for I was troubled in heart when I saw you fasting and suffering, growing light in flesh and thin in body. Now you have gained great honor, for I have taken pity on you. I am going to give you this war bundle to use upon the earth. You shall feed it, and give sacrifices to it for my sake and in my behalf. You shall be empowered to use this thing at your desire. It shall protect you, and your children and grandchildren, so that you and they shall live to see your gray hairs. I command you to use it in the way which I shall make clear to you, and if you obey me, it shall obey you.
>
> Tobacco shall be the chief thing to please it, and when you give it tobacco you will delight us, its masters. You shall take these things that I have here back to the earth again, and when you reach your home, you shall make some others according to my instructions.

MENOMINEE BUNDLE CEREMONIALS

Here is an egg, put that in the bundle. Here is a powder, put that in the bundle. These two articles shall enable you to set fire to the earth at your desire. Here is a little bow, the image of an arrow, and a scabbard to carry. Here are all the birds of the air, that are after my kind. They will lend their assistance when trouble overtakes you. Take this red paint along, that you may apply it to your men who accompany you when you go to war, and the sight of it will please me. It will put new life into you and your men. Through my magical power I gave you the dream that called you here to see me; through it you shall be able to destroy the enemies that intend to kill you. You shall conquer, and victory will always be yours. The enemies that you shall slay will be food for me and for the war bundle.

When you return you shall carve my image upon a board and place it in the bundle, in order to please me. You must take two plain square blocks, and upon each of these outline my figure in sacred red paint, one shall represent me as a Great Powered Bird, and one shall represent me as a man with a flintlock gun in my hand. I am of dual nature. I can change myself into either a bird or a man at will.

(And indeed the Thunder-bird-beings have been known to come to earth in human form. They have appeared as homely men, short and thick-set, with heavy muscles in their arms and legs, and bearing a bow and arrows in their hands. Ordinary persons can scarcely recognize them as Thunderers, but those who have received power from them in their dreams know them at once for what they are.)

I give you the power to know and see me in your night sleeps. You shall be forewarned of your enemies' plans. You shall know beforehand whether you shall win or lose your battles. You shall do all your fighting at night, and you shall destroy your enemies during their sweet sleep.

Before you go out to war you shall first prepare and give feasts to the war bundle. You shall sacrifice to it in behalf of the Thunderbirds. You shall receive that for which you ask us, for I shall assist you. Call on me through those sacred things that I have given you, and you shall have the thick fog settle down and hide you from the enemy so that you may escape under its cover. You shall have the lightning and hail to cripple the wicked foe when he troubles you.

You shall seek your enemy in the night through this bundle. You shall approach him with the stealth of the snake in pursuit of its prey, and encircle his village. Let each warrior carry the image of one of the medicine birds with him, with a single quill feather fastened in his hair, and as the hummingbird is so small in flight that none can hit it with a rifle ball, so shall each warrior be. As it is impossible to strike the edge of a knife blade ground sharp and held off edgewise from the body, so shall you and your warriors be. These things I say to you that you may understand the power of the medicines that I have placed in the war bundle.

You shall make incense of a portion of each of the sacred roots that I have included, and you shall purify yourselves with the fumes. You shall carry a little of each in your mouth, and you shall chew some of them and spray yourselves and your warriors with your saliva, that they may elude the keen vision of the enemy, for the eyesight of the enemy shall be destroyed when they approach.

When you have drawn near and surrounded the village, you shall signal on the war whistle, and you and your warriors shall rush to the attack. You shall destroy the sleeping enemy with tomahawks and war clubs that have been kept in the powerful medicine until they are saturated. Those who awake shall try to escape, but cannot, for the medicines that I have given shall sap their strength and benumb their minds. When a warrior takes a scalp he shall lick the fresh blood from it; this he must do as a sign that the enemy are devoured in behalf of us, the Thunderers.

When the fighting is over, then you shall make a great ceremony with dancing, for the war bundle and for us, the Thunderers. You shall thank us for the assistance we have rendered you. Then you shall sing songs for the scalps that have been taken with valor.

Always respect the war bundle we have given you. Be careful to keep it tied with a string, and keep it hung in a place by itself, outside of the house, away from the women, and the maidens who are just arrived at the threshold of womanhood. Especially keep it concealed from those women who are having their monthly courses. The bundle must never be opened for nothing, as that would be a serious offense to it, and to us, the Thunderers. It may only be opened in time of peril, or when you sacrifice to it in the spring or in the fall of the year for our sake. Yet this I say, in case of an accident, even in peace it may be opened and the roots it contains may be used to stop the bleeding, but you shall not forget to pay us in tobacco for our help.

And this is not yet all that I have to say. One thing that you must make when you get home, or which the women may make for you, is a wampum belt. This you shall make of coarse long beads. It shall be put in the bundle to be kept as a reward for the brave warrior who kills a chief or leader among the enemy. It shall be given to him as a great honor.

When the Thunderer had finished speaking, he called to his servants to fetch food, prepare it, and place it before Club-in-his-Hand and his followers. The servants departed immediately and soon returned bringing a quantity of sturgeon, which they cooked and set before their guests.

"Now, eat and depart," said the chief of the Thunderers. "This is the only food we can offer you. For ourselves, we may not touch it, for we feed upon the horned snakes and evil monsters of the underworld, which in their turn cannot be food for you."

So Club-in-his-Hand and his followers obeyed and when they were filled they took their leave of the islet and its inhabitants. As they entered their canoe the water lay still as glass, the sun shone brightly, and they soon reached the shore from whence they started. The overland journey from that point was equally devoid of its former perils. Food was abundant and they had never need to draw their bows, for game they met fell dead before them, so powerful was the spell cast by their war bundles. So at length they arrived among their own people again and imparted to them the story of their successful venture and from that day to this, the war bundle has been on earth among men and its powers are granted to the worthy in their dreams.

Menominee War Bundle Ritual[8]

The ceremonies for the war bundles occur in the fall and early in the spring when the voices of the Thunderers are first heard. The bundle is opened and the leader says to his company: "My grandfather, I make you this sacrifice."

A feast of meat is prepared meanwhile, not a great deal, but enough for two or three mouthfuls, and this is placed in the little wooden bowls that usually accompany the bundle for this purpose. When the food is put in the dishes these songs are sung. Twice is enough, but they may be repeated indefinitely. Each one represents a stage of action at the feasts.

> I am the first brave man to kill you,
> I am truly the God.

> All day I tell you
> This earth I tell you.

> In fog where I walk.

The owner of the bundle is fed by an attendant who takes the food from his dish with a wooden skewer and places it in the leader's mouth with these words: "Now then, we sacrifice to you Thunderbird who have given this war bundle. This man shall eat what is offered to you (in your stead)."

At the conclusion of the feast, tobacco of two kinds, both plug and smoking, is given to the bundle with these words: "Now I sacrifice tobacco to you, white mat, and to the great thunderbirds that made this and gave it to man and this earth."

The owner now passes out to the people the stale tobacco of former offerings saying, "O war bundle, handed down to us poor Indians to use when we are in trouble, we now sacrifice to you in behalf of the people," and turning to those assembled says, "Take part now."

Should the owner be alone at the sacrifice he must attend to the renovating of the tobacco and the other details himself.

---

8. From Skinner, *Social Life and Ceremonial Bundles*, pp. 106–117, with editorial changes as in the previous selection.

Casting the weed on the flames he says, "Here is the tobacco that was offered to you, but I now give it to our grandfather, the fire." He throws the tobacco and addresses the fire, "You consume it in behalf of the Thunderers and I pray that they may grant me long life, and, in addition, happiness for my family."

The tobacco is placed in the bundle, and it is consumed by the Thunderers, although in substance it remains unchanged. It is well to remove this old sacrificial tobacco from time to time, putting back some that is fresh. The old tobacco may either be used at the place where the bundle is stored, or it may be taken home by the owner and his friends and consumed at their leisure. It may be smoked in their pipes, or cast on a dish of coals, or on the fire. In the latter case, the sacrifice should be accompanied by these words: "I give a general smoke to all the manitous and it shall be consumed according to the way of the olden times."

In the old days, when the head men of the Menominee villages decided to declare a general war for any reason, runners were sent to the other districts, or, in more ancient times when the clans[9] lived apart, to territories of the various clans. Each messenger carried tobacco and a string of wampum, "as long as a man is high," painted red as a symbol that blood was to be shed. Wherever these tokens were delivered they were instantly recognized by the recipients as an invitation to war, and the people either refused them, or gathered at some designated spot.

General wars were infrequent, and were called only in extreme cases to retaliate for tribal injuries. Small war parties were organized to settle some old score, or to furnish excitement for the young men. Sometimes the sun would appear in a vision to a bundle owner, saying: "I am going to feed you. You shall eat.[10] I shall feed you and this war bundle. Go and eat up[11] the enemy."

9. See chap. 6.
10. See chap. 3, note 30.
11. Literally, "Take your war bundle and attack such a tribe."

Word was sent among the young men, who prepared to set forth.[12] It was customary to pluck out all the hair except the scalp lock, which depended in a thin braid from the crown, and a large round patch covering the top of the head, save for a wide margin from nape to forehead, something like the roach of the Sauk and Fox, but much broader. This was to render the taking of the scalp easier should an enemy be brave enough to slay the wearer. The removal of the hair at the back of the neck and particularly the base of the skull is said to have been the most painful part of the process. Two long thin braids dangled from the crown. The owner of the bundle, or leader, preceded the party with the war bundle slung over his back. He was not allowed to deviate from his path or to turn back while he bore the bundle. As he marched along he sang:

> The warrior of the sacred bundle now starts.
> As he walks he is seeking for the enemy.

After they had gone forward for some distance they halted and the leader caused a long lodge of boughs to be built. He entered the structure, opened the bundle, and spread out its contents. Then the pipe was passed. It was filled and lighted by an attendant who handed it to the leader, who held the bowl in his hand and revolved it slowly so that the mouthpiece described an arc through the air. This was done so that the spirits might partake. After this he made the following speech: "Now, Thunderbirds, you have created this war bundle for us yourselves. You have given us this power to use with these birds and roots. You have told us to use them in this way, and we now place our tobacco upon these tokens, praying that you will now give us power to defeat the enemy." Whereupon the pipe was handed to his followers and passed from left to right. Then a dog was slain and eaten.[13] Some of its flesh was offered to the bundle with tobacco and a war song was sung in praise of the contents of the palladium. It was as follows:

---

12. Destroy.
13. A dog feast before starting out for war is also reported for other tribes in the Upper Great Lakes area.

These things we use are truly of god power,
Powerful are the things that we use
God said to us they shall be powerful.

The war dance was next enacted. It was a spirit spectacle. The warriors threw their bodies into dramatic postures, giving the war cry and singing the war song to the thumping of a drum. With this dance went the following three songs, which were sung before the party proceeded.

Where I volunteer to fight
As I am walking along.

Savage I am
As god I am.

Brave I am called.

When the country of the tribe to be attacked was reached, scouts were sent out to report the whereabouts of the enemy. As soon as the village of the foe was located, the war party approached during the night according to the instructions of the Thunderers. Just before daybreak, at the hour when sleep is soundest and man's vitality is said to be at its lowest ebb, was the favorite time for the assault, from which circumstance war parties are often referred to as "night warriors." When the marauders had drawn near, the leader opened the bundle and sang this sacred war song to the accompaniment of the deer hoof rattles:

I myself, I am surely,
Over and over, God, I am.

This song stupefied the enemy and caused him to sleep more soundly.

Then the leader distributed the sacred medicines among his warriors, according to the instructions given by the Thunderers, giving to one the skin of a bird or weasel, to another a tiny carved war club, or a feather, until each one had some charm. The men bound these on their heads or bodies and slipped out to surround the village. When the camp was encircled, the leader gave the signal on his whistle and the warriors began the combat.

The fighting was done principally with bows and arrows, but men who had received promises of protection from the Thunderers often carried clubs alone. Some of the old men say that small round shields of buffalo or other ruminant hide were carried. Many wore arm bands to which were attached metal jinglers. The sound of these was thought to be efficacious to lull the slumbering enemy. There were songs for dealing the death blow, of which the following is an example:

I grasp you now.

While the members of the party were fighting, the leader stayed behind with the bundle and took no part in the fray. Indeed he was often unarmed. As fast as scalps were taken, they were brought to him by the successful warriors, who received some present from the bundle as a reward. If a brave found and scalped the body of a man he had not killed, it was not considered such a feat as though he had slain the foe himself. He announced the fact and received praise, but no compensation.

When the fighting was over, the party returned. On the way back the warriors spent their leisure time stretching the scalps on hoops and drying them in the sun. The bundle contains a noxious medicine that was rubbed on the inner surface of the scalps, so that if anyone had been scalped and still lived, he would die, no matter how far away he might be. As the party drew near the village, the people came out and met them with great rejoicing.

When they reached the place where the ceremonies had been held on the outward journey, the scalp dance was given to proclaim the miraculous power of the war bundle. In the bough lodge, the leader announced the tidings of victory, reciting the brave deeds done and the names of the heroes. Some of these men were entitled to have their names changed by the act of the council, as an honorary distinction, and others were given the right to wear the eagle feather on their heads. Only those who had killed an enemy were allowed this appropriate insignia of bravery, and the feathers of no other bird had any meaning except for ornament. Sometimes at this juncture a brave man was given a new suit of clothes by some well-wisher. The donor usually addressed the crowd as follows: "This man must now wear these clothes forever. He shall always be brave since he is dressed in clothes of Thunder power."[14]

14. Commonly those who wished to join the war party would make a present to the owner of the bundle in return for the privilege.

VI. Fox Clan Ceremonials

Among some Indian peoples, bundles may be owned by what are most often called "clans"[1] in the literature. This word does not refer to a group of relatives, friends, or associates, as it is so commonly used in everyday conversation, but has acquired a technical meaning in anthropology. It refers to a named group (often, but by no means only, the name of an animal) whose members may not marry each other[2] and in which membership is ascribed at birth—in some societies, children become members of their father's clan and, in others, members of their mother's clan.[3] Members of a clan do not necessarily reside together, and in most North American Indian societies they do not. Rather, members of the same clan

1. Sometimes termed "sibs" or "gentes" (sing., gens) in more recent literature and "tribes" or "nations" in the older literature. In the literature on the Fox, they are often termed "gentes."
2. More technically, clans are by definition exogamous, although in recent times this rule of exogamy may be a remembered practice only.
3. More technically, clans are unilineal descent groups. They are termed patrilineal if descent is traced through males only and matrilineal, if through females only. It is often also stated in the anthropological literature that members of a clan consider themselves descended from a common ancestor although they cannot trace this rela-

164

are apt to be scattered through a number of villages and this provides the basis for one of the important foundations of clans among North American Indians: the obligation to provide hospitality (food and shelter) to visiting members of one's own clan.

Among a number of North American Indian peoples, but not all, the clan is also a religious group, having its own rituals and traditions regarding their origin. One such are the Fox Indians.[4] Each Fox clan has at least one ceremony centering around a "sacred pack" or bundle that belongs to it and that by tradition originated in a direct revelation.

The following is such a tradition of the Wolf clan, which explains (i.e., gives) the ritual. Its length may be a consequence of the fact that it was written down in the Fox syllabic script rather than being dictated in Fox and then transcribed—a tedious procedure that tends to induce some brevity into the text. In any case, it will serve as illustration of the richness of Indian tradition too infrequently recorded.

This myth essentially has three parts. It begins with some description of the various contacts with spirits experienced by the man who introduced the ceremony, including those in which he was given the speeches and songs to be used in it. This constitutes the first two-fifths of the text. Half of the text in the next section is an account of the first performance of the clan ceremony, and so an account of how it should be performed in the future. The final tenth of the text describes a war expedition led by the visionary.

---

tionship genealogically. However, although members of a clan may address each other by kinship terms, such as "mother," "father," "brother," and "sister," belief that all members of a clan are descended from a common ancestor is often lacking in North American Indian societies (see Elisabeth Tooker, "Clans and Moieties in North America," *Current Anthropology* 12 [1971]: 357–376).

4. See, for example, Sol Tax, "The Social Organization of the Fox Indians," in *Social Anthropology of North American Indians*, ed. Fred Eggan (Chicago: University of Chicago Press, 1955), pp. 241–282. Tax (p. 263) states that Fox clans "function as ceremonial societies rather than as hereditary social institutions" and notes that a child may belong to another clan in addition to his father's (Fox clans are patrilineal)—a practice also reported for some other North American Indian peoples. In fact, clans in a number of other Indian societies may be more religious groups and less descent groups than is commonly supposed.

A Fox Wolf Clan Myth[5]

It is said that there were twin boys. One was born first and one was born afterward. Both were members of the Wolf clan. Their appearances indeed closely resembled each other. Their eyes were alike, and their statures were the same.

They were never told to do anything. They were loved by their mother and also by their father, indeed by all their relatives. They all loved them alike. Indeed the pair were clad in regalia by them, yet they were boys.

Then, it is said, the man was told by his fellowmen, "Come, make your sons fast for a little while at least." It is said that that was what he would be told. Indeed it was not to be. "Impossible. It is not my heart's wish that I should make my children hungry in such a way," it is said that he would always reply. Finally the people took notice of him. Indeed the two were the only children he had. Always he would be told to make them fast, and always he would refuse. "No," he would indeed always reply.

And then, it is said, one of his children became ill. He did not become sick suddenly; he began to get sick gradually. Yet he became increasingly ill. His father went and besought one who knew much about medicine. He asked him to make his son well. "I will not say 'all right' to you. I do not know what effect this medicine of mine will have on him. After I have found out what effect it has on him, then I will tell you. I will tell you in four days. I will indeed tell you if he is to get well at all," the one who had the son was told. The skilled doctor slept at their home. The man was worried over his son. And, when the four days were up he was told, "It is impossible. I cannot make him well. Indeed it is very difficult. Your son will succumb." When

5. Truman Michelson, *Fox Miscellany*, Bureau of American Ethnology Bulletin 114 (1937), pp. 18–62. The Fox speaker who made the English translation of this text based it on one written by another in the Fox syllabary. It was subsequently slightly revised and edited by Michelson. It has been here edited principally to eliminate some literal translation of Fox stylistic conventions; that is, "indeed," "it is said," "he was told," etc. have been deleted in some places where they occur in the text to reduce their number, and hence the seeming awkwardness of the text to those unfamiliar with Indian conventions. "Gens" has been changed to "clan" throughout. Most of the notes have been taken from the original.

he was told that, he wailed. He wept. "Well, you may try to doctor him as long as he is alive," the skilled healer was told. "Very well," he said.

Indeed, his patient lost strength. Soon a young man came to look at him. After the one who was doctoring went out, the man was told, "Perhaps I can make your son well. I will not say that I can certainly do so. I said, 'Perhaps.' This is what is the matter with him. He is tubercular. The one who has left will not know that that is the matter with him, that he is tubercular. I am the only one who can heal those who are so afflicted. That is why I have said to you, 'Perhaps I can heal him for you,' " he said to the father.

"Now you have gladdened my heart," he was told. "The one who has left will stop giving him medicine to drink," he said of the one who had been doctoring his son. It is said that when the doctor came back he was told that. "Now then, I shall again search for someone to try to doctor him," he was told. "Why, to be sure," he replied. The doctor departed. It is said that that young man doctored him. He healed him rapidly. The father was very glad.

It is said that he was told by the one who had cured his son, "Now you had better make your sons fast. You know how you have felt in your heart. I have indeed made your son rise. No one else made him rise for you. I have now told you to do that. That is the only way their lives will be made strong. Only this. If you do not make them fast they will always indeed get sick. They will be sickly. This medicine is the thing that will always make them well. There are many of you who can doctor. Indeed I do not think at all in this way of them, that they must be made hungry. As for myself, I simply went hungry and did not have any kind of a dream."

Then, it is said, soon afterward the people became ill, and that man became sick and also one of his sons. His son died first and he died a little while afterward. And one of them did not become ill at all. It is said that the one who did not die commenced to fast. He was yet only a boy. He was a pretty good-sized boy. He would continually fast. Indeed he even fasted during the summer. He would not take food, nor would he be tempted to eat early. The aged took notice of that boy and observed that he fasted earnestly after his father had left him. He now lived only with his mother.

Now it is said that once during the winter he was seen weeping. Behind him stood a buffalo. The buffalo was green. The boy did not see him at all. He did not know that the buffalo was there. It was then wintertime. After the boy had departed, one who had spied him went over to where the boy was weeping. Indeed he could not track the buffalo. That boy was the only one whom he could track. The man indeed could not even track the buffalo. "Why, it is very certain that I saw a buffalo whose fur was green," he thought in his heart. Then he untied his Indian tobacco. He scattered it by dropping it upon the spot. He was offering a smoke to that buffalo.

He then departed. When he had come over yonder he told about it. "I saw a buffalo where the twin was weeping; it was back of him. As for him, it is very likely that he did not know about the buffalo. Still, I could not track the buffalo. After he left I went over to see where his tracks led to, but I could not track him," he said to those to whom he was relating this. "It is very likely that he was a manitou buffalo," he was told. "It is very certain that he will be blessed by that one. Or it may be that it was himself. It is one way or the other," the old men said. "I went there and cast tobacco. I offered him a smoke unknowingly," he said. "Oh, you have done rightly. That is the reason why he has shown himself to you," he was told.

Then, it is said, later when the people were traveling there was a swamp in precisely the direction they were to go. Indeed it was the only direction they could go. Still, it was very difficult. Even when they threw wood there, it would gradually sink out of sight in the mud. "Why, what can this be?" they said. Then they thought of that twin. A warrior went over to speak to him. He came to where the twin was. "Why, my grandchild, a difficult task is desired of you. You will do what is desired of you. That is what the men say. Our chiefs also have thought of you in the same way. You must try to do so," he was told. "This is what has been desired of you. It is very difficult for us to go through this swamp at the present time. It is desired that you take the people through. Indeed our chiefs have desired you to do that for them. That is the mission I have been sent on, and that is the reason I have come to you, my grandchild," the warrior said to him. As for the young man, he sat just as he had. He did not speak. Then, when the warrior started to depart, the young man asked him, "When shall I take them across?" "You are to say when. At the time you name we will move. You can suit yourself. I shall not say to anyone, it will be at this time. It will be for you to say it, and just as you say so, that will be the time when the people will move," he was told. "Well, it will be tomorrow at noon. Still, you ought to come here again. You should come here very early," he said to the warrior. "Very well," he replied.

It is said that the warrior then departed. He returned very early in the morning, indeed it was when he had finished eating. He had already told the chiefs, "The twin has consented." And when it was nearly noon, the young man told him, "Now you may say to them, 'Let us move.' They must be quick when they take the coverings off their houses. You must say to them, 'It has been said that you must be in haste when you take the coverings off your houses.' " So the warrior was told. "Very well," he said. He went outside. "Oh ho! It is said that we are to move. It is said that you must be in haste when you take the coverings off your houses," he said to the people. Indeed they were in haste when they took the coverings off. Indeed every one of them took their coverings off.

Then, it is said, that boy said, "A member of the War Chiefs clan must paint me. He is to paint me green." Then he was painted by a member of the War Chiefs clan. He was painted green all over. He was even painted green on the soles of his feet. After he was completely painted green he said to the people, "Now, we are all to step on the same track. I am to make tracks as I go. You may follow my tracks. Those who are members of the War Chiefs clan are the only ones who can follow close to me, all of them, as many as there are. Then when their tracks disappear anyone can follow. Still, they must follow my tracks in a line. Their tracks must follow mine. Let no one go on the side. You must go in the same path upon which I go. Whatever path I shall take, that is what we are to use the remainder of this evening. Indeed, if someone has forgotten something, he may go back and get it. That is what I have to say to you," he said, and he departed.

Then the members of the War Chiefs clan walked along in the rear. After some time they came where the solid earth was. They then camped. Others were just starting to come. Then the members of the War Chiefs clan were told, "You are to cook for our friends. You are to build the camps." "Very well," they replied. The women then started to cook. The men went out to cut poles. They built camps for every one of the people. After they had cooked all of them came and ate what was cooked. They did not have to say, "Eat!" to them. They simply cooked for them.

The people had now camped in safety. The next day they were forbidden to go back and try to walk on the route they had come. They were told, "This is very terrible. You know this very well, that even the sticks sink in there. Those sticks float on the water, yet they sink here. But I have carried all of you across. Very likely something would happen to you should you turn back. "It may be that we should all be killed by some people. Indeed that is what would happen to us if we did go back there. Now we shall not meet any misfortune. If it had turned us back, we should have been an easy prey to those who speak alien languages. That is what our fate would have been. Now it will not be that way. We shall not be easily killed. Indeed, every one of us who call each other 'people' have been led or have tried to be led through something difficult. The one who goes through this will be the one who is strongest among his fellow people. Here is where every one of the people will turn back, but we have already gone through this. Indeed it has ever been so. Everyone fears this. Even a little bird, even ducks, indeed all who fly fear this. Should they alight here, then they would sink down. Even if ducks should alight here, they would sink down. Even fish would be killed. That is what I have to tell you." The people were frightened for the first time. "The manitou and others have called this the 'War-lake.' That is the reason why these members of the War Chiefs clan were the first to follow me. As for the manitou, he does not forget the members of the War Chiefs clan. Here is where those who have been made members of the War Chiefs clan by their fellow manitous will stay. This is their lake. No one is treated gently by this. Indeed if you even throw snapping turtles in it they will die here. And we all know that snapping turtles live in mud. Yet they would be killed here as anything else. That is the reason why I tell you when speaking to you that I have brought you through difficulty," he said to the people.

Then he said, "We are to stay here for eight days. Then we can move. This is the trouble with this ground. This ground has a hole in it as far as yonder. That is the reason why it is this way. That is the reason why anyone may be killed by it."

After eight days passed, the people moved. Then, the people offered it a smoke. They all cast tobacco for it as they started to move.

"Tonight you must look backward," he said to the people. When night came they looked backward, indeed everyone did. They saw fire sparkling. "This is like that every winter. It is doing so simply to show you," he said. They again cast their tobacco in that direction. "This we now offer you to smoke, our grandfather. As soon as I see my fellowman, may I slay him. That is what I ask of you," said those who sacrificed tobacco. That was what every one of them said.

"You did not ask for long life. You have asked for something which is frightful. You were to have asked for something right," the young man said to them. "The manitou made it to be peaceful for us. And we did not lose each other there. We have safely crossed the hole in the earth. We went across because he told it to be peaceful. If he had done what you ask, we should have all sunk in the swamp. We should not have been able to crawl out at all. Indeed it is very certain that this miry mud would kill us," he said to them.

"As it is, this one who is a member of the War Chiefs clan may tell him that. He may ask for that very thing. But as for you, you cannot. Your pleas are in vain. He is the only one to whom that manitou will listen. How can it be otherwise? He belongs to the same clan. For that manitou is declared to be a member of the War Chiefs clan by his fellow manitous. His life indeed is the same as that of the members of the War Chiefs clan: Indeed he is made so that he will not treat anyone kindly. That is the reason why he will not listen to you others," the twin said.

It is said, the men now began to consider him unusual. "It is very certain that he will be greatly talked about for something," they said of him. "He even knows about this place where he carried us across. He even knows about the manitou who must dwell there. Indeed he knows how that manitou came to be a manitou."

It is said that from then on they were afraid of him. Whenever there was a clan festival, the best food was served that boy. Moreover, when only warriors were invited he also would be invited by the one who did the inviting. Whenever he was gone, they would come to his dwelling and invite him. He usually sat with the leading warriors. He was always treated like this.

It is said, when he was a little bigger he began to understand wolves of every kind. His mother noticed that whenever a wolf howled he would listen very attentively to it. Sometimes he would laugh. The wolves would make him laugh. Also her son would always tell what kind of a day was coming, and the days would be just so. Once when the woman and he were sitting down she said to him, "Now, my son, I have desired in my heart to know something about you. Why is it that you seem to know about the future weather?"

"This is the reason why I know. These wolves always tell what kind of a day it is to be. That is why I know. When they talk about anything I understand them. It seems as if it were people calling. I seem to hear them in that manner," he said to his mother. "So I have observed, my son. Whenever our grandfathers howl, I think, 'My son understands them.' Indeed it has happened that you do. That is all I am going to ask you," the woman said to her son. "I have now told you, mother," he said to her. "Well, my son, cease telling that you understand your grandfathers," he was told by his mother. "What have they to do with you?" "Those wolves are they who look after us. If someone comes, for example, a scout, they are the ones who would tell me of it. They would indeed tell where he is. They would also tell when the scouts would be sound asleep. These wolves look after us that way. That is the reason they howl so loudly at times. Sometimes they howl loudly because they ask tobacco from us, for they are in need of a smoke. Yet they obtain their smoking from here only. They are not given a smoke from elsewhere. They are not even given a smoke by those whom they have blessed. And they are not given a smoke by those who speak a different language. It is only us by whom they are given a smoke," he said to his mother.

The woman's heart was relieved. And it is said she took good care of her son. It happened that he was a handsome young man. The girls all loved the twin, but he paid no attention to them. The old woman would always forbid her son to court them. Finally the old woman was told, "It may be that you do not understand me. I have said that I shall not go courting. Still, you do not cease to tell me that. I surely would listen to anyone if he said 'Don't' to me." She then ceased to say anything further. "I must yet do much fasting," the old woman was told. "That is so," she only replied to her son.

And during that winter he fasted very earnestly. Very earnestly he fasted. Finally he had a dream. Someone spoke to him, "Now, my grandchild, you have more than made yourself hungry. After you have grown older all the manitous will indeed know you. Still, they will not be those who are seated up above. Those who are seated underneath this earth are they who will remember you after you have grown to be a young man. They will especially bless you. You will not be blessed with poor blessings. You will be blessed with whatever is in their power to bless. If the manitou is allowed any amount of power, your blessing will be very rich. The Great Manitou has the power in his heart, and the manitous conform to this in whatever way they bestow blessings. You had better, therefore, cease to paint yourself with charcoal. You have done your duty long ago. Still your blessing will only be conferred when you have grown up," he dreamed he was told.

Then he told his mother, "This is what I have dreamed: It

is said that I am to cease fasting. I was told in my dream, 'The manitous are thinking of you. Indeed when you have grown up you will know your blessing.' That is what I was told in my dream," he said to his mother. He ceased to fast.

It is said, later on, during the summer, the people went on a buffalo hunt. They went in boats when they went on the buffalo hunt. They rowed upstream. After they had gone a long distance, they started to drag their canoes up the banks. From there they all went overland. Then, he had a vision of the buffaloes, and that he was not to eat them. The young man found this out. He told his mother, "It will be improper for me to eat buffaloes any more. Indeed I shall merely see them for you." And after they had gone a long distance in their hunt they saw buffaloes. The next day the men gave chase. They ran on foot. Some jumped astride of the buffaloes and rode them as they shot them. Indeed the men killed many buffaloes. The young man also shot at them, but he did not like their smell. The women roasted the meat on spits near the fire; and the people also roasted the meat over the fire. They prepared much buffalo meat. Whenever they would start to waste the meat he would go off somewhere else.

After they had been on the chase four times the leader said, "Now then, let us stop killing them." "Very well," they said to him. Then they learned that the young man did not eat buffaloes, for he could not eat them. They helped him as he went out to shoot some little birds or anything else. He was to eat these little birds or whatever else he shot.

It is said his mother continued to scold him. Especially when many women were around he would be scolded as if he were a child. The scolding he received embarrassed him.

When they had come to where their canoes were they started to load them. They departed. They now went downstream. The river was very wide. As they paddled along one entire night they saw many canoes afloat. They had met their foes. After they had gone through them they paddled fast. They seemed to be very helpless. Then they were told by the young man, "They will not know anything of us." They then camped far off. They paddled by on the other side of the stream. Some of the women even cried, for they were badly frightened. They even went and besought him that they might live. He told them, "Come, cease bothering me for a short time. They will know nothing about us. We have met them and they will not know we have passed them."

And when they had moved again, he said to the people, "You will now see the one who watches over all of us. You must all burn tobacco for him. Let no one refrain from burning tobacco for him. That is the one who blesses me. If you give tobacco to the one who always watches us wherever we go, he will be very proud. We have now already passed through the spot that is feared. That is the reason you will see him. I shall not say, 'Here he is.' You will know him as he will be conspicuous. You will then think in your hearts, 'Why, here he is.' You must look ahead." Indeed they always looked ahead. Soon they saw a wolf going across their way. The wolf was walking on top of the water. He walked along very slowly. Everywhere the people untied their tobacco and burned it for him. The wolf walked on ahead very slowly and unconcernedly. And just as soon as he came upon the land he howled. They saw wolves running all about them. Some of them ran across the river. And some of the wolves ran along on the top of the water. "The tobacco you have burned is now being offered. Those who were told to watch us are given an equal amount. You know how many there are. Those are they who watch. They are of such a nature that they will not tell a falsehood," he said to the people.

Then, it is said, they ceased being in any way afraid. They ceased to think in their hearts about their enemies. When they reached the place from where they had started, their belongings had remained unmolested. And those who had stayed where they were living were unmolested. These were told of what had happened and they were frightened. "Very likely they may have happened to row by here during the night. Quite a while ago it rained here every night," they said. "Very likely it was during the last time that they passed by here," said one who usually kept track of affairs. "Or, it may have been that they thought we were very numerous, and so passed by in the night. As these dwellings are many in number, they must have been deceived by them," they said among themselves.

Then the twin dreamed, "You will now travel about. You must depart tomorrow and exercise your legs," he was told. As soon as he awoke he went outside. He ran in no fixed direction. It happened that at first he ran toward the east. He came to find himself standing at the edge of the great sea and facing the east. He did not know from whence he had come. "You may stay here four days," he was told. He could not see the one who had spoken to him. "Very well," he said. And after four days he was told, "You will now run toward the south." He started to run aimlessly. He again soon knew that he was standing. He was standing near the edge of the great sea. It was in the south. It was hot. Then he was told, "You must remain here four days." He could not see the one who had spoken to him. He again said, "Very well." Then again he ran on after four days. And as he ran there was a path ahead of him. That is what he would think in his heart. And he again soon knew that he was standing. And indeed just then the sun glowed red as it went down. Then indeed he was told, "You must remain here for four days." He again said, "Very well." He could not see the one who had spoken to him. And after four days he ran on. He started to run aimlessly. And he again suddenly knew that he was standing. He could only see. He was told the same thing. "You must remain here indeed for four days," he was told. "Very well," he thought in his heart. It had happened that he was completely frozen. His eyes had good vision. After four days there came a green buffalo. It spoke to him, "My grandchild, your heart is also my heart," he was told. The buffalo took him underneath the earth. "It is I, my grandchild, who have wished you to run around this island," he was told. "I am the one who has tried how fast you are," he was told. "Indeed, nothing will be the matter with you. Thus, you have thought in your heart, 'I am frozen.' I have made you to be as my hoof. You have never known a buffalo's hoof to be cracked open by freezing. My grandchild, nothing will happen to us." That which had befallen him ceased. He was no longer cold. He now also ate. After he had eaten some meat, "Do you know what you are eating?" he was asked. "I have fed you human flesh. I have fed you this because you are very hungry. You are eating for your meal a chief only. Whenever you go any place you will kill a chief. That is the aim of your meal," he was told. He was exultant. "You will now return. I shall take something to you later on," he was told by that green buffalo. "It will not be at the present time. Indeed you own it. No one else has been so blessed. It is your possession. Yet, my grandchild, it will be only at that time when you will see it," the twin was told. Then he was told, "Now, my grandchild, I am going to take you."

It was during the night. Just as soon as they were outside he recognized their dwelling. He went there. He lay down just as he was. The next day there were loud sounds of those who were weeping. "The twin, the twin," they said. They mentioned him many times. He went outside and someone saw him. They ceased weeping. "Gracious!" he said to them. He then told his mother, "Mother, I was made to run in a circle over this earth." "Oh," she replied. "You did not finally run yourself to death?" she asked. "I did not know what I was doing. When I ran I ceased to know anything for a while. Then I would suddenly know when I would be standing near the edge of the great sea. That is what happened to me," he said to his mother. "Why, good gracious, it must be that a manitou is thinking of you. Who is it that has the endurance to run to the shore of the great sea? Very likely you are blessed by one who is called a 'manitou,' " she said to her son.

Then, it is said, the people moved. They were moving off toward some unknown place. After they had moved four times the leader was killed by a deer. Then they did not know in which direction they should move. That deer escaped from them. They did not kill it. Then the young man was wanted in order to kill the deer. "It is just to try, for it is not likely that I shall overtake it," he said. He ran where it had run. In a little while he saw it running. He gave chase. After he had pursued it hotly it changed into an Indian. He saw it was a Sioux. The young man caught him. After he had bound him securely he took him back. After he had brought him back he said to his fellow Indians, "This is that deer. It was a Sioux Indian." They then tortured the Sioux. The young man looked on as they tortured the Sioux. Suddenly, after the Sioux was dead, a warrior came rising from his seat. "You have now made a capture, my grandchild. You have captured a manitou who had come on the warpath against us. You are to be dreaded indeed," the young man was told. He said nothing and departed. When he came to their dwelling only those who had been in severe battles came to him. He had beaten them in all courage. They started to talk to him. They told him that he had done the hardest thing. After they had told him that, he said to them, "I only went to overtake him for you. I do not wish in my heart to become a warrior."

"You will have full control as to where we shall have our town," he was told. "I cannot consent to this. You are much older. I do not yet know anything in advance," he said to them. Then someone agreed to be the leader when moving. He was the one who had full control as to where their town was to be. After he selected it, he moved. The people truly camped there in safety. There was no one who was ill. Again they had plenty of meat as they went along. They killed game easily. Indeed it seemed as if the game were getting more plentiful as they moved on. They finally came to their destination. Just as soon as they had finished building their town dwellings some people who were their enemies came upon them. Then they began to hold a council with those who spoke different languages. Indeed every one of them spoke different languages. They were holding a council regarding this earth, to determine who had been sent here by the manitou to own this earth. Everyone said, "I." Then the Meskwakies[6] were just sitting down. It is said that the Indians were seated in different groups, each group being composed of those who spoke the same language. And they would always take that young man. They would always tell the things the manitou had wished them to do. Then that young man said to every one of those people,

---

6. The Fox name for themselves. In Fox it means "Red Earths."

"Though we are now holding a council here, it seems as if we were holding this council secretly. No one has as yet said anything about it to the manitou. As for me, I would mention the manitou, I would do that so he would know." Then he was told by the people, "You may tell the manitou. You may tell him in such a way that he will know about us." "I shall do that tomorrow. Yet the one who is right will be then known. Tomorrow we shall see what kind of a sky there will be overhead. There is going to be a chieftain sky.[7] Again, a chieftain's fire will be flaming. From there we shall light our pipes. I have now spoken. When I talk about this earth of ours I shall be right. I shall be the one to speak especially rightly. Still, you who speak these different languages must now speak. I shall speak the last," he said to them.

The next day when they woke up the sky was entirely green. Again the fire was very large and was burning a green flame. There was no wood there at all. They only saw the fire. And they held a council there. The young man started to talk to the men. After they had all gathered they began to talk. And the young man spoke last. "My friends, the manitou also knows me. He has made me to stand on top of this earth. He has made me the owner of the things on and under this earth. And he has not lent them to me. I am the owner. That is why I can say 'I am the owner,' " he said to the people. They were all then very angry. And the people began shooting in lively fashion. Then he told them to loosen the ground around the fireplace. Also he told them that no one should spit in it. He told this to a messenger, and the messenger ran on giving instructions. He was not shot while going about giving instructions. After he had finished telling them and after they had fixed their fires, their fires suddenly indeed burned a green flame. As for those who were shooting at them, they suddenly lost those at whom they were shooting. Those dwellings had sunk down into the earth. And where the dwellings had stood there now remained only red earth. Indeed where the dwellings had stood the earth

---

7. I.e., the sky will be clear and green, for green is the color (paint) of the Bear clan in which the chieftainship is supposed to be hereditary.

was in the form of paint. Those people were then frightened. "Why, those people must be manitous," the people said. They soon feared it and all moved away. They moved off to some unknown spot.

After four years the dwellings that had sunk came up. Then he was told, "Well, you must go after something." He was told that plainly and did not dream it. He indeed started off aimlessly. Suddenly he saw someone standing in the middle of the hill. He saw the being was large. He was in no way afraid of it. He went over to where it was. When he came close, he saw it was a large buffalo. It was very large. Indeed it was of an enormous size. When he was yet some distance from it the buffalo began to diminish in size. It had a green coat of fur. When the young man came on the spot, he saw there remained the good-sized hide of a young buffalo. It indeed had green fur. That was what he had beheld as a buffalo. He picked it up. When he picked it up it shot out little sparks of fire. Nevertheless he picked it up and carried it with him. Underneath it was painted red. Then he thought of placing it far off. "No, you must take it with you," he was told. He indeed took it with him to where he lived. When he had brought it there he wrapped it up carefully and put it away carefully.

Then, it is said, the people became ill. Yet they did not think of coming to the young man to have him doctor them. It is said that the people would desert the sick. Just as he fell sick the people were moving. So he and his belongings were deserted. His mother had already died among the first. The reason he was deserted was so that no one might worry over him. Later he was able to be up. He lay sick there for a long time. And he was brought food to eat by the wolves. Those people now thought of him after they had ceased to become ill, and all were well. They all lamented him. He was now told by his buffalo hide, "Let me take you on. You are to have me as your sacred pack." So he was told. Then there stood a buffalo. "My grandchild, get on top. I shall carry you on my back," it said to him. The young man rode it. After he had seated himself comfortably, the buffalo began to run slowly at first. Indeed his grandfather was fast. As they went he could see the people who had died. At the time when the people were dying they would die from sneezing. Indeed whenever anyone began sneezing he would be at it constantly. He then would die. That is what happened to them.

And, it is said, he overtook them in the night. "You must go forward and sleep," he was told by his grandfather who was carrying him. "They are going that way. Whenever they see you they will camp. Every one of them is wailing for you," he was told. He then slept very soundly. While sleeping he was awakened. All around there were many people. They camped there. They were very glad.

He no longer had any mother. He stayed in a chief's dwelling. He felt lonely in his heart. "Now I have ceased to have a mother," he thought in his heart. He could not forget it in his heart.

They lived there permanently. Finally he began to sleep far off. Whenever he slept there, it would be known because usually the wolves howled very loudly. In that way those with whom he was staying would know it. Those with whom he was staying loved him. Still, it was his mother whom he desired. Soon the one who had blessed him said to him, "I have blessed you justly. Your heart's desire is very difficult. You will see your mother," he was told by a wolf. "If you should do the same as we, she would live a long life, that is, if you wish that in your heart. She also will be told the same thing. We should indeed stay right here for four days," he was told by the wolves. There was nothing to stop him. "I shall do whatever you tell me to," he replied. "That is right," he was told by those wolves.

It is said that just as they were on the point of instructing him further the buffalo by whom he had been blessed came. "My grandchild, you must go to the other side of the hill. There you will see your mother. You then will take her. These wolves would have told you something vulgar. But I do not say anything vulgar. 'This is what you must do to her,' you would have been told. But I am not going to say anything to you. I have simply told you that you were to see her and to take her to the dwelling," he was told. He was glad. He departed for the place. He saw there his mother sitting down. He ran toward her and kissed her. "Oh! Mother!" he said to her. He was treated by her the same way. She kissed him repeatedly. Then they departed, and went to the dwelling. He now had a mother. Moreover, they were given materials by all with which they could build a dwelling. Again, they were given things to use when cooking. Everyone on all sides also gave them food to eat. And when they had a dwelling by themselves he was suddenly awakened. When he awoke it was late at night. It was the fire that woke him up. After he was awakened by it he was told, "Now you must listen closely to me. I am going to tell you exactly what the Green Buffalo ordered me to," the fire said to him. "I am now going to begin telling you these songs. You must catch on to how I sing them," it said to him. "Very well," he replied. The fire started to sing. After it had sung, he was told, "You must catch on." He tried hard to catch on to as many songs as the fire had used. He knew them. Then he knew the speech that the fire had given.

"Tomorrow the Rock-Man will talk to you," he was told. "If I have made a mistake in any way, he will tell you," he was told by the fire. "That is all."

The next day he departed. Suddenly someone called him from the other side of the hill. He went over there. He saw there was a large boulder in the middle of the ravine. "This is the place that was selected for you," he was told. He began to be given instructions. "The way the Green Buffalo has blessed you is not easy. He desires that you will not end here. We two only have been named to keep track of your songs. That is another thing we were told to do. We are to continue to carefully sing them to you. Now, if I make a mistake you will hear and know it," he was told. That rock began to talk of the songs. That rock told in every detail exactly what the fire had told him previously. "As for myself, I shall never end as a being. As for that fire, you will always continue to use it as long as you live. You will be using it at that time when your life will end. You cannot leave it before. The same will happen to me. Indeed it seems to me as though I were going along with you all," the rock said to him. It started to sing the clan festival songs. Indeed the rock sang them just as the fire had sung them. It sang them just the same. Then it started to give a speech. It was indeed just the same speech. It was given exactly the same way as he had been told it previously.

"That is the way I appoint it for you. In what regard have I told you falsely? Those are the same speeches to which you have listened. And the songs that you have heard are the very same."

"I think in my heart that no one has told me falsely in any way. It must be that both of your lives are right. Indeed that must be the reason why you did not mix some falsehood with this," the young man said.

"We are indeed righteous. That is why we are ordered to do these things," the other said.

Then after the young man had been instructed he was also told, "You must not start to use these songs at once. It will be indeed some time from now. That is the desire of your grandfather. You will not forget these. You will know them whenever you begin to celebrate clan festivals. This desire is only heaped upon you gradually. It has not been desired to heap it upon you all of a sudden," he was told. "Gradually it will continue to strongly affect you." And after he had been instructed he departed and went to where they lived.

He already knew the clan festival songs. And later on during early spring his mother was boiling sap for sugar, and after they had cut wood he went walking about. The sun's rays were splendid and the wind was blowing quite hard. The young man was lying on his back looking at the trees. "Why, these are very strange," he thought in his heart. The trees spoke to him, "Our grandchild, cease looking at us, for we are courting," they said to him. "We also are making our offspring," they said to him.

He then must have fallen asleep. Just as soon as he was asleep he saw his grandfather, the Green Buffalo. He was taken by the latter. "You must go and see the house of blessings," he was told by that buffalo. "Very well," he said to it. They went there. There were four doors in the dwelling. One faced the east, one faced the south. Bearskins were the door-flaps. And the door on the west had a flap of deerskin. And the door to which he had been taken had a raccoon skin for a flap. And he was told in his dream, "This is where you are to sit." There was a little rise of earth where he was placed. Then a man came in. He came in from the south door. Then another came in from the west side. It was a man. They did not look at the young man. Then another came from the north side. There were now four of them.

And the one who blessed him began to talk. "Men, I have brought our grandchild here. That is the relationship we have been given toward the people. The one who has seated us all around has told us that. The reason I have blessed him is because he fasted. I have done so because I knew he was more than in despair over the death of his brother, his fellow twin, and also his father. That is the reason why I have blessed him. I am indeed going to give him myself. That is the reason why I have wished this in my heart. I have given him myself. Indeed I have also given him my own songs," he said to them. "That is what I have to tell you," the men were told.

Then one of them began to speak. "I also wish the same for our grandchild," he said. "As for me, I am going to wish in my heart that he may have a good life. That he may live on to the full span of his life is what I wish for our grandchild." Then another spoke to him. "I also shall wish the same thing for our grandchild. I shall wish for him only that which is right. Also, that disease may not enter his chief's town is what I wish for him. Also, I wish that whoever from without ever speaks evilly against their town may cease to do so. It will be even more as regards one who is constantly doing so. Whoever does so will instead curse himself. That is what I shall wish for him. Also, I shall remember all who belong to the clan of which he is a member. That is what I shall wish for our grandchild," he said.

Then the fourth time he was spoken to by the buffalo who sat in the north end. "I also will bless our grandchild. I shall merely wish him this indeed. That he be considered a man is what I shall wish for him. And also this, that he may associate with all until old age. That is what I shall wish. That they never be smitten by disease is also what I wish for him. And I shall place last for him this, namely, what we consider in our hearts as 'one slice.' I wish to give him this in return for his kettleful.[8] That is what I wish for the one who continues to think often of our blessing. He is the one I shall especially remember. The present time will not be as far as I shall think of him. I shall think of him until this earth ceases to be an earth. That is how long I shall wish that for our grandchild.

"We must be quick to hear these clan festival songs that they are to have. They must tell each other to be in earnest in thinking about them. That is what he must tell his fellow clansmen. Indeed he must tell them this in a straightforward manner. He must think in his heart to never forget this that we have wished for him. He must also tell this as a message to those who are to listen to him. Those who listen attentively to him are they who will be remembered. That is what I wish our grandchild," he said.

"Yet, men, if there are to be only as many as we are, our words will not come true. You must go yonder and summon the Great Manitou so that you may tell him how we have blessed this mortal. Our wish for him does not end at the present time. When we wish him to live until that time where old age is, our wish is indeed difficult. We have wished to see our wishes continue to where old age is and lie about for a little while. Then the Great Manitou must come and see the one who made us sorrowful.[9] And also if he is to talk he must say what he thinks of him. It will be all right if he only knows about him."

Then the Great Manitou came. The Green Buffalo informed him, "This our grandchild has made us sorrowful. He has made me to be sorrowful. These men who are here have already extended their wishes to him. No one has wished that which is wrong. We alike wished him what is right," the Green Buffalo said to the Great Manitou.

"I shall wish the same for our grandchild. That is the reason why I have always told you to bless our grandchildren. You have pleased me in blessing him. I too will place my

---

8. I.e., kettleful of offerings.
9. I.e., our grandchild.

blessing with yours. This is what I shall wish him. I shall only wish that which is peaceable. I shall not wish him that which is frightful. I shall only wish him that he live a good life. Indeed my wish for our grandchild is only a good quiet life. Why I have blessed our grandchild is because in that way I shall always be able to obtain a smoke from him. I wish that disease shall not strike him, and that his chief's village be not stricken with disease. This is what I wish him.

"You have pleased me in holding a council over our grandchild. You have believed me when I told you to bless the people, and have so pleased me. And now you have come to a decision over our grandchild. Whatever your wishes have been they will be valid. But you must not think of taking back from him what you have wished him. You have already given him your wishes. I too have given him my wish. I shall not take it back and think about what I have wished him. I have already given it to him.

"The reason I have said to you, 'Be careful,' is that you are not to think of conferring this blessing on simply anyone. If you should think in your hearts, 'This one is probably living rightly,' he is the one whom you should bless. And the one who fasts, the one who fasts earnestly is the one whom you should continue to bless. That is what you should do with regard to our grandchildren. Now this one has truly fasted earnestly. Also, he surely has been in despair when his father and brother died. Surely you have blessed him justly. I am indeed of such a nature that I shall not wish anything evil for anyone. I should bless anyone in the way I have done," he said. He then departed, speaking for the last time: "Tell him how those who are to dance shall dance. And this. Tell him the speech that we have hung.[10] When we say, 'So be it,' I shall remind you," he said to the young men, and the Great Manitou departed.

Then the buffaloes began to instruct the young man. "This is how you must make the people dance. You dance in a circle. Also, sweet food must indeed be eaten first. That is what we will regard highly when receiving it from you, maple syrup

---

10. I.e., spoken.

and maple cakes. Also pumpkins. These are things of which we shall think highly.

"You must always worship in earnest. Do not think of anything else. You must think in your hearts of worship for one day. That is what you must do. Do not think uselessly of yourselves or friends. It seems as if you would have to put woman away for a short time. All that you must think of for one day is this. The next day you may think about the one whom you had put away. In that way you would conduct your life rightly. That worship is the only kind that is right. If you do not do this, you yourself will ruin your sacred pack; you will ruin your worship. There will be no one who will think about your worship. You must forbid your fellow clansmen to act lustfully toward each other and to look at each other in a flirtatious way, and to jest with anyone. They must talk quietly to one for a while at least. That is what you must tell them. And if one has many jesting words within him, he will make his life wretched. If even a woman should do so the same would befall her. She would make her life wretched. She would not bring the blame on someone else, it will be herself," he dreamed he was told.

He awoke. When he awoke the sun was hanging just where it was when he fell asleep. The limbs of the trees were thick. There were many flowers. He woke up in the midst of flowers. They smelt fragrantly. His sleep had made him drowsy.

He now had within him those blessings. He then departed to where his mother was staying and boiling maple sap. The dwelling had disappeared. Then he went to where they formerly had lived. That was gone. Then he noticed that bones were lying around where they had had their town. The bones were bones of human dead. He departed aimlessly. And a wolf came to him that night. "They have had a fight. Those bones that you have seen are the bones of your enemies. Your friends were not killed. But you have been lost. They did not know what had happened to you. They considered you dead. You have been asleep for four years. It has now been four years," he was told by that wolf.

He could just now begin to feel hunger. His desire was for some sweet corn together with beans. Then that wolf said to him, "I could go and tell your mother." "You might speak to her with difficulty," he said to it. "She might come at full speed." "That is so," said that wolf. Now the young man gave out traveling on foot. "I shall take you. I shall use medicine so that you will be strong," the wolf said. And he was given medicine. He ate it. As soon as he had eaten it he was as he had been. He was able to travel. They went on. "Perhaps we shall have to sleep four days on the way," the wolf said. "Very well," he replied. They walked on slowly. The young man had ceased to desire the sweet corn cooked with beans. And after four days they arrived and he was led to where his mother was. He saw here his mother sitting with blackened cheeks. "Mother, what has been the matter with you?" he said to her. "It is my son," she said to him. His mother ran toward him. The young man was petted. He then told her what he desired to eat, sweet corn cooked with beans. Shortly after nightfall the food was cooked. Then his mother questioned him. "I must have been asleep," he said to her. "The manitous truly have told me what they wish for me and how I am to conduct my clan festivals. I have been told how I must think of my clan festival. So therefore we had better build a large dwelling, mother. Soon I shall try to have the people dance. Do not go about saying this in the future, Mother," he said to his mother. "It cannot be that I will go about talking about it," he was told.

Then he began to look for good upright posts. He found them that evening. They were just the way he desired them to be. And he again went out the next day. He saw some also that evening. He would find some more every evening. On the fourth day he had found the desired number of posts. Then he went and chopped down those which he had found at first. He kept on chopping them down for four days. That is what he did. It took him four days to chop down one kind. It took him sixteen days to do all the chopping. Later on he prepared them all. They were cedars. And his mother helped him. She cut the poles. They would work on those green trees for four days. Even if the trees had large trunks it took them just that length of time. They had been told by the manitou to do this, and that was the reason they did so. Then the young man thought in his heart, "What must I do to carry these?" He had cut the trees down here and there. Then he thought in his heart, "Why, the manitou has really blessed me." He went to where they lived. When he came there he lay down to sleep. And he thought in his heart as he was lying down, "If indeed the manitou really knows me, those poles on which I worked so hard to cut down will come over here." Sure enough those poles were lying there the next morning. Then he began to implant them in the ground. And the men began to help him. They thought something of him. The women also helped. In a little while they had made a large dwelling.

"Now you may summon a young man who is a member of the War Chiefs clan," he said to them. He was summoned and came. "Now, my friend, what I am going to say to you is somewhat of a nuisance. You are to walk about as a ceremonial attendant. You must go about and summon only my fellow clansmen. Indeed every one of them must come here," the youth was told. "Very well," he replied. Then he was told, "You also must come here." "Very well," he replied. He departed summoning them. "You are to go to the twin's dwelling," he would say to them. He would call women or any members.

They had now gathered together. As for the ceremonial attendant, he was the only one who did not belong to that clan. The twin started to speak. "Men and women, children, girls, today this our ceremonial attendant has gone about summoning you to come to where I dwell. This is the reason why we are gathered here. We shall try to hunt. We are to give a clan festival. That is why we have gathered here. In eight days you should gather and bring here by noon something. If you have anything you should bring it, sweet food or anything. We are going to worship the manitous who bless us," he said to those who were seated about him. "Still, this member of the War Chiefs clan is the one who is to act as our ceremonial attendant always. It shall not be anyone else. Indeed we shall always have this member of the War Chiefs clan to be our ceremonial attendant. Do not think in your hearts of ever changing this rule. This is the one whose services we shall always continue to ask. This one has been made by the manitou to touch the surface of the earth. He was one of the first. Again, he was the first to be made to see all things—the sun, and this sky, and the stars. That is the reason why he will act as our ceremonial attendant, this one who is a member of the War Chiefs clan. The manitou has given us members of the Wolf clan all that remain under this earth. There are many things under this earth. It has been decided that we should own those things. Whenever we imitate something it will be exactly that way. The manitou has desired that we should always tell the truth. That is what I want to tell you," he said to them.

They then departed to their homes. Then some moved off. They were hunting. Every one of them obeyed. And when the appointed time had come, they began bringing in the where-withal to celebrate a clan festival. Indeed there were all sorts of fresh meat—prairie chickens, quails, pheasants, squirrels, and deer meat, a bear, and harvest-crop food. And they brought in maple sugar cakes, and maple syrup, and corn dumplings. There was abundant food. And the youth acted as the leading ceremonial attendant.

After the youth had come, he was told, "Ceremonial atten-dant, you may now go and get anyone whom you wish to act as your fellow ceremonial attendants. For you are to be the lead-ing ceremonial attendant. You will only have to stay around here tomorrow. You will smoke our sacred pack. That is all you will have to do," he was told. "Very well," he replied. Then he went around summoning those who were to act as ceremonial attendants. He went about summoning many. And it was getting to be evening when they came for their duty. They plucked the feathers off the pheasants and quail, indeed all the game. They singed the hairs off the squirrels. A little later on, the one who was to give the invitations was summoned. "Now, member of the Feathered clan, you may go and give invita-tions," he was told. "Very well," he replied. He then went out to invite the people. "You may invite anyone, women and also men," he was told. "You may also invite girls." "I shall do so," he replied. "And you, ceremonial attendant, you go directly from your dwelling and summon those who are to give the clan festival. Go out as soon as you awake. You must say to the men, 'You are to go over early to sing.' And you are to say to the women, 'You are to go over early and sit at your places.' You do not need to first come here," he was told. "Very well," he replied.

He went home. He told his parents what he had been told. "Then you must wake up early. You may depart from here before you have eaten," he was told. He straightway went to bed and woke up early. He departed calling those who were to give the clan festival. "You must go early to sing," he said to the men. And he said to the women, "You must go over very early and sit at your places there."

After it was daybreak he went about, eating heartily. A little after sunrise he had summoned all who were to give the clan festival. He then went over to where the clan festival was to be held. And he went after some earth. He put loose earth around the fires. After bringing it, he was told, "Now, ceremonial attendant, you may spread this out," and he was given a matting. "You are to make a mound of earth. And you may stick my feathers on top," he was told. After making the little mound of loose earth, he stuck the feathers on it. After sticking them upright he placed the sacred pack on it. "You may also tie up the drum," he was told. "One man is to be a member of the Feathered clan, one of the Bear clan, one of the Eagle clan, and one of the War Chiefs clan," he was told. After they had tied it up, they placed some Indian tobacco in a pile on the middle of the drum. The attendants had already placed the game in the kettles to cook.

After the attendants had everything boiling, the one blessed jumped down and said to them, "Men, you may listen to me. Eventually I am going to try to speak to our grandfathers. You must catch on how I speak," he said to them. "I do not say this to one only; I spoke to every one of you when I told you to catch on to what I was about to say. I have been told by

191

the manitou to tell you this. I have told you that," he said to them, and he began to give his speech.[11]

"Our grandfather, you have been told this by your fellow manitous, namely, that you were to be here, where you could watch over us. You are the first beings to whom we scatter our tobacco. You are to tell correctly in which way we extend our tobacco. You have been named as they who shall not fail to utter our wants to your fellow manitous. First of all we remember the Green Buffalo. He is the one to whom we first raise our hands. We extend to him our cooked food, and also this sweet food. He was the one who spoke to me first. He has mentioned life to me, and what he wished me. Also he has wished me pleasant association with my fellow people. And he will think this because of our tobacco. He must bless us who belong to this one clan in that way. You must tell him this for us.

"Also you must tell the one who sits yonder under the earth and who sits in the east. You also must tell him the same thing for us. Therefore we speak to him in the same way so that he will wish the same for us because of our tobacco. That we may associate with our people till old age is what we say to him. That is what you must tell him for us. And that we shall not have weak lives in any way.

"Then also we ask from the Sunny Buffalo who dwells in the south under the earth the same thing. May our children continue to live in good health. He must wish them this for us. That is our prayer to him. That is what you are to tell him for us who are now made to use this wolf name.[12] That he think intently of us is what we ask you to tell him for us.

"Then also the Buffalo who sits yonder, straight toward the west, is also one to whom we raise our hands. Our grandfather, you must wish that our lives reach old age because of the tobacco we have given. That is what we say to him. That is what you must say for us, our grandfather. These who sit with me are they to whom the tobacco belongs.

---

11. This speech has the words "so be it" inserted after every few words of the English translation; they are omitted here although they indicate the special character of the speech.

12. I.e., those who belong to the Wolf clan.

"Then also the Northern Buffalo, who sits yonder in the north under the earth. That indeed is what you must tell him for us. We ask the same thing from him. He must wish life for every one of us who belong to this clan. We implore him that it strengthen our lives. That is what we pray as we now raise our hands toward the manitous who dwell beneath this earth.

"We have now named them in a circle. And we are all to plead with them. These pleading all belong to this town of ours. That our lives will not be weak in any way is what we ask. And may our town be well. And also if evil disease stands about, may our dwellings stand unmolested. And may no one be afflicted with disease. And, again, may whoever from without goes about speaking evilly against our town, may his desire end prematurely. May he cease to think evilly against us. That is what we say to them. And if he does not cease thinking against us, may he at last demolish his own town. And we ask especially from them that which was wished me last and which was placed last, one slice. May they give us life in exchange for our kettleful.[13] These are our fervent prayers we ask because of our cooked food. That is what you must carefully tell for us, our grandfather.

"And also we beseech The One Who Sits In The Smoke Hole the same way. Moreover, may you all bless us that our heart be with your heart. That is what we beseech of you. And may your heart be with our heart because of our cooked food. That is what we beseech you. That you will tell the manitous whom we worship. How can it be that they will not hear our prayers? How can it be that they will turn their heads from us? You, Spirit of Fire, our grandfather, must insist on them hearing our prayers."

That, it is said, is what the speaker said in his talk.

Then he said to his fellow clansmen, "This speech is indeed very difficult. If anyone utters this from his mouth he thereby obtains life. If anyone knows the songs, the same will happen to him. Because our grandfather has shortened our lives too much, he has granted us to worship one day. We must

---

13. I.e., kettleful of food.

be gentle whenever we worship. That is what the manitou expects of us. We must put aside for a short time our lustful manhood. Also, we must also put aside our funny sayings. We are only to think quietly of the manitou, and of him alone. That is what he expects us to do. The one who does that is he who will be successful in his prayers. He is the one who will be remembered by the manitou. For he will be living as the manitou desired. How could it be that he would not be remembered by the manitou? Indeed the manitou will remember him.

"We do not worship him long. It is just as long as these ceremonies are being performed. That is how long he must be thought of. That is why the manitou is here who knows every inner thought. He is seated here where he cannot but know what we think in our hearts.

"And this Spirit of Fire does not misutter our prayers to those whom we worship. He speaks all the languages the manitous speak. We see this Fire plainly. He cannot be held by anyone. We who are mortals fear him. Still, we will not cease to take care of him. Every one of us must continue to take care of him. That is what we must do. He is the one who will look after that which we are to eat. It is not only here when we are celebrating our clan festival. It is anywhere. He helps every one of us. It is only after he has chewed our food that we can eat it. He has been told to do that. As many of us whose heads are covered with hair will use this Fire that way," he said to his fellow clansmen.

"Now then, at last we are to begin singing. We shall not continue to sing very long," he said to them. He then sang:

> When I arise here;
> When I arise here;
> When I arise here;
> When I arise here, I;
> When I arise here;
> When I arise here, I;
> Upon this earth, my horns are fixed;
> When I arise here;
> When I arise here;

When I arise here, I;
When I arise here;
When I arise here;
When I arise here, I.[14]

The Buffaloes here tell me, "I fear you," yes; they fear
me;
The Buffaloes here tell me, "I fear you," yes; they fear
me;
The Buffaloes here tell me, "I fear you," yes; they fear
me;
The Buffaloes here tell me, "I fear you," yes; they fear
me;
The Buffaloes here tell me, "I fear you," yes; they fear
me;
The Buffaloes here tell me, "I fear you," yes; they fear
me;
The Buffaloes here tell me, "I fear you," yes; they fear
me.[15]

This is why I have spoken, so I may be quoted;
This is why I have spoken, so I may be quoted;
This is why I have spoken, so I may be quoted;
This is why I have spoken, so I may be quoted;
This is why I have spoken, so I may be quoted.[16]

The buffaloes here call me "the Green Buffalo";
The buffaloes here call me "the Green Buffalo";
The buffaloes here;
Sacrifice a dog to me;
The buffaloes here call me "the Green Buffalo";
The buffaloes here;
The buffaloes here.[17]

---

14. The meaning is "as soon as the young man was blessed he went to war."
15. The buffaloes say the young man is brave.
16. The young man was blessed by the manitous so that he might slay his foes.
17. The chief Green Buffalo who conferred the blessing is supposed to be speaking.

They were to dance again. "We are now going to make you dance again, our leaders," the member of the Feathered clan was told. "You must invite your woman who is to follow you," he was told. "Very well," he replied. He said to the woman, "Now then." They went and stood in position where the sacred pack was. This dancing song was sung:

> I make it dance for you, I make it dance for you;
> My father, I make it dance for you, I make it dance for you, I make it dance for you;
> My father, I make it dance for you, I make it dance for you, I make it dance for you;
> My father, I make it dance here by the fireside, I make it dance for you, I make it dance for you;
> My father, I make it dance for you, I make it dance for you, I make it dance for you;
> My father, I make it dance for you, I make it dance for you, I make it dance for you.[18]

> Then, my fellow buffaloes, refer to me;
> Then, my fellow buffaloes, refer to me;
> Then, my fellow buffaloes, refer to me;
> In the wilderness my fellow buffaloes refer to me;
> Then, my fellow buffaloes, refer to me.[19]

> Father, I speak to you from afar;
> Father, I speak to you from afar, do I;
> I speak to you from afar;
> Father, I speak to you from afar, do I;
> Father, I speak to you from afar, do I;
> I speak to you from afar;
> Father, I speak to you from afar, do I;
> Father, I speak to you from afar;
> Father, I speak to you from afar, do I;

---

18. The one blessed dances around the fire, thus showing his blessing is valid.
19. The Green Buffalo says, "My fellow buffaloes have aided me in blessing the one I blessed, so that he may slay his foes far off and in lonely places."

FOX CLAN CEREMONIALS

I speak to you from afar;
Father, I speak to you from afar.[20]

He is instructed, he is instructed;
He is instructed, he is instructed;
He is instructed; he is instructed;
He is instructed, he is instructed, is he;
He is instructed, he is instructed, is he;
He is instructed, he is instructed.[21]

They had now danced. "These are the songs that we are always to use. I wished that you take these songs on and on. The manitou has desired that I take these songs on as long as there shall be an earth. You had better do so, my fellow clansmen," he said to them. Then he began to tell them to partake of sugar, maple cakes, syrup, the sweet foods of any kind. And after those whom he had told to partake of the food had gone out and invited others, he began to give a speech: "These are indeed that which we first hand to the manitou, those buffaloes who dwell, who sit fixedly under the earth. They themselves have already said that they would think highly of this that flows from the trees. We desire life from them in return for our tobacco that we have given. We first mention the Buffalo who sits permanently in the east. The Sunny Buffalo who sits permanently in the south is also one to whom we hand this. And the Buffalo who sits in the west is one to whom we say the same when we mention them collectively, 'Pray, think of us in return for our tobacco and this sweet food.' That is what we say to them. And that is also what we say to Wintry Buffalo who sits in the north. He must wish us good health in return for our offerings. That is why we have handed him our tobacco. And therefore you should have good health. Wherefore you should eat. Eat, women and men," he said to them. That is what he said in his speech.

---

20. The esoteric meaning assigned this song seems out of place. The Green Buffalo says, "You know how I have blessed you."

21. The one blessed is told by the buffaloes that they have completed this instruction.

"This is the way you must speak at this time, that is, when eating the sweet food. And you also must try hard to catch on to this other one after they have eaten," he said to them.

After they had eaten he said to them, "Sit down where you were seated." Then he said, "Our chief must come here." Then he told the chief to serve the meat food. The chief then gave invitations. He invited anyone, but two from each clan. After indeed all had come, then the chief began serving them. After he had served them, he said, "It is done," to those celebrating the clan festival. "Very well," he was told.

Then the young man began to make a speech:[22] "We have offered this separately to the Green Buffalo. It is life that we mainly desire from him. He should wish this for us because of our tobacco. Pray, wish old age for us because of our cooked food. That is what we implore him. We do not desire anything that is frightful. We ask him only what is good. That is why his fellow chief sits down at his feast. That is why you should eat. Eat," he said to them.

Those who were eating ate slowly. They put away slowly the bones that were left over. After they had eaten the chief himself went to gather the bones. Then the ceremonial attendant put them away carefully. He placed them out of the path. And after the ceremonial attendant had returned, he began to serve the pumpkins. There were four bowls. And one member of each clan was told to participate. They went out and invited others. Each one invited many. Then they told when there was a sufficient number. "We are now of a sufficient number," the ceremonial attendant said to those celebrating the clan festival. Then the leading ceremonial attendant said to the leader of those giving the clan festival, "They have now all come."

Then the one blessed said, "From the buffaloes, whom we worship, life is what we desire it. We have talked of ourselves. We have asked them that the manitous may take us on to old age. He, the Spirit of Fire, no doubt began long ago to tell our grandfather about this. We also extend our hands to the buffaloes who are here on this earth with our tobacco and also this,

---

22. See note 11.

our cooked food, this pumpkin soup. They themselves stated that they would think highly of pumpkins. They should bless you accordingly, you who have invited each other. They have already said this with respect to those who shall eat these carefully. They must wish old age for us who eat carefully. Therefore, you must eat, you women, and you men. Eat!"

They ate. And after they had eaten he said to them, "Now sit here where you have been seated, you women, and you men. There is much of this 'So be it' when the buffalo speech is given,"[23] he said to them. "You should carefully catch on to the times when it is used. Now we had better start in singing," he said to them. "These are the same songs that we are to continue to use. There are not many of them, youths. This indeed is how we shall sing," he said to them:

[The first four songs with slight variations are given here.]
They danced.
[The final four songs with slight variations are given here.]

"We have now made them dance twice. There are yet two more times to make them dance. They will now eat some more food. They shall invite each other. They must place some more food in the kettles in place of the food that has been eaten. The men will now cook in a hurry," said the twin.

Then he said to the ceremonial attendants: "You who are a ceremonial attendant may eat from anywhere you desire. You ceremonial attendants must first have your bellies filled. After your bellies are filled, you will begin to be busy. You are then to serve the food to the women and children. You will feed them."

The attendants then stopped to eat. And after they had eaten they started to serve the food. They went about it slowly. They started to serve the food beginning at the east, and they did so slowly. Moreover, one was outside inviting. A ceremonial attendant was inviting. There were many to eat. After the attendants had served the food to those sitting inside they then began to serve the food to those who had been invited. Later on they had served all the food. "That is all," the ceremonial

---

23. See note 1.

attendants said to the twin. "Very well," said the one who was giving the clan festival. He then began a speech.

"Women and men, we have first scattered our tobacco to the Spirit of Fire that he may tell for us in the right way what we ask from the manitous. We ask from them good health for our entire town. That is what we ask them to wish because of this, our cooked food. Should disease stand around, may our dwelling remain as manitous. That is what we ask from those who are now seated about conspicuously, our grandfathers. They must think alike of our lives. That is what we say to them. That is why you are to eat, women and men. Eat!" he said to them.

The people now ate. They indeed consumed much food. Still, the ceremonial attendants put more food into the kettles. Then the young man said to those who were celebrating the clan festival with him, "Now we must sit quietly for a while." They sat still. "This sacred pack does not belong to me alone. We alike own it, even a little baby. It owns it in just the same way that we own it. I have been instructed with regard to it, but nevertheless I do not myself own the sacred pack. What it thinks of you it thinks of me. It does not love me alone. It loves you also just as much. How could it be that I should think that I claim the manitou's desire? It will not claim me alone. It has been placed here by the manitou so that we may worship it earnestly. Our grandfathers think the same of us. That one yonder is our greatest grandfather. At the time when he ruled our lives to be too short, he called together those who are called manitous. He told them what they must think of us. 'You must always love and bless the people.' That is what he said to them. Still, those who are blessed by those told this, are taken up there. They are taken where the Great Manitou dwells. And when one is not taken up, the Great Manitou is summoned. He looks at the one who has been blessed. The Great Manitou is simply of such a nature as to be shown the people. He will not refuse. He too must talk to one. Yet he is not to tell anyone that which is frightful. He must wish for the people that which is right. That is how he is. It is against his rules for the Great Manitou to wish the people that which is frightful. His wish for them is alone peacefulness. These others, however, might wish that. For it seems as if they have been made to wish for you whatever you may desire. 'You will continue to wish for them,' they were told. It is impossible for the Great Manitou to say, 'You must not wish this for them.' That is why our grandfathers here continue to wish for us this, namely, 'I wish you to be a warrior.' The manitou has simply granted us that we make each other wail, back and forth. That is how he has arranged it for us. Even indeed some other little beings will do that to each other. They kill each other alternately. Indeed it has been fixed so for even the different kinds of little birds. One kind flies about at night. One kind flies about during the day. The one who flies about has enemies in accordance.[24] And we speak all sorts of different languages. That is how we have our enemies. That is why I say we take turns in making each other weep. No one alone will always make his fellow people weep. We are considered alike by the manitou who thinks over us. Yet our fasting is of different kinds. Our fasting does not think of us alike. Our way is very hard. Whenever our women-folk stay outside,[25] they must stay outside. We must never eat with one who is staying outside. That is what is expected of us. That is against the rules of these sacred bundles. And a woman who is staying outside would be ruined by these sacred bundles should she go inside where they are hanging. It is not only here where our sacred single bundle hangs, but also where any sacred bundles hang. That is how the manitou has preserved us.

"And also this. She must not look on during a clan festival such as we are holding. It is not that way. Indeed the same is so with every other clan festival. The one celebrating the clan festival should not allow them to look on. That is a thing that will be against our rules so long as there is an earth. It is said that soon we shall get so that we shall not care anything about this. When we cease to care anything about this, something will happen. It will be so if no one gives any clan festivals. It

---

24. I.e., with his time to fly.
25. I.e., when they are menstruating.

will not be so if one goes on and gives clan festivals. It will be after he ceases to think about it. Then the manitou will be ruled by it in turn. The manitou will call to this. If at that time the manitou has already called to it, then the things here will cease to grow. We then cannot eat anything. Indeed even this one who flies with wings will be gone. The little game will be gone. And the rivers will go down, indeed gradually. Now, what is there for us to eat? That which has made us to cease to think about our sacred packs will be around in abundance. It will then lie around everywhere.

"Still, we cannot do anything about that at all. That will happen to those who will come far off from now. As it is now, it seems as if we have just come to a hill for the first time. And we shall try to carry our sacred bundle over it. I am now taking care of it. If I die then we shall carry it further. Finally we shall bring it up to the top of the hill. As soon as we have taken it down a little way, there is where one dwells who cares nothing about it. From there it will be rolled down the hill. After rolling down to the base, it will unwrap. That is the time when we shall fall here and there from hunger. And we cannot eat anything else," he said to them. "That is why I coax you to think about what I have told you. If some of our friends who sit yonder know anything about a sacred bundle they would tell this same thing. Indeed they would not tell you anything different. They would say the same thing. I am telling you the plain truth," he said to his associates. "So I have once told you a tale."

Those who were invited were now through eating. "Now then, you may go to the places from where you were invited, for a while, women and men," he said to them.

The ceremonial attendants had now boiled food again. They had now cooked everything. They now were finally well filled. Then he said to them, "These songs are the ones we shall always use. These are those we shall use at first. Later on there will be many of them. These will not be the only songs we shall continue to use. Indeed these songs will increase just as long and as many times as we are victors on the warpath. It is not that we shall use all of them here at once. If the Buffaloes who are under the earth so desire we shall do that. Indeed he who goes out as the leader of a war party is he who will know what songs are to be added. I alone will not name them. He who heads a victorious war party is he who will be made to know by the manitou. That is how it is. I tell it to you in advance so that you will know what we are to do, and that you know what a difficult time we shall have in obtaining these songs. The songs of our friends are like this here and there. But ours are very difficult. If you desire to use them in a hurry you must fast. You will know the songs that we are to own at that time. Well, I am enjoying talking too much; we had better start to sing," he said to the fellow members of his clan. "Very well," they replied. They started to sing. They again used the same songs that they had used.

[The first four songs with slight variations are given here.]

They had now sung. Then he said to them, "We are to be seated for a while," he said to them. "This is why we are to be seated a while. Our offerings have just been put in the kettles a short time ago. That is why I have said, 'Let us be seated for a while.' " Then he said to them, "Well, our leaders, eventually we are to dance."

[The final songs with slight variations are given here.]

"You are now to eat," the dancers were told. "Now, ceremonial attendants, they are all to eat. You must all withdraw the kettles from over the fire. Since you are ceremonial attendants you may see whether you want to eat or not," the ceremonial attendants were told. "You indeed must serve them slowly. Do not be in a hurry while serving food to those who sit about. Indeed be slow. Again, those who are to issue invitations are to be two in number. The Toohkaana may go toward the east, and the Kiishkooha toward the west.[26] That is what they are to do. One of them must be a member of the War Chiefs clan and one of them must be a member of the Bear clan. There will be exactly two of them. They will not walk as if they were trying to beat each other. They are to walk around

---

26. These names refer to the two divisions of the Fox. Children were alternately assigned to these divisions: The first child of a couple was assigned to the division not that of the father; the second, to the father's division; and so on.

slowly when they walk to give invitations. The only persons whom they are not to invite are those who are disabled. The food may be carried to those who are disabled. They may eat yonder. They may say to the children, 'I invite you.' Indeed they must say that to them. That is what the manitous say to each other. Just for fun they say to each other, 'I invite you.' For that reason they may go about saying that to them. They must even say to babies in their cradles, 'I invite you.' They must say that to them and mention their names. They are to walk around slowly. Wherever they happen to meet each other, there is from where they are to return. And those of you who are here may then begin serving the food to those who have been invited. That is what you must do. You are not to serve them in a hurry. You must serve those who are to eat slowly. You may eat after they have all come. You must not proceed to inform us. Every one of you must indeed think about life. You must think about it in your hearts. 'I wish I could live to that time.' That is what we are to think. 'I wish that I may reach the full length of my life.' That is what we are to think in our hearts. Also 'I wish that disease may not strike me.' That is what we must also think in our hearts."

The one celebrating the clan festival said the same things to all. And, those invited began to come in. As the people came in they were served food. Then there was no more room inside the dwelling and they had to sit outside. And, after the people had started to sit outside, the leading ceremonial attendants went outside to serve the food. The people who had been invited came continously. There was humming everywhere as the people talked to each other.

Some time later they saw the inviters coming as a pair. Then the one celebrating the clan festival said, "Now you no doubt are keeping track of what we are doing. You must keep track very carefully of what we are to do. These people are to eat all at once. We shall do this so the food may be eaten all at once. Our offerings must not be left over. That is not our way. The manitou has desired us to do it this way. It seems as if this worship were spilled. Then the lives we were to get were thrown away. That life which is thrown away is not somebody else's but our own. It seems that should someone have a weak life, then his life would end indeed quickly. Indeed his life would go backward. That is what would happen to him. Also, our children would be those who would continue to die. It seems as if a child's life is weak. Because it is a child is why it barely lives. That is why it would continue to die. It is the same with regard to the life of the aged. That is precisely my reason in forbidding our offerings to be left over. That is why I tell you that. When you hold your clan festivals have the right amount of offerings. Do not be dissatisfied with the amount of your offerings in the clan festivals. As it is now, it is very likely that we have the right amount for this clan festival. If they could barely consume it, then we should offer less in our next clan festival. Then we shall know the amount we are to offer in our worship of the manitou. The manitou himself does not desire that we offer him much food in our worship. It makes no difference if the offering is little when we worship him. He would consider it much. It is then made into any amount that is desired. If the manitou desires that there be much of it, he can make much from it. When he is offered much of it, it is considered the same. That is why you should continue to tell one another. You should continue to tell each other. Indeed the manitou is truly a manitou. We should do whatever he has wished. If he blesses us he will never forget us. We shall be remembered just as there is a people. We see this earth and this sky as reminders. We do not know when they are to go to ruin. Very likely later on it will be desired that they change. Even in the same way you who are still remembered will see each other. And you will not see each other in few numbers. Still, it is very hard indeed to have the manitou pity you and to have him think about you. That is what you should continue to tell each other. Why should you lie to each other about this? It is all right," he said to them. "That is what I have to say to you," he said.

Then he was informed, "We have now served all the food to all. Indeed the food was exactly enough. There was not too little, and there was none left over."

Then, it is said, he said to them, "Now when I begin to

give my speech this time, you must all think alike in your hearts about our offerings. Every one of you has been made to sit down to this offering by the ceremonial attendants. You are not to talk to each other for a while. Do just whatever I have told you, that is, think alike in your hearts. This is what you must think, 'I wish I could reach old age.' You must think that as you sit down with this offering. That indeed is the way. And also this. 'I wish I could become a man and could easily deal with my enemy.' That is what you must think of. 'Think of me in the same way as you think of the one whom you have blessed.' That also is what you must think. That is what I have to tell you. If you think in your hearts, 'Who is there who will know what we think in our hearts?' There is a manitou called 'He Who Lies With His Face Bulging In The Smoke Hole.' He is the one who will know what you think in your hearts. That one was told to come down here and live with the people. He was instructed to come here so that he might know what we think in our hearts about our lives. Indeed he is the one who is to tell all our hearts' desires. That is what he has been told. He will not tell falsely what we think about our lives. He will tell all of the manitous who have blessed me. There will be none of them who do not know about us. So indeed think that way," he said to them, "women and men." "All right," they replied. Then he began a speech.[27]

"When I made the manitou take compassion upon me he did not wish me that which is evil. He wished me that which is good. This is the first time we will worship him. He has stated that I would tell the truth in here. So if all of you who are tasting my offerings for the first time, if you think alike, then his life will be exactly the way he desires. We shall chew the war enemies soft of the one whose relatives have been wronged. This is what we shall wish for such a one, that in return he will make them sad. That is what the manitous who sit under this earth told me when they blessed me. We speak first to the manitou buffalo who sits facing us in the east. He must wish life for us in return for our cooked food. And we

---

27. See note 11.

have also raised up our hands collectively with tobacco. 'Wish that for us because of our tobacco.' That is what we say to him. And again, wish that some of them be men.[28] That is what we say to him. Again, may our entire town never be entered by this disease. That is what we say to him. Think and wish life only for our town. That is what we ask from the buffalo who sits facing us from the east. He himself has promised what we would think about us, so that he thereby might derive his smoke from here.

"And also the one who spoke to me the second time, the Sunny Buffalo who sits in the south has also spoken that way. 'When you first worship me I will think of every one of you in your town.' That is the way they spoke when they first blessed me. He also has told what he would wish for us. 'I will wish life for every one of them who has been affected by your worship.' That is what he also has told me. 'And again, if he desires, the enemy from without who has made him weep, I will chew him soft for him.' That is what the Sunny Buffalo has said. That is what we ask from him. Also, that he think quietly of our town. That is what he has said. And if disease should pass by, may it not enter here. That is what we ask the Sunny Buffalo to wish for us.

"And the Buffalo who sits facing us from the west has also told me that. I ask from him that which he has told me. When he said, 'When you first worship me and someone is first made to realize this by your worship, he will reach old age.' That is what we ask from him, that which he has already said. 'And if he desires his war enemies in any way I shall wish that for him or whatever he desires. If he only desires old age, I shall wish for him that which he has asked.' That is how he spoke when he spoke to me. 'And when this disease stands around your town, your dwellings will stand as manitous. It cannot enter your dwelling. I shall only quietly wish it away for you.' That is what the Buffalo told me when he spoke to me. He must wish us that. He must wish us that because of our tobacco as we raise our hands upward with it. And they must also think the same because of our cooked food. They have already said that them-

---

28. I.e., warriors.

selves. That is the reason why I have confidently reminded them thereof.

"Then the Wintry Buffalo who sits facing us from the north has also told me the same. 'When you first worship me, why I shall indeed bless every one of your fellow people who is first affected by your worship.' What we have now told them is what they must wish us. And if someone's relatives have been slain, the slayer will be chewed soft in return. That is what we desire the Wintry Buffalo to wish for us. 'And if anyone wants old age only, indeed I shall wish him that.' That is what the manitous who blessed me said. And this Spirit of Fire must so remind them. He has been named as the one upon whom we are to depend, our grandfather.

"That is what our grandfathers also must think of us. We do not only ask them what they must think about us alone. Indeed they must think that of every one of us, children as well as women and men. Whatever we desire them to wish for us is now granted us. We have now implored the manitous what to think of us. After all they will be reminded of it as they smoke our tobacco. That is what we say to them. They may speak to each other. We are then to do whatever we have desired for ourselves. That is all. They will not merely say this. They are not too small to think. We shall now all alike request the same from this Spirit of Fire. He has probably begun long ago to tell his fellow manitous. And the one called 'He Who Knows Inner Thoughts' will begin to tell what we think about our lives. Again, those who desire to become warriors will be granted their desires by the manitous whom we worship. The manitous must think that way of every one of us. They are those who own those desires. They must think that of us. They themselves, our grandfathers, have already told me. You women and you men ought to begin eating. Eat!" he said to them.

The people ate slowly. There were many. They ate for some time. Their bellies were exactly well filled. No one was too full. The eaters had their bellies filled each alike. There was much food that they had eaten. Still they had consumed it all.

Then the one celebrating the clan festival said to his fellow members while the eating took place: "I have now just told you about this. We shall now each alike have strong lives. I have told these people what they must think in their hearts about their lives. Some of them have desired what I have told them. And some did not think about that at all. Still, they will be thought of in the manner the manitou thinks of us. They will not be thought of in the way they desired. It is only he who has thought in the way I have indicated who will be thought of in whatever way he desired. He who has desired to be thought of in another way will not be thought of at all. The manitou has told what we must desire from him. He who desires this is he who will be thought of by him. That is the only way I know how to be blessed by him. If one has the privilege of desiring to be thought of in another way, he will not be thought of. Only he who thinks about his life in exactly the way I have said is he who is known by the manitou, and by those leading beings whom I have mentioned in a circle.[29] They are the leading ones who have been made to watch over our desires. They have mentioned that they would all join in thinking about us at this time. This day we have thought of them for the first time. They told me to tell everyone what to think. That is indeed why I have told everyone. At this time we shall begin singing. Yet we shall stop to tell them and thereby remind them. It is a rule that everyone must dance. That is what we must stop to tell them," he said to them. He spoke to them himself.

"This time you must all dance for us," he said to them. "After we sing we are to sing dancing songs. You must then think about what I have told you. You must do so," he said to them. The people everywhere replied favorably. They were willing to dance. "Our leading ceremonial attendant, we shall want your servies for a while right here," he said to him. Then he said to the attendant, "These are not to return home after eating." Then he informed those who were seated about outside. "It is said that you are not to return home," the ceremonial attendants said to them. They indeed remained seated. Then at last they began singing.

[The first four songs with some variations are given here.]

---

29. I.e., in east, south, west, and north.

"At last we are going to make you dance, our friends. You will make us willing if every one of you dance," he said to them.

[The final four songs with some variations are given here, and another song sung.]

"We have now made you dance," he said to them. "And when dancing songs are used for the third time, these dancing songs are used. That is the way it is. You should keep track of how they all are. The third time only three dancing songs are used," he said to them.

There were many people. He was yet seated. "Now, my friends, I have told you some time ago what you should think of yourselves, what you should desire to be thought of by the manitous who blessed me. You did not all alike believe me. Some did not think in their hearts what I said for them to think. Some thought about something totally different. They did not desire what I told them to desire. They have disbelieved me. And if we were to see the manitou suddenly, we could not indeed tell him our desires the same way. This, it seems, would happen to us. Our desires would be strung all over. We should not do what would please the manitou. It seems that we shall only ask that which will make our lives good. That is what we alike say to the manitou. He would not refuse us. And if we desire from him different things he would not know whom to believe. Very likely the manitou would be discouraged if we asked too many things from him. Very likely someone would ask for something that he hates. He would not be told 'I dislike that,'[30] if he said to him, 'this is how you will bless me.' That is how it now looks. Some ask that all sorts of things may be granted them. Even some old men ask for women. And a woman asks the same thing. He does not like that very well. For somewhere there is seated one who bestows such blessings. That is what I have to stop to tell you.

"Now who is there who would think in his heart, 'Gracious!' when his worship has just been completed? Perhaps we thus have pleased our grandfathers. They probably would not

---

30. I.e., I dislike that to be your wish.

think in their hearts, 'It shall not be.' We no doubt have made our grandfathers' hearts glad because we have eaten this, which is extended to them with our hands. We have raised our hands up to those manitous. You have probably thereby pleased them. They will always be that way. That is what I wish these grandchildren of mine. That is what they should think of us. As for you, our grandfathers should think the same of you. And they think indeed the same of these ceremonial attendants. They should wish them to reach old age after carefully handling all of our offering. We all have worshiped them. We alone did not worship them. Indeed we pleaded that they think of all of us alike. We were to have desired the same. Yet we did not desire the same. Therefore you had better depart to where you live, women, and also you men."

Then the people walked off in different directions. When they came to where they came from, those who believed thought in their hearts, "This is what he has said."

It is said that they would know that as soon as they went to sleep. Some indeed obtained what they had asked.

Then that member of the Wolf clan led a war party. He too thought in his heart, "I shall carry my sacred bundle about. It may be that there will be no one who will carry it for me." He said to them, " 'Very likely someone will carry it off,' I thought," he said to them. Then he was informed by many who desired to become warriors. And he addressed them: "Now men, I do not want many, I want only men from four households. There must be just that number—four. Our enemy will not harm us in any way. They will all alike be brought here. It seems as if this that I am to carry about will bring them. Let no one be afraid of those whom I have already eaten. They are those whom I have already eaten. What is there then that will make you fear them? Let no one think of fearing them. I am now telling you what you will do to them. You must not stop to deal gently with them. That is why I have told you. There will be four households of them. There will be precisely so many. And you must go about and beat our enemies' heads until they sound. Even if they have something that hurts, it will be nothing. It will be ruined before they have a chance to use it on us. That is what will happen to them. That is why I tell you that you can go at them to your heart's desire. What is there then that will make you fear them?

"If you should turn and run, then they would see just which of us they shoot at. That is what I have to say to you. Should they even hold knives in their hands they will indeed drop them when they start to take after us. That is what I have to tell you. You must think earnestly of what I have told you. You must do what I have told you. Still, it may be that we shall not return for a while, or we might come upon them easily. We might come to them later on. Where they will stay will not be in this direction. If you think in your hearts, 'We shall come upon them quickly,' we will quickly come upon them. You may do as you desire," he said to them.

The one who carried about the sacred bundle with him was the ceremonial attendant who belonged to the War Chiefs clan. And he told his ceremonial attendant, "You must inform me what they have to say, ceremonial attendant." Then he listened while they counselled. Some thought they should search for them slowly. And some thought they should find them quickly. And those who thought they should find them quickly were believed. "We shall do that. We shall see them quickly," they said. "Very well," they were told. They then told that ceremonial attendant so he might tell about it. And he told the leader of the war party. "They said that they would see them quickly," so he said to him. "Very well," the other replied. "Then you must go hunting very early tomorrow. If you kill an elk before sunrise, then it will be so. It will not be so if it is killed later. The one who kills the elk will be the one to kill the enemy first. You will bring the elk in quickly. Then you will butcher it. If you dress it carefully and without trouble we will be masters of what we are to do. At this time they may go hunting very early in every direction. Why, they have wished us to see the foe quickly," he said to them.

Then that ceremonial attendant was told to go over and tell them that at least. He told them just what he had been told. Those people, those belonging to the war party, were proud. And the hunters went out early in the morning. After they had walked a little way, a man killed an elk. He was proud. He already thought in his heart that he would be the first to slay a foe. Some of them envied the man. They brought the large elk in. "You must butcher it quickly," the men were told. And the ceremonial attendant was awakened after it had been butchered. "You alone must roast and eat it," the ceremonial attendant was told. He started to roast much of it. After he had cooked it, he started to untie that sacred bundle. "This is what I am going to worship," he was told.

After he sat down to his roasted meat, then the one whom he served as a ceremonial attendant began to make a speech. This is what he said: "Now we shall rely on the manitou who sits in the east. He will indeed bring the hearts of those whom I shall attack. You will therefore eat this. Eat," he was told.

The ceremonial attendant ate heartily. After he had eaten alone he was told: "Ceremonial attendant, cut it up in pieces." He cut it up in pieces. Then he was told, "Ceremonial attendant, go around and give it to our friends. I also will even eat. Every one of us may eat, for you have eaten the one I offered in my clan festival. We shall now eat this one." That is what the young man said. "You may give everyone the same amount. Each clan shall have the same amount. We shall eat that way," he said. They then, every one of them, ate with the members of their respective clans. For example, the ceremonial attendant ate with the members of the War Chiefs clan. They sat in no particular places. And after they had eaten they were told, "Now you will put out the fire every place." And those whose business it was put the fire out everywhere. Then they were told, "We shall listen very quietly." They listened to learn who was going on the warpath.

Suddenly they saw where there was light. There were four lights burning. "There it is, men," they were told. Then the ceremonial attendant was told to go and watch as a scout. "Very well," he replied. He departed. He came to where the Sioux were staying. He counted how many men there were. And he also counted the number of women. He departed. He returned to the place from which he had departed. "Well, ceremonial attendant, what did you observe?" "I could not look

at them closely, that is, I could not go inside their dwellings."
He started to tell how many Sioux there were, and how many
in each household. Then he was told, "That is it, ceremonial
attendant. You please me. I thought in my heart as you walked
away, 'I wish he could count.' You have done just what I
desired you to do," he said to him. "You shall indeed kill one
who has the nature of a manitou. I have told you to do this so
that I may always think in my heart, 'This ceremonial attendant is one who has a being who has the nature of a manitou,' "
he said to his ceremonial attendant. The ceremonial attendant
was proud.

Then they started to creep upon their foes. They lay down
close to them. Just as soon as it was light enough to see they
attacked them. They whooped at them and knocked them
around until their heads sounded with each stroke. The scouts
were all struck down. Then the war party went home. They
were joyous on their way. They had not been harmed by their
foes. And they were cheered on their way. No one felt sad in
his heart as they were returning. And when the men returned
everywhere their relatives were proud. "That is it," the men
were told. Every one of them became warriors. Every one of
those young men now loved the one whom they accompanied.
They would always invite him whenever they ate. They always
did that to the one by whom they had been made warriors.

And later on the man again departed. "Now, men, where I
am going is dangerous. Very likely you will indeed shoot each
other's flesh back and forth until it sounds," he said to them.
Then some returned. They were afraid. That was why they
returned. There were many who had been made afraid by his
talk. That was why they returned. Finally those who were not
able to return came to the spot. "You now know how many of
you there are. You may go and cheer the food that I have left
over where I have been summoned to eat. There is not much of
it now. There is but a single one whom I am going to attack.
He who has gone home has simply gone home. There is one
person whom I shall go to attack. It is one that is lost. So that
he will not simply starve to death is why I am to attack him. It
has been said that he is thought of evilly by a manitou. That is

the only thing that is considered best for him, so that he will not be worried any more by traveling. He would always think in his heart of where he came from. After he is gone, he will remain just in one place. That is considered best by the one who thinks of him. If he is killed he will not die naturally. It would be shameful for him to starve to death. He would be in shame. Therefore, I shall go and be fed. I hold him in my mouth. You are not to fear him. I have already dissolved him in my mouth," he said to those whom he accompanied. "This is the way he will come. He will have only a single weapon. He will be satisfied with it. He is the one who has been starved. That is the one I am to attack. And you will get him unmercifully," he said to those whom he had taken.

Those who accompanied him were few in number. He told them what they had to do. And they did exactly so. They waited to see where the foe would come into view. They really saw that man. When he came close they whooped. He only looked at them. They all ran toward him. He threw away his bow and jumped on this knees. He raised his hands upward. He then was not killed. He was taken. They fed him well. That is what they did to him. And they took him along. And indeed during his stay he learned to talk Indian.[31] After he could speak Indian well he began to relate what had happened to him during the time he was lost. He never mentioned who his parents were. He was asked, "Have you any parents?" "No," he replied. "I was wretched when I was a child. My fellow Indians deserted me when I was sick. Whenever you go on the warpath I will go with you. I am going to capture those who deserted me."

And one man who desired to go on the warpath fasted. That Indian went with the one who took care of the sacred bundle. And later a war party went on the warpath. He accompanied them. The man who took care of him stayed at home. The captive now could speak Indian well. He also walked along anywhere when they went on the warpath. Later on they attacked, and he captured those who had deserted him. Later

---

31. I.e., Fox.

they recognized him. He cheered against them. He captured those who had treated him so very cruelly. He took along those whom he captured. He brought them to where he was staying. He gave his fellow Indians to the one with whom he was staying. "I went after them because they treated me very cruelly. I did not go after them for no reason. They deserted me when I was disabled. So you can do with them whatever you desire. If you wish to club them to death right here, you may club them to death," he said to him. And the other replied, "The ceremonial attendant is the one who should club these to death." The ceremonial attendant was summoned. "Ceremonial attendant, you are to club these to death. You must wait and bring them inside my dwelling. After you have brought them inside, then you will club them to death," the ceremonial attendant was told. Then they were taken over there to him. The people were many. He took them inside. After they were taken inside he went to kill them. There was a soft sound. Later, a scalp came out; and then another. As many as there were were all clubbed to death. All he did was to throw out the scalps. Whenever he threw them out the men would seize them from each other, and he became a warrior. And at last he said, "Where are the warriors?" "These are they," they said to him. "They are to take these whom they have killed and throw them away," he said to them. They took them off.

Then the member of the Wolf clan spoke: "This ceremonial attendant of mine has been made a man[32] by the manitou. He will always do that to his fellow people. He will not wish to deal gently with them. He is not made to do that. He will not deal gently with any little thing. That is what he is to do. If he tells about the time he was spoken to, we would hear horrors." That is what the member of the Wolf clan said. And when he came yonder he jumped and lay down. They did not know what the matter was with him. He had died. "It is too bad," the people said. This is the end.

---

32. I.e., a warrior.

VII. Winnebago Clan Ceremonials

Like that of the Fox Indians, some Winnebago ritual centers around bundles associated with the clans, that is, thought of as belonging to the clans. These rituals are of two types. One is the clan feast, a ceremonial at which offerings are made to the clan animal. Only members of that clan are invited and may participate in this ritual. The other is the winter feast for the clan war bundle, a ritual that also has something of the character of a general ceremony of thanksgiving to the spirits and to which members of all the clans are invited.

Descriptions of both types are given here. The first is of the clan feast of the Snake clan; the other is of the winter feast of the Thunderbird clan.

Clan Feast of the Snake Clan[1]

When a person wishes to give a snake feast, four chickens must be obtained. The nephew of the feast giver is then told to prepare these chickens and make the general preparations.

---

1. From Radin, *Winnebago Tribe*, pp. 325–328. The notes are from the original text.

The feast is given in the fall, just as the snakes are supposed to go into their winter quarters and close their doors. The winter is their night, and then they go to sleep.

Shortly before the feast begins the host takes out a bundle containing four snake skins—a yellow-snake skin, a rattlesnake skin, a blow-snake skin, and a bull-snake skin. In honor of these he gives his feast and makes his offerings.

As the fall of the year is to the snakes the same as our evening, the Winnebago give this feast in their honor then, in much the same way as we have our supper before retiring for the night. The snake skins are representatives of the first four snakes Earthmaker made and that he pierced through the earth in the direction of the east. The snake skins are kept to represent the four original snake-beings and to keep evil away from homes. That is why offerings are made to them. Four men only are invited to this feast,[2] and they must each eat a chicken.

The host himself opens the door for the snakes. In front of him, next to the fireplace, he makes four holes in the ground, thus opening the door for them. There he likewise places tobacco for them. First he pours tobacco in the fire, for the fire is the mediator between the people and the spirit. The fire tells the spirit the wishes of the people and is, in general, in charge of the members of the tribe. For that reason they always pour tobacco upon it.

Now the host rises and speaks. "Grandfather,[3] you who stand in the center of the lodge, I offer you tobacco, for you are the interpreter,[4] and I know that you will deliver the requests I address to our grandfather-who-crawls,[5] just as I have said to them. I offer you tobacco.

"To you likewise, grandfathers, you whom Earthmaker created first and placed within the earth, you whom Earthmaker placed in control of abundance of life and whose war clubs were made heavy, so that nothing could miss them;

---

2. As main participants.
3. Fire.
4. I.e., the interpreter between the spirits and the human beings.
5. Snake.

to you we offer these things. Whatever you can give us, we ask of you in return. Here are our offerings of food, tobacco, and eagle feathers. We place them here at your door. We ask that you bless us with victory in war. We know that the weapons you carry make you invulnerable, and we wish likewise to be invulnerable. You never fail to obtain what you desire with your clubs, and we ask that the same power be bestowed upon us. As the years pass may the blessing we obtain increase in power. When you look out upon the world, life emanates from your eyes. May this life be given to our posterity. As we strut about in the short number of days allotted to us may you keep out of our path, so that we may not be frightened. Yet should we cross any of your paths may we be strengthened thereby. It is said that you are the grass, and that is why we ask you to bless us. Bless us because you are in possession of the life we desire. For these reasons do we offer you tobacco, feathers, and food."

Then the host pours tobacco into the four holes that he has made in the ground and places feathers there. Then he takes a little food from each of the kettles and pours it into the four holes. After that he greases the heads of the snake skins that are lying before him with kettle grease and pours tobacco on the heads of the snakes. He asks all his relatives to offer tobacco likewise and he puts tobacco into the holes again and pours some upon the heads of the snakes.

When those invited have arrived, someone who is a good speaker sits near the entrance, while another good speaker sits near the farthest end. After all have entered, the leader of the four participants makes the circuit of the fireplace four times. He then sits down, and the host greets each one in turn, as follows:

"I greet you all. It is good. How could I say aught but that it is good? I am a poor worthless fellow, yet you have remembered me. It is good. You did not look upon my unworthiness and think within your hearts, 'He is a worthless fellow,' but you thought of the spirits, and therefore you came to sit with me so that I might see your face. It is good. I have obtained four chickens, and the attendant is now cooking them. I suppose he has cooked them by this time, and we will soon be able to eat them.

"I am attempting to cook water for the beings first created, so that we might be blessed with victory in war, and with life. That is what we are asking and what we would like to obtain from them before they[6] retire for the night. It is our desire to be blessed year in, year out.

"Your plates will be filled soon, so let me greet you again, you[7] who are taking the place of the spirits. All you who are present I greet."

The attendant now takes the kettles from the fire and takes the plate of the first of those sitting in the row. Then he takes the sharp stick that he holds in his hand, sticks it through one of the four chickens, and puts it in the plate of the first man. He passes the plate around the kettle four times, going from right to left, and finally he places it before the feaster. The feaster then says, "I thank you all," and the attendant passes on to the next one, and so in succession until he comes to the last person. Then the one first invited rises and says, "All those present, the host and the three other guests, do I greet." Then the speaker addresses the one sitting next to him, who greets him in return. In the same way he greets the third and the fourth one. Then he speaks as follows:

"It is good. Who would not be thankful for this? The host and his relatives present here are praying for life and victory, to the four greatest spirits Earthmaker ever made, to those spirits whom he pierced through the earth so that it might hold together. All the snakes whom we see on the earth are ruled by these four. From them have they asked blessings. The first human beings on earth saw these spirits face to face and, we are told, they used them for protection. These we see before us as the host has laid them out. We are told that blessings can be obtained by the use of these snakes.

---

6. The spirits.
7. Humans.

"I am indeed not a fit person to be invited to such a gathering as this, but the host has kindly overlooked my faults. My grandfather fasted and thirsted himself to death and he was blessed and his spirit taken to a spirit-home. That is what happened to my grandfather, for he told me this himself. The place where he was blessed was at Red Banks at a place where a creek flows into the sea.[8] At the fork of this creek there was a hill lying east and west. It is there that the yellow snake-chief lives. To the home of this snake-chief my grandfather was taken. This snake was at this place gathering tobacco for all the spirits. There my grandfather was even blessed with their bodies. For this reason I always pour tobacco for them. And I have been given to understand that the spirits do not overlook the least fault.[9] They are always in our midst just as even the grass and the dust represent snakes. They know everything, they say. It is not safe to cross their path. As, however, the host is now making an offering to them, should we cross their path now it would even strengthen us. It is good. These clubs are heavy and they will not fail to strike everything within their reach. The host has asked for that power so that he might have victory in war. They, the spirits, also have life to dispose of and that we ask of them also, giving them these offerings of tobacco, feathers, and food. They will bless us I am certain, for I am told that they even know our thoughts and wishes before we express them, and are willing to grant them if we pour tobacco while making them. However, today we have done more. We have openly made a great offering to them. How could any spirit fail to see such an offering? For that reason I know they will surely bless us. And the blessings asked for the posterity will surely be granted. I feel that when I go home and talk to my children afterwards, they will be strengthened by the fact that I have taken part in the feast. All who are present, I greet. You, the host, I also greet. I greet you all."

Then the second one invited rises and speaks. He thanks

---

8. Green Bay, Wisconsin.
9. In the performance of the feast.

the host for the privilege of having been invited and encourages him and assures every one that they will surely be blessed, telling them why they should be blessed.

Then the third one rises and says approximately the same as his predecessor. He also tells how his grandfather was blessed by the snakes, and so forth.

Then the fourth one speaks, telling what the snakes do and that he himself was a member of the Snake clan and was consequently descended from the snakes. Inasmuch as he had partaken of the feast, all who were present would surely be blessed by the snakes. He assured them that what they asked would surely be granted. Then he greeted them and concluded.

After that, all the four participants greet each other in turn again and when this is over they sit down and begin the feast. Each person must eat a chicken apiece. They must not leave anything on the plate, for it is a sacred feast. After they have eaten the chicken they are given soup to drink.

When the feast is over the host throws cedar branches into the fire and the plates and the spoons are held over the smoke in order to purify them. The host then rises and says:

"You, the first invited, and you, the second invited, and so forth, I greet you all. It is good that you have come and occupied seats at my request and I am grateful to you for it. Even were that all the blessing I was to receive, it would be enough. But you have assured me that I would receive the blessings I longed for. You truly encouraged me. You told me of your grandfathers' blessings, so that I feel positive that I am blessed, for your grandfathers' blessings were surely great and I am sure everything could be obtained with them. Surely your grandfathers' blessings were equal to those of the spirits. It is good that you have indeed partaken of my feast. This must be what the older people said: 'Your life is naturally weak and you can only be strengthened by the counsel and advice of brave men.' Truly you have counciled with me and given me enough to live on. I thank you for the speeches you have delivered, for it is life to me. It is good. I greet you all."

Winter Feast for the Thunderbird Clan War Bundle[10]

This description of the Winter Feast for the Thunderbird clan war bundle—a one-day affair that is preceded by a sweat bath the night before—consists for the most part of speeches. They include both the speeches of the host and the principal invited guests.

The main day's events are divided into two parts, each with its own feast. The opening speech of the first part is that which accompanies a tobacco offering to the spirits and the second, one that accompanies the buckskin offering to them. The next set are principal speeches by the host and the final set are those of seven of the eleven invited guests. The latter speeches follow the feast and conclude the first part of the ceremony.

The second part of the ceremony opens with another tobacco offering to the spirits. Then more speeches are given by the host and guests. The ceremony concludes with speeches after the feast by the remaining four principal guests and a final speech by the host. The night before the ceremony proper is to begin the owner of the bundle (host and leader in the ceremony) and others who are to take part in the ceremony go into a sweat house[11] and make offerings of tobacco to the various beings. The speech of the host is as follows.

---

10. From Radin, *Winnebago Tribe*, pp. 447–527. This text consists mainly of the speeches given at this ceremony with some brief description of other ritual actions. None of the songs are given either in text or translation. In the following, the major speeches are reproduced. Transitional passages between the speeches are based on the text and Radin's introduction to it (pp. 427–445). Some of Radin's labels for the parts of the ceremonial have been changed. The text is in ritual language, that is, it employs special words and phrases not used in ordinary speech. The self-depreciation so apparent in the speeches is customary in such speeches. The notes are taken from Radin.

11. The sweat house is a small lodge into which hot stones were brought and splashed with water to produce steam. The practice of taking sweat baths in such houses was common but by no means universal among the Indian peoples of North America, and a more prominent practice among some than among others.

Sweat Lodge Speech

I greet you; I greet you all, war bundle owners.[12] My grandparents,[13] especially my grandfather, had concentrated their minds upon this for me. The fireplace[14] with which they blessed my grandfather, that I am going to ask for myself. However weakly I may wobble about,[15] my elders will aid me. I am now going to pour a little tobacco and offer, my elders, whatever feast I am able to. War bundle owners, I send forth my greetings to you. War bundle owners, I greet you. You elders, I am about to pour tobacco for them.[16]

Hearken, Earthmaker,[17] our father, I am about to offer you a handful of tobacco.[18] My ancestor Jobenangiwingkha[19] concentrated his mind upon you. The fireplaces with which you blessed him;[20] the small amount of life you granted to him; all, four times the blessings you bestowed upon my ancestor, that I ask of you directly. Also that I may have no trouble.[21]

To you, who live in the west, our grandfather, chief of the Thunderbirds, a handful of tobacco I am about to offer you. My grandfather, Jobenangiwingkha, you strengthened. The food, the deer-couple you gave him for his fireplaces, that I ask of you directly. May it be a fact that you accept this tobacco from me and may I not meet with troubles.

You also, Great Black Hawk, blessed my grandfather. Whatever food you blessed him with that I ask of you directly. Tobacco I am about to pour for you that you may smoke it. May troubles not come upon me; that I ask.

---

12. Literally, "children of the bundle."
13. Meaning "elders."
14. Literally, "that one throws with something, i.e., an offering." It is a ritualistic word.
15. A metaphorical expression.
16. The spirits.
17. The Winnebago culture hero comparable to Iroquois "Sky-Holder." He is called by words that are translated "Creator" and "Great Spirit."
18. I.e., the regular offering.
19. An ancestor of the speaker. Radin gives no translation of this name, and hence it has been retained here although respelled to eliminate the technical linguistic orthography used by Radin to transcribe Winnebago.
20. "Fireplaces" here means "blessings," for only those who had blessings could erect fireplaces, and as a fireplace was erected for each separate spirit, the greater their number, the greater the number of blessings.
21. In life. Throughout, "troubles" refers to troubles in life.

You on the other side, who live in the east, who walk in darkness,[22] tobacco I am about to offer you to smoke. Whatever you blessed my ancestor with, whatever fireplaces you blessed him with, those I ask of you. If you smoke this tobacco, never will I be a weakling.

You who live in the south, you who look like a man, who art invulnerable; who on one side of your body present death and on the other life, Disease-Giver, as they call you. My ancestor in the daytime, in broad daylight, did you bless. With food you blessed him. You told him that he would never fail in anything. You told him that you would avoid his home.[23] You placed animals[24] in front of him that he should not be troubled about obtaining them. An offering of tobacco I make to you that you may smoke it and that I may not be troubled by anything.[25]

To you, Light-Wanderer,[26] an offering of tobacco I make. May it be my good fortune that you accept it. Whatever fireplaces you blessed him[27] with, those I ask of you directly. May I not be troubled by anything in life.

You also, Grandmother Moon, blessed my ancestor with food. With whatever you blessed him, that I ask of you now directly. An offering of tobacco I am about to make for you now, so that you may smoke. Whatever blessings you bestowed upon my grandfather, I pray you to give me now, so that by reason of it I may never become a weakling.

To you, too, South Wind, I offer a handful of tobacco, that you may smoke it. May it so happen that you accept it and that I am spared troubles. With whatsoever you blessed my ancestor, that I ask of you.

For you likewise, Grandmother Earth, will I pour tobacco. With whatever blessings you blessed my grandfather, those I ask of you. May I in that way never become a weakling.

---

22. I.e., the Night Spirits. "Those who walk in darkness" is the ritualistic name of the Night Spirits.
23. I.e., that you would not permit disease and death to enter it.
24. I.e., food.
25. In life.
26. The sun.
27. I.e., my ancestor.

To you, a pair of Eagles, my ancestor prayed. The blessings you bestowed upon him, those I ask of you. I am about to pour a handful of tobacco for you. May you accept it and ward off trouble from me.

Hearken, all you spirits to whom my ancestor prayed; to all of you, I offer tobacco. My ancestor Jobenangiwingkha gave a feast[28] to all those who had blessed him, and we are repeating this now. However, as it is about time to proceed to the next part we will ask you once again to bestow upon us all the blessings you gave our ancestor. That we may not become weaklings, I ask of you. I greet you all.

Ritual Feast

On the following day, various preparations are made before the ritual proper begins. The buckskins, which have been bleached as white as possible by the women and which are to be offered to the spirits, are marked by the host, each buckskin receiving a special paint marking. For example, that to be offered Earthmaker is marked with a green cross; that to the Thunderbirds with three semicircular lines, one red, one white, and one blue, to represent a rainbow; and that to the Night Spirits with four parallel charcoal lines.

There are eleven such buckskins, one each for the following spirits: Earthmaker, the Thunderbirds, Great Black Hawk, Disease-Giver, South Wind, Sun, Morning Star, the Night Spirits, Moon, South, and Water. (As will be seen, other beings are mentioned in some of the speeches, but these are not given buckskins.) Each buckskin is given to one of the special guests during the ceremony who represents (impersonates) the spirit. And, as each special guest is from a different clan, all twelve Winnebago clans are represented (at least in this idealized version of the ceremony)—the host's and the eleven other clans.

While the host is marking the buckskins, the women put meat into the kettles to cook. The meat is deer. After the custodian of the bundle has decided to give the feast, he asks his

---

28. Literally, "tobacco pouring."

nephews to kill as many deer as they can so that all the clans can be invited and offerings made to a larger number of spirits. A total of eleven such kettles is prepared. Seven are used for the first part of the feast and are for Earthmaker, the Thunderbirds, Great Black Hawk, Disease-Giver, South Wind, Sun, and Morning Star. (The name of the first part of the ceremonial is taken from the first two kettles; this part is generally known either as the Feast in Honor of Earthmaker or the Feast in Honor of the Thunderbirds.) Four kettles are used in the second part of the ceremonial and are for the Night Spirits, Moon, Earth, and Water. (The name for this part of the ceremonial is the Feast in Honor of the Night Spirits.) Each of the special guests, as each represents one of the spirits, takes charge of one of the kettles.

A dog is also ritually strangled—with a rope so that no blood is shed—as an offering to Disease-Giver, and a pouch of tobacco and red feathers is tied around the dog's neck, and a tobacco pouch and feathers around each of its legs. Before the sacrifice, the dog is addressed thus:

> My younger brother, you are to go to the south; to the Disease-Giver you are to go. There you will live better than here. War powers and life we wish to have and that you should ask for.

The dog is laid before the war bundle, which, in this case, contains the following: bodies of an eagle, a hawk, a pigeon hawk, and another bird; a deer-tail headdress; eagle feathers; a war club; flutes; and medicines. The bird bodies gave the owner of the bundle, in times of war, the characteristics of these animals. The deer-tail headdress, eagle feathers, and war club were war paraphernalia always worn on the warpath. The flutes were used during the ceremony to accompany certain songs.

After the buckskins have been marked and arranged, the guests enter in no particular order. When all have taken their places, an old warrior gives a tobacco offering to the spirits. Then the host distributes the buckskins to the various guests and sings two songs. Next the buckskins are hung up near the fireplace and the host opens the war bundle. He gives tobacco to each invited guest, pours some tobacco on the war bundle, and then some into the fire with the following speech.

Tobacco Offering to the Spirits

Six white buckskins, with enough material for as many pairs of moccasins, I am going to send to our grandparents. They will be able to recognize the buckskins by the marks upon them. If you[29] recognize them, it is our desire that you take these buckskins. That is why I am doing this. I hope, also, that our grandfathers will accept our food offerings. That is why I am making them. Many are the war bundle owners who are sitting here; the lodge tent is full of them. I am thankful for it. I am going to make you very tired; I am going to make you very hungry; but I know you never thought of that. You are thinking only of our grandfathers, the spirits, and that is why you have permitted my lodge to become filled with people. It is good. All you war bundle owners who are seated here within, I greet you. I am now going to pour tobacco.

Listen, Father who dwells above,[30] all things you have created. Yet you said if we would make an offering of tobacco you would accept it with thankfulness.[31] So it has been said. I am about to offer a handful of tobacco and a buckskin for moccasins with it and a white-haired animal[32] to be cooked so that you may have a holy feast. These things I turn over to you. If you accept them, the first thing I wish to ask for will be the honor of killing an enemy outright,[33] of leading warpaths, and

---

29. Spirits.

30. I.e., Earthmaker. No Christian influence is to be suspected in this term of address.

31. According to Winnebago tradition, Earthmaker first created all the various spirits and bestowed upon each one of them certain powers. When finally he created man he noticed that he had nothing left to give him, so he decided to give him tobacco. This was to remain his exclusive possession, and not even he, Earthmaker, would be able to take it away. It was finally agreed that man would offer it to Earthmaker and the other spirits and receive in return specific blessings. See also above, chap. 2, "A Winnebago Father's Teachings to his Son."

32. Deer.

33. I.e., killing an enemy in the midst of his own people and without the assistance of anyone else. It was the highest war honor a Winnebago could obtain.

of obtaining life honors.[34] That is what we would like to lead.[35] That is what I would ask of you. My relatives, as many as are sitting around here, even that many ask the same things of you.

Those in the west, our grandfather, Thunderbird Chief, you blessed grandfather, and I am now going to offer you a handful of tobacco. With thanks you will accept it, it has been said. Buckskin for moccasins, also, I am sending over to you. A feast made from one whom we regard as one of yourselves, whose body we are like,[36] I am sending along for you. Indeed a sacred feast I am offering you; that I am now sending toward you. As many of our clan members as are here, they all desire to make these requests: To kill an enemy outright, to lead a war party, and—Oh, grant it to us!—a life honor. Life, that is what I pray for to you—that we ask of you. Our clan has put itself in a pitiable condition,[37] so that we may live a good life. That we ask of you.

You who live in the east, you who walk in darkness,[38] you directed your minds toward grandfather, and for that I will pour tobacco for you, now and forever, so that you may bless me. A handful of tobacco, if we pour for you, we know it will make you thankful, and for that reason do I offer you some. A buckskin for moccasins and, together with it, a sacred feast that I am about to send toward you. With whatever you blessed grandfather, that I and all my clansmen who are here ask of you. This request, we make, that one of us lead the war party you have predestined for us.[39] Pitiable we are making ourselves in life, that we may live a good life.[40] That we ask of you.

For you who live in the south, Disease-Giver, my grandfather Jobenangiwingkha thirsted himself to death[41] and put

---

34. "Life honors" always refer to war honors.
35. I.e., a war party.
36. A dog. In offering up the dog they wish to imply that they are offering up themselves.
37. I.e., a condition that calls for pity.
38. I.e., the Night Spirits.
39. A person may be blessed with victory on the warpath directly or he may be entitled to war blessings to which near relatives were destined but which they were deprived of by an early death. The present prayer is directed toward both things, that he may enjoy the "unused" blessings of his relative and that he may not be cut off by an untimely death from the fulfillment of his own.
40. By obtaining blessings from you.
41. I.e., fasted.

himself in a pitiable condition. Then you who are in charge of great war powers blessed him. For you control a greater amount of war powers than any other spirit. A great amount of life you also control, for you are said to possess two sides, one side of your body containing life and the other death. You told grandfather Jobenangiwingkha that you would bless him at noon, in broad daylight,[42] and thus indeed you met him. There you blessed him with war powers; and with whatever you blessed him, that we ask of you now. Whosoever of my clan are present they all pour an offering of tobacco for you and also give you soup.[43] The Creator made animals for us, white-haired animals for food, and these we send to you; together with buckskins, that you may have moccasins. We also send toward you a head ornament of eagle feathers, that also. We offer you tobacco and we ask of you to bestow upon us that with which you blessed our grandfather Jobenangiwingkha. Grandfather Jobenangiwingkha had had war powers and life, it is said; and those we ask of you. And it is said that you told grandfather that whenever you go on your warpath you will not walk upon the descendants of Jobenangiwingkha wherever they breathe.[44]

You, grandfather Who-Bring-Day,[45] who come every day, you blessed grandfather Jobenangiwingkha with war power and life and I am therefore offering you a handful of tobacco. All the war power the Creator controls he delegated to you and for all of that which you blessed our grandfather, as many of my clansmen as are present, we are about to pour tobacco to obtain. Tobacco, here it is.

It is said that you will do what we ask of you. You yourself told that to grandfather, it is said. War powers and life, that we ask of you. Tobacco, food, and feathers we sacrifice to you and if you accept them, then we will assuredly wear war honors some day. That we may pass through life without any troubles

---

42. To be blessed in the daytime, especially at noon, was considered as particularly holy. Generally a person was blessed at night.
43. Literally, "hot water."
44. I.e., when Disease-Giver deals out death he will avoid all the descendants of Jobenangiwingkha.
45. Sun.

and that we may live long, we ask of you and offer you tobacco, grandfather.

Grandmother Earth, you blessed Jobenangiwingkha with whatever the Creator delegated to you. With everything that exists on the earth, for all eternity, did you tell grandfather you would bless him, and this is what we ask of you and that for which we will forever offer you tobacco. You will do it, he told us you had said. A handful of tobacco we are about to send toward you, we, as many of our clansmen as are here. Tobacco do you accept from us, grandmother. A handful of tobacco there, upon him who stands in the middle of the lodge,[46] do we pour. Give us war powers and life; for these we beseech you. Here it is, the tobacco.

Soup, vegetables, together with maple sugar we are about to send you.[47] If you accept them, life we will obtain; that we ask of you.

Grandmother You-Who-Come-at-Night,[48] grandmother, you blessed Jobenangiwingkha and now all his descendants, as many as there are, are about to offer you tobacco. Now when we come to a tobacco offering we will certainly offer some to you. And you will be cognizant of it, you assured us yourself, it is said. Whatever you are in control of and with which you blessed our grandfather Jobenangiwingkha for all eternity, that we are to ask for at all times, they told us you had said, and you will assuredly give it to us. The tobacco, here it is.

I am using the tobacco as a means of obtaining life for myself and my relatives. The Creator gave it to me and I am offering it to you. As many of our clansmen as are here we beg of you war powers; and that if we ever go on a warpath there we will obtain the war honors. Soup and the animals the Creator made for me,[49] the black-furred one[50] we are offering

---

46. "He who stands in the middle of the lodge" is the ritualistic name for the fireplace. He is always personified and the tobacco is generally conceived of as being poured on his head.

47. As the offerings are made to the earth, vegetables and maple sugar are selected.

48. The ritualistic name for the moon.

49. I.e., what the Creator had placed in his way and permitted him to catch and prepare for this feast.

50. Bear.

you; soup of bear ribs. A sacred feast we are about to hold for you. A buckskin for moccasins we are about to send out to you. War powers and life we ask of you; that you give us life, so that our days may be happy. Truly, grandmother, did you bless our grandfather Jobenangiwingkha with whatever powers the Creator put in your control. That with which you blessed grandfather it is said you would give us, too, when in the course of time we would pray to you to bestow them upon us. So it is reported our grandfather Jobenangiwingkha said. A handful of tobacco we place for you in the fire. You would smoke it, it is said that you, yourself, told grandfather. Tobacco you told him you would always accept, it is said. Here it is, the tobacco.

If you smoke the tobacco for us, war powers and happiness in life we will ask of you. Soup, vegetables, rice, and maple sugar we send out to you, and buckskin for moccasins likewise. If you accept these things from us, it will be ours to use, war power and life. That we ask of you, grandmother.

Chief of the Eagles, you who walk on light[51] up above, you yourself said that only you are the greatest one in control of war powers. That you are thus, you said of yourself. Life also you are in charge of. You blessed our grandfather Jobenangiwingkha with whatever powers the Creator put you in control of. You blessed grandfather for all eternity,[52] and for those powers we are now about to offer you tobacco. It is for that purpose you told grandfather we should have a tobacco pouring. So grandfather told us, it is said. Grandfather also made a sacred bundle[53] and to this you also added your power, grandfather said, it is said. The tobacco, here it is.

To you, Chief of the Eagles, grandfather, do we pour tobacco. With whatever you blessed grandfather, that we ask of you. All the members of the clan offer you tobacco that you may have knowledge of it[54] and bestow upon us who dwell on

---

51. The ritualistic name for any bird.
52. The set phrase here and later translated as "eternity" is literally "as long as the earth lasts, that long."
53. Literally, "he tied up the spirit mind or manifestation," i.e., he made a bundle of the blessings he received from the various spirits. Jobenangiwingkha is the individual who is said to have received the war bundle used in this ceremony.
54. I.e., the tobacco.

the earth, war powers and life. That is what we ask of you, grandfather.

To the Day[55] I pour tobacco, also soup, and a rib of a white-haired animal.[56] A sacred meal we are about to offer to you. Grandfather Jobenangiwingkha you blessed and you also added your thoughts, it is said. If you accept tobacco and the feast, war powers and life we assuredly are going to obtain. For that we ask, grandfather.

South Wind, to the bundle grandather Jobenangiwingkha made, you added your power, so grandfather Jobenangiwingkha said, it is said. That which the Creator put you in charge of, and with which you blessed grandfather Jobenangiwingkha, as long as the earth lasts, we are about to pour tobacco for, as you yourself told us. The tobacco, here it is.

A four-legged animal, a coon, that the Creator made for us, we are going to give you in the form of a soup. If you accept the soup and likewise smoke the tobacco, then the first request we wish to make is that it might be our fortune to obtain war powers and travel safely on the path of life. That is what we ask.

Wind who lives in the north, you said "I am the equal of the spirit of the north";[57] so grandfather Jobenangiwingkha said, it is said. Tobacco, soup, vegetables, what a tree bears, fruit, as we call it, and maple sugar, that also we send toward you. If you accept them, the request we make is for war power and life; that we ask of you. To kill a person outright is an excellent power to have, grandfather Porcupine,[58] you said of yourself. So grandfather Jobenangiwingkha said, it is said.

Black Hawk, you also added your powers for grandfather, it is said; and a handful of tobacco I am pouring for you for that

---

55. Although, according to the Winnebago conception, the light of day is associated with the sun, yet the sun is not regarded as causing the light any more than the absence of the sun is thought to be the cause of darkness, but both light (daylight) and darkness are associated with special deities.

56. I.e., a deer.

57. I.e., cold does not affect me. The North Wind and the spirit of cardinal point north are entirely distinct.

58. No reason is known why the spirit is here addressed as porcupine.

reason. Whatever war powers and life the Creator put in your control, that I ask of you. You blessed grandfather Jobenangiwingkha for as long a period as the world would last, and you said that you would always smoke tobacco, it is said. If you are cognizant of this tobacco, let us obtain life and war power. For these we ask.

Grandfather Thunderbird, you added your power also, it is said. Tobacco we are about to pour for you. Tobacco only we are giving you, so that we may obtain war powers and life; that with which you blessed grandfather Jobenangiwingkha for all eternity, may we obtain from you. If you accept the tobacco may I and my relatives live well by reason thereof; that we ask of you. That is all.

You, Big Black Hawk, who are in charge of war powers,[59] blessed grandfather Jobenangiwingkha with war powers and life, and these we are to ask of you, you told grandfather, and pour tobacco at the same time. As many tobacco offerings as grandfather would have liked to have had and as many buckskin offerings as he would have desired, that many there will be for you. If you accept the tobacco and feast and all the offerings, you will assuredly give us blessings. Thus you told grandfather Jobenangiwingkha. Tobacco, here it is.

If we extend toward you a handful of tobacco, you said you would always smoke it. If, at a tobacco offering, you smoked the tobacco, the requests we might make are these—war powers and life. A feast of one whom you look upon in the same way as ourselves,[60] one whom I have been treating like a brother, with whom the children have eaten the soup of such a one, we are giving you. An offering of buckskin for moccasins and of one like ourselves,[61] whose body is well prepared, do they offer you. Food they are offering you, asking in return for life.[62] You are the only one in control of great war powers. The Creator placed you in charge of life; above the Creator created you. With that you blessed grandfather Jobenangiwingkha for

---

59. Literally, "in control of grass bundles."
60. I.e., a dog.
61. A dog.
62. Literally, "light."

all eternity. We will have a tobacco pouring, that you may give us these things. If you take cognizance of the feast offerings, the buckskin offerings—if you will take them; then we will obtain the war honors and then we will obtain life. We, as many older people as we are here, beseech you for those powers you added to the spirit bundle of our grandfather Jobenangiwingkha. We will not have enough food to go around, but if we offer you tobacco, it will not be an offense thus to act to you, we have been told.

*   *   *

After a song and the pouring of tobacco by the guests on the bundle and into the fire, the buckskins are offered to the spirits with the following speech by the host.

Buckskin Offerings to the Spirits

War bundle owners who are seated here, I greet you. We are endeavoring to prepare footwear for our grandfathers,[63] but we did not really accomplish it. Spirit footwear we tried to make, that is what we were doing, but our work was lacking in every respect. However, our grandfathers[64] would not take offense at the inadequacy of our work, it is said. That we may not be weakened, for that reason it is that we are preparing the moccasins for our grandfathers. Up above we are going to send them.

Grandfather Thunderbird, our clan is sending you moccasins. War powers and life are the requests we make in turn.

You who live in the east,[65] moccasins do we send you, and the request we make is war power and life. That we ask for.

Disease-Giver, grandfather, moccasins we send you. Grandfather, life you possess on one side of your body, and death you are in control of on the other side of your body, so

---

63. I.e., offer buckskins to the spirits.
64. The spirits.
65. The Night Spirits.

our grandfather Jobenangiwingkha told us, it is said. War power and life, that is the request we make.

To you, grandfather South Wind, here is the tobacco for our grandfathers. You blessed grandfather Jobenangiwingkha with war powers and life and you said yourself that you would bless his descendants whenever they offered you a handful of tobacco and you accepted it. Moccasins we are sending you. Food we are about to offer you. Whatever you blessed grandfather with, that we ask of you.

Grandfather Light-Wanderer,[66] you said that if at any time we poured a handful of tobacco for you and smoked tobacco as an offering you would give us that with which you blessed grandfather Jobenangiwingkha whenever we ask for it. So it is said. Moccasins we are sending you. Soup, vegetables, and maple sugar also we are about to send you. Tobacco is what we think of in connection with you. If you take cognizance of it, war honors we will assuredly obtain. Life, that is what we would like to obtain.

You who are above,[67] our Father, we ask life of you, extending tobacco. You made this for us; you let us have it. Indeed it is you that made it and yet you will take a handful of it that we extend to you and accept it as an offering. That is what you said to us. So grandfather Jobenangiwingkha said, it is said. You blessed grandfather Jobenangiwingkha with war powers and life. Bless us in turn now that we are about to offer you a handful of tobacco. We, as many clansmen as there are here, are about to send to you moccasins so that we may obtain life from you. Tobacco, deerskins as offerings, food of the white-haired animal, of a male animal, we are about to offer you.

Grandmother, the Moon, moccasins, soup, and tobacco, these we are about to offer you. Our request is for the things with which you blessed grandfather Jobenangiwingkha. That we ask of you.

---

66. Sun.
67. Earthmaker.

WINNEBAGO CLAN CEREMONIALS

You who are above, Morning Star, our request is that you bless us with that with which you blessed grandfather Jobenangiwingkha. Tobacco and food and a buckskin offering we are about to send you.[68]

Grandmother Earth, you also added your power to the spirit bundle that grandfather Jobenangiwingkha made. The powers Earthmaker put you in control of, and with which you blessed grandfather Jobenangiwingkha, those we ask of you. Tobacco, soup, and a buckskin offering we are about to send to you and the request that we make of you is war power and life.

Water-Spirit, grandfather whose body is of water, tobacco, food, and a buckskin offering for moccasins we are about to offer you. I and my relatives desire to lay our hands on war and life.

Grandfathers,[69] we have probably been very remiss in what we have done, but do not hold it against us, grandfathers. We greet you, war bundle owners. The life[70] that those who have gone before us had, the songs that they handed down to us, not in their manner will we be able to sing, but still, however it be, it will be our best. It has been said that nothing will provoke you,[71] grandfathers. Well, however, that is the way we will do it. I greet you.

*   *   *

A song and a ritual filling of the ceremonial pipe follow. Then, after the appropriate songs have been sung, the pipe is lit and passed around so that all the men may smoke, a ritual that is repeated three more times. Then the host begins the principal speeches, each of which is followed by songs.

---

68. That this spirit was not mentioned before is an oversight on the part of the man who gave the text to Radin.
69. Here referring to the spirits generally.
70. Blessings.
71. I.e., that no inaccuracy or ignorance on their part will anger the spirits and cause them to refrain from bestowing their blessings.

Principal Speeches

Host's First Speech

War bundle owners, who are sitting here, I send forth my greeting to you. It is good that you have come in response to my invitation. It is my purpose to make you tired from sitting, but do not for that reason think any the worse of us. We will make you hungry, hungry to the point of starvation, but we know you came for the sake of the spirits, not for our sake. It is good. We are not going to do anything in the correct manner, but our grandfathers who live in the west taught our grandfather Jobenangiwingkha some songs and these we are going to try and repeat. We will now sing the songs just as they taught them to grandfather. We may perhaps sing only one song. However, if you know only one song and take pains about it, it will suffice; so grandfather said, it is said. Anyhow, if we try to cry, in our efforts of singing, our grandfathers will take cognizance of it, it is said. That is what we are thinking of when we try to get the spirits' attention by singing.[72] We will do our best to sing the songs,[73] and we will sing four of them; and when we have finished then it will be time for us to eat. Warriors who are sitting within the lodge, we send forth our greetings to you. [Was bundle song.]

First Guest's Address to the Young People

War bundle owners, young men, those who are the proxies of spirits, are about to use a song for you and start a dance in your behalf; and when they do it, get up and try to obtain war powers by dancing. Women, you should also try to obtain war powers for your brothers by dancing. Now we are not able to obtain the number of men that our ancestors used to obtain in the beginning. Then, if in a speech they asked for them, as many men as there were around would immediately begin to dance. Not one of them would remain in his seat. Young women, they used to act in that way in order to obtain life also.

---

72. Literally, "by voice to attract attention."
73. Literally, "to make one's breath visible in the form of a song or speech."

All night they would dance and not a single one would tire of it. We encourage you to do thus; that is why I am saying this. That the obtaining of life may be easy is the reason they told us this. Because I believe it likewise is the reason I am telling it to you. War bundle owners who are seated here, I greet you all.

Host's Second Speech
War bundle owners who are sitting here, I greet you all.

Our grandfathers knew that one of a different tribe had had a vision and obtained material for use in life. They tried to obtain it and finally asked him to pity them. They made the heart of the man of this other tribe sad.[74] He had obtained it in the following manner: A woman fasted[75] and one of the Water-Spirits whom the Creator had placed there for all eternity, a Water-Spirit for keeping the earth quiet,[76] blessed her with the power he had been placed in charge of. The Water-Spirit had himself died and the woman there took the material.[77] That it is good, they knew. Then she tried her medicine. The first time she did the following: Up above, almost near the sky, a hawk stood whirling around. The woman dipped her forefinger into the medicine and then she pointed it at the hawk and it fell dead; she made it fall through the top of a house; right in front of the woman it landed. She wanted to use it as a medicine bag. Then she dreamed that they had taken a man from his home that he might fast. She said to the man, "Put forth all your strength and don't try to come here." She also told his relatives to watch him. "Tonight I am going to sing a paint song and if he comes he will die. Take care of him that he doesn't come." That night she sang a paint song and the man came running to her. She forbade him but he came anyhow and he died dancing. That is how it acted.

---

74. I.e., at the idea of parting with it.

75. Literally, "thirst oneself to death."

76. Referring here to one of the four beings Earthmaker placed at the four ends of the world to prevent it from moving continually.

77. I.e., the remains of the Water-Spirit. The "bones" of the Water-Spirits possess powerful qualities when powdered and mixed up into medicines. All "paint medicines" are made of Water-Spirit bones.

They[78] knew that it was good paint and he[79] tried to get him[80] to bless him with the paint.[81] When they obtained it, they never used it in their own midst.[82] They made a medicine bundle of it. The paint medicine, it is good to use in war. That they knew very well. They were very sparing in their use of it.[83] They placed it in their war bundle. Paint songs we are about to use, yet we are singing for the war bundle. If, indeed, we had paint medicine we would amount to something. We are not going to sing as if we thought ourselves in possession of paint medicines nor will we sing them correctly. Yet if we knew only one, if we could in singing this one bring ourselves to the state of crying, it would be all right, it is said. That is why we say it. [Paint song.]

Host's Third Speech

War bundle owners who are seated here, I greet you. I know that I am causing you to famish with hunger, but we are doing this in an attempt to get the attention of the spirits. One in control of death who dwells in the south[84] and who of himself possesses greater war power than all the other spirits that exist, blessed grandfather Jobenangiwingkha. He is in control of life and in control of death. He met grandfather in the middle of the day and blessed him with war powers and life. He said to our grandfather when he blessed him, "If I should ever go on the warpath, your descendants, as many as they are and wherever they live, I will not tread upon, should they get sick.[85] However, your posterity never will get sick. Should they ever have a bad illness, they have the means of obtaining life by praying for it, by offering tobacco and a flute."[86]

---

78. Our ancestors.
79. One of them.
80. The man of the other tribe.
81. The latter had obtained from the woman.
82. I.e., among themselves.
83. Because it was so valuable.
84. I.e., Disease-Giver.
85. See note 44.
86. I.e., by playing on a flute.

Disease-Giver himself made these things holy. Thus they would obtain life, if they had any illness, by offering you reed flutes, food, tobacco, feathers, a white dog, and by making you at the same time an offering of buckskin hides. Thus Disease-Giver spoke to our grandfather when he blessed him: "A holy flute I made for you, and I forbade you to blow upon it, yet you did it. Now, hereafter, if you offer me a sufficient number of buckskins, you may blow upon it. A different life from that of others will you lead, if you do that. You will be able to cut off[87] a bad disease caused by someone else. Nor will this one who was ill ever have another disease."

Thus Disease-Giver spoke. This is what the one who causes disease said. That is how they blessed our grandfather Jobenangiwingkha. A song I am now about to start. War bundle owners who are seated here, I greet you. [Disease-Giver song.]

Host's Fourth Speech

War bundle owners who are seated here, I greet you. The last song we will now finish. You who are in the east, Night Spirits, you also added your blessing to the spirit bundle of grandfather Jobenangiwingkha. So that he might know[88] the spirits, grandfather Jobenangiwingkha starved and thirsted himself to death[89] and made himself pitiable. At first he fasted four nights and the Night Spirits came to him; with mighty sounds they came.[90] There they stood and said, "Human, you have thirsted youself to death and we bless you for that reason. We who speak are the spirits who are called Night Spirits." They blessed him with war power and life, they said. Then he looked and said to himself, "I wonder whether these really are the Night Spirits that speak." So he looked at them and they were small birds. They had fooled him. Then once again was his heart sore. "Well! I will die," he thought.[91] So he fasted

---

87. Stop.
88. Be blessed by.
89. I.e., fasted.
90. All powerful spirits are supposed to approach with loud voices.
91. Fasting.

again and once again he rubbed on the charcoal. For six nights he continued to fast. And again from the east the Night Spirits came. They came making a great noise and they stood near him and said, "Human, we bless you. You have thirsted yourself to death and you have made your heart sore. We felt sad on your account. With war power and life we bless you," they said. Then he looked at them. "I wonder whether they really are the Night Spirits?" he thought. They were not the Night Spirits who were speaking to him. The birds that spoke fooled him. Instead of feeling sad this time, however, he thought to himself, "I don't care what happens; I am willing to die."[92] Then he began fasting again. He rubbed the charcoal over his face again. Seven nights he fasted. And once again from the east the Night Spirits came singing. They came and stood before him and they said, "Nephew, we bless you. So long have you been sad and cried to us piteously that we will bless you. No one did we ever bless before. In war and life you shall do just as you wish," they said. Then he looked again. "I wonder whether those speaking are really the Night Spirits?" he thought. But they were not the Night Spirits. As many of them as they were, their breasts were dark. As many birds as there were, they were bad. "My oh my! How they abuse me!" he said. At first Jobenangi-wingkha had thought in his fastings that just to spite them he would fast again. Now he rubbed charcoal on his face again and wept bitterly. Both hands contained tobacco and he stood in the direction from which the Night Spirits came and, weeping, put himself in the most abject condition.

Now, indeed, to its very depths did his heart ache. Ten nights did he fast. Finally the Night Spirits came after him. "Human, I have come after you." He followed the spirits and they took him to the east; to the site of a Night Spirit village they took him. The chief of the Night Spirits had sent this one to go after him. In the village was a long lodge standing in the east. There they took him. As many Night Spirits as there were in control of powerful blessings, of that many the lodge was

---

92. In order to get the blessing.

full. When he entered he walked in white feathers up to his knees.[93] Many kettles and much food he saw stretched right across the lodge. On the outside, a buffalo hide stretched almost across the entire lodge. Then they said to him, "Human, without giving up, long you have suffered; your heart has, indeed, been sad. They, as many spirits as there are in the lodge, that many talked of what was to happen to you. And I, I am the chief of the Night Spirits. This creation-lodge[94] just as you see it[95] I give to you. You will never be in want of food. You are to offer as many buckskins as you see here and tobacco for all time. Thus it shall be. The creation-lodge of the village of the Night Spirits I give to you. You can go on as many war parties as you wish and obtain as much life. As many tobacco offerings as they[96] continue to give, all the tobacco, food, buckskin offerings, red feathers, as many as there are, they will all come to the creation-lodge that you see, and we will accept them."

Thus did they speak to grandfather Jobenangiwingkha. So he said. We will do this that we may ask blessings for our relatives and sing songs. Even if we do not perform everything in just the manner that the spirits in the east told our grandfather Jobenangiwingkha, we know that our grandfathers[97] will not be offended. So they say. Even if you know only one song, if you bring yourself to the point of crying in your efforts, it will be all right. Thus we mean to say it. War bundle owners, who are seated here, I greet you. [Night Spirit song.]

*   *   *

After the host has made another offering of tobacco into the fire and four special songs have been sung, the Feast for the Thunderers (also called the Feast for Earthmaker) is given—

---

93. The lodges of the Night Spirits are supposed to be strewn with white feathers.

94. The lodges of the spirits are always called "creation-lodges" in reference to the fact that it was by the assembled spirits in these lodges that at the beginning of the world everything was set in order.

95. I.e., with all it contains.

96. I.e., you and your descendants.

97. The spirits.

each of the seven kettles is in charge of one of the guests. Each distributes the contents to his band, the warriors getting the heads.

The feast concluded, the guests speak.

Speeches of the Guests

Speech of the First Guest

Councilors[98] and relatives who are seated here, I greet you all. As many war bundle owners as are seated here, I greet you all. The councilors of the clans have enjoined upon us earnestly to offer up sincere prayers to all the different spirits who are seated here.[99] It is good that our war bundle owners offer up prayers in this way. It is for this reason that we are still living. Some of us cannot accomplish much in that line and that is why so many of us are gone already.[100] This ritual was made for one who is the very greatest of all the spirits, for whom they have offered tobacco and food and offerings of buckskin. Thus they have done. Earthmaker, who dwells above, they have asked for war power and life. Indeed, how would it be possible for the spirits not to take cognizance and accept these offerings?[101] If we follow the preaching of our host, life we will obtain; life we will feel ourselves in connection through the food that they[102] have offered up. We have had the honor too of impersonating the spirits, I and my relatives. The meal likewise was excellent. It is good that they have brought us in connection with so much life and it is to thank them that I am saying this. That one of their ancestors whom they called grandfather and whose place I am taking was not one to speak foolishly, it is said, and still his place they thought of for me, unworthy as I am. They have given me the part of a councilor

---

98. Literally, "enjoiners"—a reference to the injunctions and instructions the elder people give to the young.

99. In the persons of the guests.

100. I.e., are dead.

101. I.e., the offerings are so wonderful that the spirits would have to be blind not to see them.

102. The host and the members of his band.

of their own clan and the privilege of impersonating a spirit. It is good. Earthmaker they have prayed to.

I greet him. To the enjoiner[103] I send my greetings; to all the war bundle owners who are seated here, I send forth my greetings.

Speech of the Second Guest

Host and relatives, as many as are seated here, I send forth my greetings to you. War bundle owners that are here, I send forth my greetings to you. Those of the various clans present have counseled me repeatedly and all the women and children have pleaded in my behalf with the spirits. What love that was! And what does life consist of but love? The clan councilor is repeating the songs that were obtained when the sacred bundle was made, so that when the time for the tobacco offering to the spirits came, they would have the tobacco that they have all this time kept ready. Now, sure enough, the time has arrived and they are sitting prepared to pray to all the various spirits. Long ago when they saw war they cooked the man they were to go after.[104] That is why they did it. A good[105] warpath they will surely have. When they are actually in the midst of their warpath and are about to rush for one another,[106] let him pour tobacco to the various spirits who are in control of war. If you say "Grandfather, thus we used to offer you," although you may not know by any word or direct sign whether those in control of war have answered you, you will know it as soon as the rush upon the enemy takes place and, although you go where the bullets and arrows rain hardest, you will pass out of the reach of the bullets and will pass safely out of all danger. If the people rush for a man to bestow the war honors upon,[107] you will be the one. If you give the sacred feast in the proper

---

103. The host.

104. I.e., the spirit of the enemy they are to kill on the warpath is present in the food offered up at this feast.

105. Prosperous.

106. I.e., the Winnebago and his enemy.

107. This refers to the custom of running out to greet the returning warriors in order to conduct them into the village and bestow the war honors upon those who have counted coup.

way, if you burn up much tobacco and food, then the various spirits, especially the Thunderbirds, who are in control of the greatest war power, will bless you for the excellent way in which you have prayed to them. Whenever the Thunderbirds come they will remember you; and when they come they will even call you by name and say, "Let us smoke here."[108] When the young begin to grow up, one of the men encourages them. Only a few, however, are like this. It is good. The host has preached and pleaded for as many men as are present. They[109] have made offerings of food to our grandfathers who live in the west[110] and pleasing offerings of tobacco and buckskin have they sent out to them. They have permitted me to impersonate this spirit and have thus given life to myself and my unimportant clansmen, who have been living in so lowly a condition. With real life have we felt ourselves connected through your actions. With life have we felt ourselves connected by means of that vessel which the Creator gave me as a measure.[111] To those preached to, who are in the west, I send forth my greetings. To the host and those of his clan who are seated here, I send forth my greetings. To all the war bundle owners who are seated within the lodge I send forth my greetings.

Speech of the Third Guest

To all who possess tobacco and food do I send forth my greetings. The means for my feeling thankful has come to me.[112] Councilor[113] and members of his clan who are seated here, I send forth my greetings. And to you, war bundle owners, who are impersonating the spirits seated here, do I send forth my greetings. In my thoughts I used to think that this is the way it was to be done, they said, but it has actually

---

108. I.e., if a person makes it a habit to offer tobacco, the spirits will say, "Let us stop at such and such a man's place as we go along and have a smoke."

109. The host and his band.

110. The Thunderbirds.

111. A circumlocution for stomach.

112. I.e., now that it is my turn to speak and offer prayers, I can thank those who have invited me and the spirits.

113. I.e., the host.

happened.[114] Thus did the clansmen, the councilors, sit acting. This [115] belongs to their[116] grandfather,[117] yet they gave me this position. If at any time a person finding me alone had asked me if I wanted to offer up thanks to the spirits,[118] how could such as I have said anything? They told me that they had thought of one of their ancestors in connection with this feast, one who had been of no importance, and that I was to impersonate the spirits in his place. It is good. How could the spirits who dwell in the west at the side of the chief of the Thunderbirds who is in control of war power help but recognize one who impersonates them, sings their songs, and whom, withal, they have blessed with control of a war bundle and given life? And if they recognize them, we, too, will follow them.[119] They have given us the place of the spirits. It is good. Most assuredly have I helped myself and my relatives in gathering around here, for we have been brought in connection with life. To those they have preached to who represent the Big Black Hawk, do I send forth my greetings. And to the host and the war bundle owners who are impersonating the spirits do I send forth my greetings.

Speech of the Fourth Guest

War bundle owners, councilors, relatives who are seated here, I send forth my greetings to you. This is indeed a marvelous performance and he who was able to do it is surely a marvelous man. Very few people listen to the counsel of their parents, but he was one of those who did, and for that reason he has done so well. The members of the clan have been sincerely worshiping the spirits. He who made the war bundle ritual was like a spirit in power and what he told them to do

---

114. I.e., in my fondest imaginings I used to think that the ideal way to give the feast was the manner in which I see it given here. How could I have imagined that such a thing was actually possible?

115. Place of honor.

116. The host's.

117. I.e., ancestor, the original impersonator.

118. I.e., take part in this feast.

119. I.e., they will recognize us too.

they are doing in every detail. It is good work that they are doing. Sufficient food they are offering to those who are in control of war powers that they might easily be cognizant of it. They have placed plenty of tobacco and different offerings of buckskin within their reach. A pleasing white buckskin they have strung out and offered to you; a pleasing red feather as a hair ornament have they also offered to you. They have offered these things, so that they might ask for war from those who are in control of war. How, indeed, would it be possible for the spirits not to recognize these offerings? And if they recognize them, then we who are impersonating the spirits will also receive the benefit of the blessings of war and life.

Long ago our ancestors asked the spirits to bless them so that, having been blessed with life, they might live happily. Here we are sitting around a fireplace and the life that they[120] have asked for, the spirits are extending not only to them but to everyone. In the early times the old men said, "You are not able to fast and offer up proper food to the spirits so as to clear away the weapons held against you."[121] Thus they spoke to the younger people. Just as the older people would have liked it so they are doing. I, who do not amount to anything, have nevertheless been permitted to take the place of a spirit to whom food is offered. This they have done for me, given me the place of that very spirit who is the very bravest of them all, the one who is in control of the power whereby one can kill an enemy outright! One side of his body controls life and the other death. Now they are about to offer him the food of a white animal, of a male animal,[122] a white buckskin, feathers, and tobacco, all objects that please him very much. To Disease-Giver they are about to extend these things, so that therewith they may ask him for war power and life. It is a fear-inspiring spirit that they have been making offerings to. I, who have listened to the spirits through the host's kindness, surely do not have to say anything in their behalf.[123] They thought of their grandfather

---

120. Host and his band.
121. By denying that they can do it he tries to spur the young people to redoubled efforts. The weapons are the obstacles encountered in life.
122. I.e., a dog.
123. I.e., this feast will speak for them, more than any words I can utter.

when they asked me to impersonate this spirit. Of all the spirits, his is the name that one cannot speak of lightly, it is said. If I greet the name and speak about this spirit whom they have asked me to impersonate, may I not be weakened by uttering his name. Those who are about to offer food to you, Grandfather Disease-Giver, send forth their greetings. To the host do I send forth my greetings. To the war bundle owners who are seated here do I send forth my greetings.

Speech of the Fifth Guest

Clan councilors who are seated here, I greet you all. All you within this lodge who are impersonating the spirits, I greet you. It is good. If we say it is good, we mean it.[124] That we are living[125] is because they have done this for us.[126] That we have been able to move about so long[127] is due to the fact that the war bundle owners knew how to offer tobacco to the spirits. It is for that reason likewise that we have not been killed. Expert in their preaching to the youths and maidens, our chiefs have also kept the fireplace for us two-legged walkers.[128] Our chiefs have piled more fuel upon the fire that it may start up.[129] And not for themselves are they doing this. What they are doing is to enable us to obtain life. The name of South Wind they have uttered, he who alone is in control of life. They knew that he was a great spirit. An old man, one who was like a spirit in his power, called Jobenangiwingkha, they are speaking of. As many good spirits as there are, that many added their thoughts.[130] Of this they are reminding the spirits whom they are worshiping. Sincerely are they saying it. The life they blessed the old man with, that life they are using. With war powers they blessed him. They did not fool him. Because they have made their requests sincerely is the reason that the spirits

---

124. Literally, "it is not for nothing that we say this."
125. I.e., have been blessed with life.
126. I.e., asked us to participate in the feast.
127. I.e., are still living.
128. "Two-legged walkers" is the ritualistic name for human beings.
129. To be taken as meaning "blessings" since in adding fuel they are cooking the sacred food.
130. Power.

have given them these things in return. I feared that they might not take cognizance of them.[131] However, now I thank them,[132] for we have been as though connected with war power and life through South Wind. Tobacco they have poured for him, and white buckskin and red feathers have they extended to him. He will smoke the tobacco and we will follow in the path of life as a consequence. As though we were a member of their clan they have made us by permitting us to impersonate the spirits. What we have done will give us plenty of life to live on and for this we are indebted to them. We are thankful for it. Those who have been preached to, the South Wind I greet. Councilor,[133] I send forth my greetings to you. You who are seated here and are impersonating the spirits, to you also do I send forth my greetings.

Speech of the Sixth Guest

Host and members of your clan who are seated here, I send forth my greetings to you. To you also, war bundle owners who are seated here, do I send forth my greetings. The members of this clan have often preached to me. My grandfather once told me the following: "Some day there will be a dearth of people for a feast. There they will offer tobacco to the spirits and as many pieces of meat as they cut that many will be holy. There also they will cook heads. Heads are not to be eaten by those wearing dresses.[134] Women are not permitted to scatter their food in eating, we are told.[135] Some day if they boil these holy pieces, the heads, they will be in need of people to invite to the feast. If they call upon you for one of the sacred pieces, even if at that time you had not yet obtained a war honor, if you had not counted coup, still if you offer up thanks to the spirits for anything—still more so, of course, if you had been able to count coup and you thanked them for all this—they will

---

131. I.e., their offerings.
132. The host, etc.
133. The host.
134. I.e., women.
135. In eating the deer head the meat is devoured so fast that the food is literally scattered in the process of eating.

listen to you."[136] My grandfather told me, "Thus they spoke to me," he said, it is said, "Little grandfather, the spirits up above gave your ancestor a war bundle to those of the Earth phratry.[137] They gave them a mouth for speaking in offering thanks, but they told him that it was forbidden to speak to outsiders about this matter. They gave them a mouth that they might speak to one another."[138]

My father gave the information to me. For that reason, they told me, I am in a position to thank the spirits. One of the greatest of the spirits they have offered tobacco to, to one of the greatest of the spirits they have prayed. Tobacco, food, a sacred white buckskin, pleasing to their eyes, they have extended to them. With offerings of life[139] they have asked for life. We have been asked to impersonate the spirits, even although there are plenty of war bundle owners. But the host is a relative of ours and therefore wishes me to live. A pitiable existence we had been living until they saw to it that we were brought into connection with life. Proud we are of it. For if the spirits accept their gifts, we also will be able to utilize the life obtained. Clan members, we did as we pleased here. It is good. Those preached to, the Morning Star, I send forth my greetings. To the host and all the clansmen sitting with him, do I send forth my greetings. To those who are impersonating the spirits I also send forth my greetings.

Speech of the Seventh Guest

Host and your relatives who are seated here, I greet you all. I am not able to say anything,[140] but I can at least thank for

---

136. The whole meaning of the speech up to this point is: Should they in the future want to give a feast and lack of the proper people cause them to call upon you, even if you had counted coup only once, the spirits would listen to you. And yet here I am and have not even counted coup once and yet I have the effrontery to expect them to listen to me.

137. I.e., moiety. The Winnebago clans are grouped into two moieties, "those who are above" and "those who are on earth." Clans with bird names belong to the first division; clans with land and water animal names to the second.

138. I.e., members of the same clan.

139. I.e., with offerings of deer and dogs.

140. I.e., I don't amount to anything.

the body.[141] It is no harm to do so, we are told.[142] That is what I mean and why I say it. To speak of life is surely no harm, we are told.[143] Thus I thought. If ever I obtained the position of one who impersonated a spirit and partook of a sacred piece of food, I felt that I would be beside myself with thankfulness and gratitude. Not of war power will such as I be able to speak. In spite of that, they have seen to it that I came in connection with life. They have permitted me to impersonate one of the spirits who is among the greatest in the control of war power. It is good to thank the spirits and at the same time to preach to one another, it is said. To speak to one another of life and of the body, certainly there is no harm in it. Thus I thought, and that is why I am saying this. I am very thankful. If I could only say something that would be of any value to the spirits I would say it. You, grandfather, who come every day, you who are in control of great war power and life, tobacco, food, an offering of a white buckskin pleasing to the spirits, and a head ornament—that is about to be sent toward you. I was to be one of those impersonating the spirits at the feast, they told me. I am deeply grateful for the honor, to all those of the various clans that are gathered together here with offerings and who are impersonating the spirits. It is good. Even had I eaten a common piece of meat I would have considered myself well repaid, but I have actually been put in charge of a spirit who controls something. We are thankful. To those to whom we preached[144] I send forth my greetings. To the host I send forth my greetings. To those who are sitting in the lodge impersonating the spirits I send forth my greetings.

Speech of the Host

War bundle owners who are seated here, I greet you all. What I long for is exactly what we have been doing. All the

---

141. Probably referring to the dog.

142. I.e., there is no harm done if even a worthless person like myself thanks for the good of the dog, even although by doing this he is actually taking part in the feast.

143. I.e., there is no harm in obtaining life for one another by delivering speeches and offering up prayers to the spirits.

144. I.e., the Sun.

members of the various clans have pleaded for us in song. Very good have they been to us. It is good. This is what I have longed for, what we have been doing and all the good they have said about us. It is good when you give a feast to do just what you wish. The war bundle owners, as many as there are here, have spoken for me. It is good to obtain something when asking for it. Very well have they spoken. It is good; it is very good. You have eaten the food in my behalf; very carefully have you eaten it up for me. All the sacred speeches that they blessed our grandfather with you have repeated so that you might obtain real life, you said. It is good and I thank you, for we have done here exactly what I have longed for. War bundle owners who are seated here, I greet you.

*   *   *

This ends the first part of the ceremonial. The lodge is then swept and new kettles of meat placed over the fire. Then the host gives another tobacco offering to the spirits.

Tobacco Offering to the Spirits

To you, grandfather Jobenangiwingkha, does the council lodge of the Chief of the Night Spirits, standing in the east, belong. Holy you have kept it. You[145] were the one who blessed him with it, he said. When the time comes for the tobacco pouring we will offer you a handful of tobacco. War power he liked to obtain by doing this. With what you blessed him, that we ask you to give us in return. Grandfather, Chief of the Night Spirits, tobacco, here it is.

Here in the fire I shall place tobacco for you at all times. Tobacco, holy food, and buckskin for moccasins, all those things I will send to your sacred creation lodge.

You who are our grandmother, Earth, you blessed grandfather Jobenangiwingkha with life and war powers. As far as you extend, that far, O grandmother, do we spread out for you

---

145. Chief of the Night Spirits.

tobacco and food and moccasins. Here is the tobacco. Here in the fire shall I place tobacco; and food and offerings of buckskin will we send to you at all times. You will always accept them, grandfather said, it is said, so that our clansmen may travel in a straight path of war and life.[146]

This we ask, Grandmother Moon, of you also. You added your power to the other blessings of grandfather Jobenangiwingkha and you said that as long as the world lasts you would willingly accept the offerings of tobacco that his posterity extended to you. Thus you yourself said, we are told. Here is the tobacco.

As many of our clansmen as are here living in an abject condition,[147] may they all follow in the direct path of war. For that we are now extending to you tobacco, food, and moccasins. And may we in the future travel in the path of war and life.

You likewise, Chief of the Water, whose body is water, blessed grandfather Jobenangiwingkha. Here it is.[148] If we poured tobacco into the fire, you said you would always smoke it, it is said. Food and buckskin for moccasins we are about to extend to you. War powers and life, that we ask from you in return, for you said that you would always accept our offerings, we are told. When you blessed grandfather Jobenangiwingkha you said that we should pour tobacco for you at all times, it is said. Here it is.

You would recognize the offering of tobacco and the tobacco with the food that we sent forth to you, you said, it is said. We desire war powers and life for our kinsmen.

You likewise, Porcupine,[149] told grandfather, "For killing an enemy outright, I am useful, it is said. I am even the equal of the one who blows from the north!" Thus you told grandfather, it is said. When the proper time has arrived we should pour tobacco. Tobacco, here it is.

---

146. I.e., may nothing intervene to prevent them from enjoying all the blessings they have received in war and life.

147. Spiritually.

148. The tobacco.

149. This section is the offering to the North Wind. Porcupine is also associated with the North Wind in the first part of the ceremony.

Our first request is for war power and life.

Here is tobacco for you, too, Pigeon Hawk. You blessed grandfather with war and life and it is said you told him that you would always give him what we asked of you.

For Earthmaker, who is the foremost, you said we should pour tobacco, so for him we pour tobacco.[150] A handful of tobacco we are about to offer to you.[151]

To you, also, Thunderbird, I am about to pour tobacco. It will be one of the foremost offerings, you said, it is said. Tobacco we pour to you.

To the Big Black Hawk we also offer a handful of tobacco.

To you, Grandfather Disease-Giver, I also send tobacco.

To you, also, Grandfather South Wind, I send tobacco. You would consider it foremost, you said, it is said.

Here I place tobacco for you, too. Grandfather Sun. A handful of tobacco I place here for you.

*   *   *

After some other rituals, which need not be detailed here, the host continues his speeches.

Principal Speeches Continued

Host's First Speech

War bundle owners who are sitting here, I greet you. The songs that the Night Spirits place within the reach of grandfather Chiwoithenhiga,[152] those he tried to learn. He fasted and thirsted himself to death for the blessings our grandfathers[153] gave him over the length of the earth. Our grandfather Chiwoithenhiga said that he had come from somewhere in the east, that a Night Spirit chieftainess was his mother and that

---

150. I.e., we even have the effrontery to offer him tobacco as if people like ourselves could ever obtain a blessing from so great a deity.

151. Earthmaker.

152. Literal translation, "Kills-within-the Lodge." This name has been respelled from Radin's more technical transcription.

153. The Night Spirits.

the son of the chief of the Thunderbirds was his father, that his parents lived beyond the confines of this earth.[154] When he fasted to be blessed by these spirits over again,[155] they blessed him. If at any time he should die he would be able to visit the earth again, he said, it is said.[156] The song he was taught, the Night Spirit song, that we will try to sing. Even if you know only one song, you will not bore the spirits with it, for if you bring yourself to the state of weeping in your efforts, it will be acceptable. If you do not put on any embellishments when you pray[157] for war and life it will be acceptable, it is said. Thus we should say it.

War bundle owners who are seated here, I greet you. [Night Spirit song.]

Host's Second Speech

War bundle owners who are seated here, I greet you. When we finish our part of the ceremony, may you help us by repeating the spirit songs your ancestors gave you to be handed down from one generation to another. That we ask of you. Now we will start a dance song and when we are finished singing, our grandfather, the drum, will start to walk in your direction.[158] That we ask of you.[159] War bundle owners who are seated here, I greet you.

Host's Third Speech

War bundle owners who are seated here, I greet you. We are now trying to do our best to attract the spirits' attention to what we are doing and that is why we are placing the drum in front of the guests. What I said about the messenger who is

---

154. What Chiwoithenhiga means by saying that these spirits were his parents is that he is a reincarnated spirit that has chosen to be born of human parents. Such claims were by no means rare among the Winnebago.

155. Before coming to the earth as a human being, he had of course been told that he would receive certain blessings, but nonetheless he had to fast for them just as a human being does.

156. I.e., become reincarnated.

157. Literally, "cry."

158. I.e., the drum will be passed from one guest to another.

159. I.e., to help us also in our dancing.

about to walk,[160] that I am going to speak of to you. War bundle owners who are seated here, I greet you. [Dance Song.]

*　　　*　　　*

When he has finished, the drum and rattle, flute, and tobacco are passed to the guests, who in turn give their speeches.

Speeches of the Guests

Speech of the First Guest

Host and his relatives who are seated here, I send my greetings to you. To you who are sitting here impersonating the spirits I send forth my greetings also. It is good. The host and our grandfathers pour tobacco for me. Those in the east, the Night Spirits, added their blessings also, grandfather said, it is said. If at any time we sang the songs and poured tobacco for them he would take cognizance thereof, he said, it is said. The handful of tobacco we poured they would smoke. The clansmen and councilors who are living in as pitiable a condition as I myself who am speaking will be helped, should the spirits accept their offering, just as I will be helped if they accept my tobacco. Thus I thought. The messenger that they have caused to come my way[161] so that the spirits might hear my words, I am unworthy of. What our ancestors have handed down I can merely guess at.[162] Oh, that it were my good fortune to say even one thing as they desire it! Would that the Night Spirits, our grandfathers, would accept the food and the tobacco and the offerings of buckskin! It is with that wish that we say this. Host, members of this clan who are sitting here, I send my greetings toward you. All who are sitting here impersonating the spirits, I send my greetings toward you. [Night Spirit song.]

---

160. I.e., the drum. "The messenger" is literally "the one through whom something is told."

161. I.e., the drum.

162. I.e., my knowledge is so imperfect that I will have to take chances at saying the right thing.

Host, and your clan who are sitting here, I greet you. You who are sitting here impersonating spirits, I greet you. The messenger of the spirits[163] they have caused to walk in our path, first.[164] This drum has brought me and all my relatives who are here in touch with life. We have done this in order to obtain war power. The messenger that has walked thus far I have annoyed.[165] That is why I am saying this. Host, I greet you and yours. War bundle owners who are seated here, I send my greetings toward you.

Speech of the Second Guest

Host and members of your clan who are seated here, I greet you. You seated here who are impersonating the spirits, I greet you. It is good. Food you have given our warriors. There is plenty of ordinary food, but you have made us eat nice food, of animals that we like very much.[166] Even common food would have been good enough for us. They are boiling food for the spirits so that they might ask them for life. You are not merely doing this for them, but you are doing this for all those people who are present in this lodge. You have filled us full of blessings and you have permitted us to pour tobacco. You have caused the messengers[167] to walk over to us. We are thankful. Do I or does anything I say amount to anything? You thought of your grandfather[168] and that is why you did it. Those in the east, the Night Spirits, taught him songs. The first nice evening that they start the songs, then I will offer tobacco for them. Even if we do not sing the songs correctly, they[169] may still take pity on us and smoke our tobacco. The host and the members of his clan prayed earnestly to the spirits who are sitting here that they accept these offerings. It is with this thought that I speak in this way. War powers let us cry for.

---

163. The drum.
164. I.e., they have given us the place of honor so that the drum will be passed to us first.
165. I.e., I have made requests of the spirits by means of the drums and the rattles.
166. I.e., we have been asked to eat the deer head.
167. The drum and the rattle.
168. The spirit.
169. The spirits.

"When they give the feast, when they see to it that the sacred criers[170] come to you, remember that you should not take things lightly on that occasion. What the host desires do you also pray for," my ancestors told me. That is why I will say it. Now we are about to drum. Host who is sitting here, I greet you. War bundle owners who are seated here, I greet you all. [Song.]

Host and his relatives who are seated here, I send my greetings toward you. War bundle owners who are seated here impersonating the spirits, I send my greetings toward you. [Dance songs.]

Host who is sitting here, I send forth my greetings to you. It is good. It is to obtain war that we accept the drum. It is to gain life that we are doing this. We are doing this because the host wishes it. Nothing can be gained by anything I would say, but, nevertheless, howsoever small its value may be, let us start the drum. Host and members of his clan who are seated here, I greet you. War bundle owners who are seated here, I greet you.

Speech of the Third Guest

Host and relatives who are sitting here, I greet you. You sitting within this lodge who are impersonating the spirits, I greet you. It is good that the drum of the spirits has been made to walk in our direction. It is good. They have sent us the means for imitating the Night Spirits who live in the east, for impersonating our grandfathers. The drum that they have caused to walk in our direction, the songs that they have handed down, we will also repeat them. Our grandfathers, who are called the Night Spirits, it is for them that these songs have been offered, he said. If at any time we sing these songs and offer a handful of tobacco, surely they will smoke the tobacco, our grandfathers said, it is said. Tobacco we place here for the Night Spirits. The tobacco that the host has poured for us, here we offer it. How could I have thought of anything else to say? That the spirits may recognize the offerings of the host—the tobacco, the food, and the buckskin—that is why I speak. To

---

170. I.e., the drums.

plead for war power piteously, that is why we speak. Host, members of his clan, war bundle owners who are seated here, I greet you. [Night Spirits' song.]

Host and members of his clan who are seated here, I greet you. You also who are seated within this lodge impersonating the spirits, I greet you. An insignificant dance song we are about to use. I know that I am unable to obtain anything by singing. However, one should not be discouraged, and that is why I am saying this. I greet you all. [Dance song.]

We have been annoying the messenger that walked in our direction.[171] As many clansmen as have taken hold of it, that many have been strengthened. Thus we have annoyed it. Host, I greet you. You who are impersonating the spirits, all of you, do I greet.

*   *   *

Next a war bundle owner, one who has very likely been blessed by the Night Spirits—one therefore to whom they are apt to listen and one regarded as expert—gives a speech before the buckskins are thrown out, that is, offered to the spirits.

Speech of the Prominent Guest

Host and members of his clan who are seated here, I greet you. You seated in this lodge who are impersonating the spirits, I greet you. War bundle owners who are seated here, I greet you. It is good that the war bundle owners have done so much for the host. He has brought us the means of blessing and caused us to come into this lodge and has fed us. He has permitted us to offer tobacco. It is good. Not insincerely should we speak on such an occasion, our father told us. If at any time the spirits pay attention to a human being and permit him to offer them moccasins, rest assured that they will not let a weakling do this. If you are of any importance the spirits will accept the moccasins you have offered them. Indeed, my son, our grandfathers on both ends of the earth will have knowledge

---

171. The drum.

of these offerings,[172] they told each other. [Night Spirit songs alternating with Thunderbird songs.]

If at any time they consider you a man and accept the moccasins you have offered them, use your power. Above all, be careful that you do not say anything in a frivolous manner. The host putting himself in a pitiable condition has with copious dropping of tears besought the spirits for war power. For life he has also besought them and has prayed to them with offerings of tobacco, food, buckskins, and feathers. Putting himself in a pitiable condition he has hunted for the spirits,[173] weakened himself through exposure to cold, and caused himself untold sufferings. Oh, that I could have done similarly! It is for this[174] that they[175] have done this. Do not say anything frivolously, for the host has offered in your behalf tobacco and tears. Cry that you may obtain life, even as the host and his people have done. Act thus so that you may be of help to one another even as our ancestors of old were. If people act together they will accomplish their purpose. That is what they did in the beginning and that is why they lived like spirits at that time. They cried and made offerings of tobacco, grandfather said. For the Night Spirits shall you pour tobacco here. I send forth my greetings to you. [Night Spirit song.]

*   *   *

The host and the others then take the buckskins and dance around the lodge. The buckskin for Earthmaker is thrown out through the top of the lodge at the end of the third circuit of the lodge and the rest at the end of the fourth circuit for the spirits.

After more speeches, the feast of four kettles is distributed. Then the guests who have been in charge of these kettles speak,

---

172. I.e., the Night Spirits living in the east and the Thunderbirds living in the west.

173. I.e., hunted the deer used at the feast both for eating and for the buckskin offerings.

174. These laudable reasons.

175. The host and his band.

in a sense a continuation of the speeches given by the guests in the first part of the ceremonial after the distribution of those seven kettles. Before these speeches end, the host takes the war bundle and wraps it up.

Speech of the Eighth Guest[176]

Host and relatives, I send my greetings toward you. You seated here who are impersonating the spirits, I send my greetings toward you. It is good that there are so many war bundle owners here. It is good that they have given me the opportunity of impersonating the spirits, by placing me in charge of the food that they offer to them. Though I am not related to the host, he has done this for me. That I may grope for war powers, feel myself in connection with life, that is why we do it. It is good. As many of my relatives as are here, they all worked splendidly so that we might be connected with life. He who is the leader of our grandfathers who dwell in the east,[177] who is in control of all things, who is in control of war powers, he blessed our grandfather and he caused him to swallow as many people of other tribes as had been preordained for him. Within his stomach our grandfather heard their cries, he said, it is said. Thus thinking of my grandfather they asked me to impersonate the spirits. How could the spirits do anything but accept the offerings of tobacco, food, and buckskin! They have had a very great feast, and surely if the spirits take cognizance of it, all those who have been impersonating the spirits will also be permitted to participate in the blessings to follow. Our ancestors handed down to us from generation to generation the following: "When you offer food to the spirits, sit down to your undertaking with the greatest possible attention and care. Try to smoke as much tobacco as possible, for if you smoke much tobacco then all the spirits who are in control of war powers will pay attention to you, it is said. If a man smokes very much tobacco in one night, then he will be able to obtain a

---

176. I.e., the eighth guest to receive the buckskins, continuing the numeration from the first part of the ceremony.
177. The Night Spirits.

war honor, it is said. Try your hardest. Young men, it is easy to obtain war powers, the old men used to say. If the spirits accept the offerings of food and tobacco and buckskins, then afterwards those who have impersonated them will participate in the blessings that follow."

We feel that we have been connected with life and war power. It is for that reason that I say these words of thanks. If you give the feast for the war bundle well, if you pour tobacco well, then, if at some time or another you have a chance to kill an enemy outright, the war bundle will strengthen you greatly. No one will be able to kill you.

Host and members of his clan who are sitting here, I greet you. You seated here who have impersonated the spirits, I send forth my greetings to you.

Speech of the Ninth Guest

Host and members of his clan who are seated here, I greet you. To you, seated here, impersonating the spirits, I send my greetings. It is good. The host has tried to make us live. All those present here have been pleading to the spirits who are in control of life and war powers. If any Indians are sick and the keepers of the war bundle give this feast, then their illness will be overcome; they will recover from their disease, it is said. My father said that the people used to add more fuel to the fireplace of our chiefs when they do this. My grandfather told me that even if I, insignificant as I am who speak, were to make an offering of food to the spirits it would be good. I knew that he always spoke the truth, yet I knew that such as I could not do anything. Thus grandfather spoke to me, "Some day when you are in the presence of war and the rush is about to be made, you will not be frightened for you can say to the spirits, 'Grandfathers, I always gave you something to smoke, boiled food for you, and gave you the material for moccasins. Now I wish to go to the fight that is to take place.' If you speak to them thus, though you do not hear them answering you, you will recognize their answer in the fact that without any effort you will be victorious." They told the truth to one another, for they were certain of these things. That is why they encouraged one another. This is what the host and the members of his band are doing. It is good. A laudable thing they have done. They have boiled food for our grandmother, the Earth. They have offered her tobacco and buckskins and have as a reward received war powers. It is good. Our grandmother whom they made me impersonate, I greet. Host and all those who are seated within this lodge, I send forth my greetings to you.

Speech of the Tenth Guest

Host and members of his clan who are seated here, I send my greetings toward you. It is good. The host has given the tobacco offerings to the various spirits at the proper time. They[178] have accomplished very much. Once long ago, four generations back, a man like a spirit in power had told them what to do and since then they have been repeating it. It is good. Their ancestors long, long ago first gave this feast and yet even today we have seen it. They[179] listened attentively to what they said and they have repeated it exactly. We, ourselves, could not accomplish anything if we gave a feast. When in former times they had feasts in honor of our grandfathers, him whom they call Jobenangiwingkha gave them tobacco to smoke and he worshiped the spirits sincerely whenever they came to him. Thus these people have done for a long time and that is why we are recognized by the spirits. As often as they gave this feast they gave it for the honor of the spirits. They have done well and we are very well acquainted with the spirits as a consequence. Yet I myself who am now speaking cannot do anything; I can hardly be said to have lived.[180] I am unable even to put on one kettle in honor of the spirits. Those who have given this feast to the spirits have done well and perhaps, as a consequence, we may be able to obtain just a little of the blessings of life. So I thought. It is good, I tell you who have made offerings to the spirits who are impersonating the spirits. He who has been given the kettle in honor of the Moon expresses his thanks. They gave this to me so that we might

---

178. Host and clan members.
179. Host and his relatives.
180. I.e., lived the life of a respectable man.

plead for them with the spirits. Not anything of consequence can we say. We are thankful. It is good, it is said. That is what I wish to say. Those counseled, I greet, the spirit who comes at night. Host, I send forth my greetings to you. You impersonating the spirits, I send my greetings toward you.

Speech of the Eleventh Guest

Host and his clansmen who are seated here, I send my greetings toward you. Those impersonating the spirits, I send my greetings toward you. The host and his people sit here crying for war powers. Tobacco they offer, asking for life; the tobacco that they possess they sit here offering that they may obtain life. They know that it is good to have war powers and that is why they ask for it with tears in their eyes. It is good to die in war. If you can kill one enemy, then you will be a brave man and all the men will say that you have done a good deed. We would all know it. However, not without effort can men become braves. They must suffer to obtain this honor. The host has made himself suffer, they have poured tobacco. If we do as they did and make feasts for the spirits and offer them buckskins, then we will be able to obtain war powers for ourselves, and only then. That is what the Creator would do. Not without fasting, not white faced,[181] are war powers obtainable. Yet the old men long ago said that if one could not fast, still if he poured tobacco for the spirits and offered them food and if he made excellent offerings of buckskin to the spirits, war powers might be obtained. Thus the elders spoke and they knew of what they were speaking. The host and the clansmen sitting with him listened to the elders and that is why they performed this ceremony so well. How could we ever obtain war powers as they have done? All we hope is that we may obtain some of the war powers that will follow.[182] We feel ourselves connected with life, for surely one of the great spirits will take cognizance of the tobacco, food, and buckskins that we who are impersonating the spirits have offered. Surely the

---

181. I.e., not without blackening one's face as is done in fasting.
182. As a result of the feast given.

spirits will not care to see these offerings lost nor let us cause ourselves to suffer in vain. Thus the Creator said. As counseled ones do, I greet you.[183] Host, I send my greetings toward you. You seated here impersonating the spirits, I send my greetings toward you.

Host's Final Speech

War bundle owners who are seated here, I greet you. It is good. We were living in an abject condition, so you performed this ceremony most carefully for us. All night have you been sitting here. It is good. With the greatest care have you eaten. It is good. That is what those who are in charge of feasts, who are in charge of war powers, counseled us, it is said. I shall now call on a man who can make himself heard by all the spirits who are in control of war power, including those who live above where the Creator lives, to those who live on the earth, and those who live under the earth. I will now sing four songs and when I begin them that will be the end of the ceremony. Then the man is to give the war whoop four times.

* * *

After the victory whoop is given four times, the dog is sent as an offering to Disease-Giver with the following speech of the host to Disease-Giver.

Speech to Disease-Giver

War bundle owners who are seated here, I greet you. In the beginning one of my grandfathers told me that the man in the south is the greatest one in control of war powers. One side controls death and the other life, he said. He blessed our grandfather and his descendants wherever they might be and he said that he would at all times remember them. Whenever we pour tobacco, then those who offer tobacco will not take sick, he said, it is said. That is the reason they pour tobacco, they said. We are extending to you one like ourselves,[184] and

183. I.e., Water.
184. The dog.

we have told all, that all who wish to pour tobacco may do so. I greet you all.

*   *   *

All—men, women, and children—pour tobacco, and all leave. The ceremony has ended.

VIII. Iroquois Ceremonials

Among those peoples who live in very small groups scattered over a very wide territory, self-reliance—the ability of each individual to deal with whatever confronts him—is cultivated. There are few other people to whom he can turn in a crisis, and undoubtedly because of this, he early comes to expect that he must rely on his own knowledge and skill. This includes practical knowledge of the animals he hunts and skill in taking them. But it also includes knowledge of himself—his soul and what information and advice it might provide. Hence the importance accorded the dream, for it is in the dream that the "soul" reveals itself. Hence also the importance attached to the cultivation of the dream—attending the dream experiences.

Other help may be sought through the vision. The blessings so received, the help of the persons who reveal themselves in the vision, supplement those accorded by friends and, more importantly, relatives. And so important may this aid be that each boy attempts to obtain it, and once obtained it serves as one of the most powerful influences on his life.

But where the community of those living together is larger

IROQUOIS CEREMONIALS

(although still small by present standards) and is relatively stable in time and space, activities involving the people generally, including rituals, assume more importance. One such ceremony common among those of this area who practice some agriculture is the Green Corn ceremony, also termed the Busk among some southeastern Indian groups—a ceremony held after the corn first became edible.

Such rituals, however, as far as our knowledge of them exists, coexisted alongside others based on individual visions and dreams. No contradiction is implied. Nowhere in North America were Indians completely dependent on agriculture. To some extent all were dependent on hunting and gathering, and often on fishing. And to some extent all were dependent on the dream and vision for aid.

Iroquois custom is a case in point. The vision and the quest for such vision were once of some importance. Of importance also was the dream—for the dream could and still does indicate what should be done to maintain or restore good luck, including health. In addition, the Iroquois have ceremonies involving the people generally. These include not only the Green Corn ceremony, but also the Maple ceremony held when the sap begins to rise in the maple trees, the Planting ceremony held when the seeds are planted in the spring, the Strawberry ceremony "when the berries hang on the bushes"—that is, when the strawberries are ripe, the Green Bean ceremony when the beans are ripe, the Harvest ceremony in the fall, and the Midwinter or New Year's ceremony held in the winter when the Pleiades were observed to be directly overhead at dusk and following the new moon when the Pleiades were so located.

Of all these ceremonies, Midwinter, which both concludes the old year and begins the new, is the longest and most important. The theme is renewal. Old dreams are renewed, including those cures effected by the so-called medicine societies. When it is so indicated by a dream of the ill person or by the dream of another seeking the cause of the illness, members of the medicine society perform their ritual for the patient's benefit. At Midwinter these cures could be renewed, that is, the individual so cured should sponsor a dance by the members of the society that cured him. Other dreams should also be renewed, for not only may the rituals of the medicine societies be used to cure, but also virtually any dance, song, or game may be so used if indicated by the dream.

The theme of renewal is also evident in the ashes-stirring rites that precede renewal of dreams. In the past, these rites included not only the stirring of the ashes of the household fires by various visitors, but also the extinguishing of the old fires and rekindling of new ones—a common practice in parts of North America and a rite that may have had its origin in Mexico.

It is also evident in the tobacco invocation—once said over the white dog that served as a messenger to the Creator—requesting the Creator that things continue in the coming year as they have in the past. The sections of this tobacco invocation are essentially those of the Thanksgiving Speech[1] to each of which is added a request of the Creator that the item mentioned in that section continue for another year—for in an important sense the Midwinter ceremony is concerned with the battle between the creative and destructive forces symbolized in the cosmological myth as the antagonism between the Sky-Holder (the Creator) and his younger brother.

In an important sense, the ceremonies given during the year recognize that the Creator has continued these things: the Maple ceremony that the sap again flows in the maple trees; the Strawberry ceremony that the berries appeared again; the Green Bean, Green Corn, and Harvest ceremonies that the Three Sisters—corn, beans, and squash—have come again; and the less frequently given Sun, Moon, and Thunderer ceremonies that these things also continue. As one Iroquois stated it, "At the Midwinter Festival we beg the Creator for everything; most of the time we are thanking him for what he gave us."[2] There is, then, an intimate connection between the cosmology of the Iroquois as outlined in the Thanksgiving Speech and the yearly round of ceremonies.

---

1. See Chapter I for a text of this speech.
2. Foster, *From the Earth to Beyond the Sky*, pp. 129–130.

IROQUOIS CEREMONIALS

The Creator, Sky-Holder, also ordained all these ceremonies, and that he did so is recounted in the following extracts from an Onondaga version of the cosmological myth.

Excerpts from an Onondaga Cosmological Myth[3]

So then now every one of you must give strict attention. Indeed, all you who live upon the earth share it equally; and the matter will continue thus in the future. They shall regard it as important. I myself too will regard as an important matter what I will leave here on the earth, the Four Ceremonies, or Rituals.[4] You shall continue to keep those customs, and the ceremony shall continue to be observed. So then I now decide that you shall continue from time to time to gather, and it shall begin at this time. That for which you shall gather yourselves is the sum of all things that grow, upon which you live. The first time you again see the new fruit of that on which you live, you shall take that which is first seen. It shall be collected and placed in a certain appointed place. Then you too shall assemble yourselves, the whole body of people must gather. So then I ordain that you shall first greet each other and mutually congratulate one another that so many persons do again see the new, and it shall be the first thing that they shall swallow again, that upon which you live. So when you will have ended mutually congratulating one another, then you shall give thanks to me. So then I leave [establish] the Four Ceremonies, or Ritual Matters, which shall continue before you. I have patterned it after the ceremony as it is being carried on in the place where the Earth, which you call the Sky, is. And it is actually so, the pleasure with which those on the upper side of the sky rejoice is most important. I patterned it so because I desire that the ceremonies that will be going on here on earth, on the under side of the sky, shall be the same as those. The ceremonies that shall continue to be carried on are, then, that

---

3. From Hewitt, *Iroquoian Cosmology—Second Part*, pp. 559–564, 574–576, 581–582. Source in editing is as described in note 9. The notes are mine.
4. I.e., Feather Dance, Thanksgiving Dance (also called the Drum Dance and the Skin Dance), Rite of Personal Chant, and Bowl Game. All four of these rituals are given as part of the Green Corn and Midwinter ceremonials.

which is called the Great Feather Dance; that which is called the Drum-Dance, that which is called the Chants,[5] and that which is called the Grand Bet, or They Strike Bowls.[6] Then, too, these ceremonies, four in number, shall be carried on at certain appointed times.

So then the first shall be when the season changes. As soon as all that on which you live will mature, at that place and time will be marked with the Grand Pleasure, which shall be called the Sharing of the Grand Foods.[7] Then all the things, though small in quantity, all the kinds of things on which you live, shall be collected from all the several families; and cooked things shall be gathered; and the flesh of game, that also shall be present. Now at that time the ceremony, the Great Feather Dance, shall start. So then all persons shall be thankful. They must keep thinking, "I am thankful that I am still alive and in health, that I have again seen that on which we live; and that I also have again seen the performance of the ceremony that he ordained for us." And then one shall say, "I thank you, you who have formed my body, you who dwells in the sky. I am thankful that it is still possible for me to perform the ceremony that you have ordained for us." Thus, will you who live upon the earth continue to do. You must perform the ceremonies, and you shall make a circuit of the fire. You shall make a circuit of the fire in a certain direction. Do not ever let anyone make a circuit of it in the opposite direction; and do not even let it be that the left side of the body be on the outside of the circle. When one makes a circuit, the right side of the body shall be on the outside of the circle.[8] And all persons shall make a circuit of the place where the two who shall sing will sit. So then the

---

5. I.e., the Rite of Personal Chant. Each man has a personal song or chant, which customarily he sang before death might be expected as before going to war, while being tortured, or in other times of danger. These songs—each man singing his own song in turn—constitute the Rite of Personal Chant.

6. I.e., the Bowl Game. This game is a game of chance played by striking a flat-bottomed bowl containing six peach stones against the floor. The peach stones blackened on one side serve as dice. In the Midwinter ceremonial it is played between the moieties; the clans constituting one moiety play against the clans of the other.

7. I.e., Harvest ceremony.

8. All Iroquois dances except a few in honor of the dead are danced in a counterclockwise direction. This passage refers to that custom.

feather headdress shall be the principal thing.[9] It is that which you will be in the habit of using, and then it will be evident what kind of persons you are. And also when the Four Ceremonies will have passed, all should be happy.

Now, another time is when the condition of the earth, and also of the days, will be changed, when it will again be cold, and when one will say, "It is wintertime." So then at that time will the matter of the Four Ceremonies be again marked.[10] The game animals upon which you live shall be one of the principal things.[11] The game animals will change themselves. When it again becomes warm and the spring season comes upon the earth, they will come together, that is then that the lives of the game animals become weaker. As soon as the summer season ends and the earth again becomes cold, then they two will again go together, when again their meat becomes fine; the lives of the game animals will become new again. That is the reason that it shall continue thus to be, so that when the life of the game animals becomes new again, then one will fell their bodies, and it is the meat thereof that will be used to form the assembly, and that too on which you live, these shall be placed together. So now when they shall have assembled themselves, the first thing shall be the Greatly Prized Ceremony. It will be called the Midwinter ceremony.[12] So then the place where lies what supports you, the fires of the several firesides,[13] shall become important places. Then one will set his or her hands to the fire; will take up and stir the fire, which has become ashes.[14] One will speak and say, "I am thankful that I am alive in health. Now the time has come in which the Midwinter

---

9. "Indian costume" should be worn while dancing the Feather Dance (and Thanksgiving Dance). A feather headdress is an important part of that costume.

10. I.e., at the Midwinter, or New Year's ceremony.

11. I.e., the meat of the animals must be provided for the feast. When game animals were more abundant than they are now, a hunt preceded the Midwinter ceremony.

12. The Onondaga word Hewitt uses here refers to distraught or frenzied minds, with the implication that they are so because of an accumulation of obligations revealed in dreams that should be fulfilled (renewed) during the first days of the Midwinter ceremony.

13. I.e., the relatives who use the same fire.

14. In the first days of Midwinter, people go about the houses, stirring the ashes of the fires, and give thanks that they are still alive.

ceremony is marked. So then now do you, Sky-Holder[15] who live in the sky, do you continue to listen. Now, I thank you that it still has been possible for me again to see the place where you have set the ceremony." Then at that time one will lament, one will sing, and then one will begin to dip up the ashes with a paddle, and then will tip it and the ashes will fall. Then one's voice will accompany that action, and all will be thankful. So, then, when all those who are alive on the earth will have performed the entire ceremony, then all will be of one mind. Then at this place, when that will become the principal thing, you will then use as a means what will be called Trussed Things.[16] So then I, personally, will continue to greatly prize that ceremony; and all the peoples of the earth will satisfy my word.[17] So then the dog whose body is purely white will be the principal matter. There shall be no black spot on it, and with that they shall again dress my person. That shall symbolize the form and kind of my raiment. Then shall come the appointment of him who will cast its body on the fire, and in the next place the native tobacco.[18] When he will direct his words toward that, then he will say, "This day is present. You who dwell in the sky, continue to listen. Now you do see clearly how many persons there are who have come to stand at the place where a fire has been kindled to you. Now, moreover, do you continue to listen. Now they who are alive upon the earth will speak. And they will speak with one voice; and they have formed their word of that matter which you highly prize, the Trussed Thing. All peoples on the earth have satisfied your word. Now, therefore, there goes the thing you do highly prize, the thing you did intend that they who are alive upon the earth shall continue to observe. Now all the many orders of those who are alive with one voice have performed their duty to you. Now they thank you that it is still possible for so many

---

15. The Creator; see Chapter I.]

16. I.e., the white dogs. One or two were burned as part of the Tobacco Invocation to the Creator; see above.

17. I.e., fulfill the dream of Sky-Holder.

18. A reference to the Tobacco Invocation that is an important rite of Midwinter; see above. "Native" because the species is *Nicotiana rustica*, called "Indian tobacco," in contrast to the *n. tabacum* of commerce.

persons again to see what kind of thing is the ceremony, which you have ordained for us. So then we beseech[19] you that this body of persons should continue thus undiminished, so that all of us should again see it when the season will again change and it will again become warm on the earth. We beseech you that you should send the game animals of all sizes, some whose bodies are small and also some whose bodies are large. Now, another thing. They again beseech you that they should see grow again the provision that you have provided for us, and that on which we live, and also that by which our children live, that it should mature and ripen. Now, again, another thing. We again beseech you in reference to all those things that grow and that bear fruit, the various kinds that you have planted for us, that all should again see them grow and see them when again all come to maturity. Now, another thing: We beseech you that still again you should send thence the persons whose lives are small, the infants, that they should stand on the earth here present, so that the purpose of your mind should be fulfilled, in that you did intend that it should continue to be thus, that persons should continue to be born anew. And so then that is what one continues to beseech you for that one should see it thus come to pass. Now, then, to you who dwell in the sky one has committed the whole matter. Now, again, another thing. Now with one voice all the persons that still are, the children to the last one, who still remain upon the earth, beseech you that still unchanged this assembly should again see that period where the ceremony is marked, and the time will also arrive wherein you have placed the ceremony, the matters you have placed before us. So then they make their word of the native tobacco that you have left to us. Now, again, another thing. So then with a single voice all those who still remain upon the earth shall turn their face thither. So then all the various orders of you who have assigned duties to perform, duties appointed you by the former of our bodies, do you continue to listen. So then that is the first thing. To you, our Mother, whereon we

---

19. Beseeching or begging that the Creator continue in the coming year what was in the past is an important part of the Tobacco Invocation; see above.

stand, this earth here present, we give thanks. Next, we encourage you, so that your mind should be firm, that thus it should continue to be, so that we should continue to think in peace day after day and also night after night. Now, then, again, there is another thing. Now do you, our Elder Brother, the diurnal Light Orb[20] going about on the visible sky, continue to listen. Now, then, you will continue to know that all those whose persons remain alive have made preparations to thank you with one voice. Now, in the next place, they have made preparation to do it, and have encouraged your mind that your mind should remain firm for so long a time as he who formed our bodies has appointed your assigned duty. Now, again, another thing. You next, the nocturnal Orb of Light,[21] our Grandmother, and now also the Stars on the sky in many places, do you know that every one of whose who remain alive has made preparation to thank you now with one voice? Now, our Grandmother, they thank you, and also the stars fixed on the sky in many places. And next they have made preparation to encourage your minds, and that thus it should continue for so long a time as one has appointed your overseeing duty. Now, again, another thing. Now do you continue to listen, our Grandfathers, whose voices are uttered from place to place, who are in the habit of coming from the west;[22] and whom he has appointed to protect us who are alive upon the earth day after day, and also night after night. Now, then, every one whose body remains alive has now made preparation to thank you now with one voice. That, in the next place, they now encourage your minds that thus it should continue to be that your mind should be firm for so long a time as he who formed our bodies appointed your assigned responsibility. Now, then, we wrap up into a single body,[23] as it were, all the various grades of those of you to whom he has assigned duties here on the earth—here also all the grasses that grow, the growing

---

20. The Sun.
21. The Moon.
22. I.e., the Thunderers.
23. In abbreviated forms of the Thanksgiving Speech, the separate sections may be combined. The speaker is doing this here, "wrapping them up in a single body."

shrubs, the growing trees, and the several springs of water, and the several running springs, the several streams of water, and the several running waters, and the air that moves;[24] this also, the present day, and also the present night, and the several fixed Orbs of Light,[25] and the several Stars fixed on the sky, and you who habitually come from the west; and now also, you who have completed our bodies and also all those things that we have indicated, now, moreover, we thank you all. Now, then, another thing. You, Sky-Holder, continue to listen. You will continue to know that the ceremony will be performed by us who are alive on earth, even the Four Ceremonies. So then you will see it clearly, when the ceremonies will start you will be the principal person, when they will thank you repeatedly. Tomorrow, early in the morning, the ceremony, the highly prized ceremonial dance, the Great Father Dance, will start. The songs of it will be repeated thrice. And, on the day after tomorrow will then start the Drum Dance and they will select one who will speak and who will give thanks repeatedly.[26] He will begin with all those things that are contained in the earth that give satisfaction to your[27] minds, and also all the various orders of those to whom he has assigned duties, and he also will be among them when he will give thanks. Now, again, another thing. The Ceremony of Chanting[28] will start. This ceremony rests entirely with each of you individually.[29] If you will desire that he should perform this ceremony, he will tell of the extent of his handiwork, and he will give thanks, and he will also continue to give thanks. Now, again, another thing. When the Ceremony of the Great Betting will start you must use whatever thing of what you are in the habit of using, you will spare that,[30] and with that they will lay wagers one against another.

---

24. I.e., the wind.

25. I.e., the Sun and Moon.

26. The Drum (Thanksgiving or Skin) Dance consists of songs interspersed with sections of the Thanksgiving Speech. The reference here is to the man who delivers these sections of the Speech as part of the Dance.

27. I.e., the people's.

28. I.e., the Rite of Personal Chant.

29. I.e., each man sings his own song as an individual.

30. It is said that wagers on the outcome of the Bowl Game should be something valuable.

That will be the principal thing, and will keep up the strength of the noise[31] when the ceremony will be in progress, when the people who are alive upon the earth will be amusing my mind. All that I have ordained shall be the means of doing, and they shall be greatly prized matters.

Now, then, I will also supplement the Four Ceremonies I gave. In this manner, then will you again do it in the days to come. When the season changes, and the spring season starts, then you will begin; when you will again see wild strawberries, the small kind, again mature, when it will have put forth berries, thus you will do. You should get berries, they shall be gathered, and then, you, the entire community, the old women, also all the children, shall assemble yourselves. When all will be assembled, then a drink shall be made of the berries; and the first thing will be done, that the juice of the berry shall make a circuit of the assembly.[32] You shall choose two persons who shall make the circuit of the assembly and who shall divide the juice of the berries into portions, to every one.[33] Those whom you shall choose shall be those whose lives are new, one person shall be a male and the other a female. They two shall have grown to that age when he will have just grown up to that point when his voice begins to change, and, in reference to the girl, she will have grown up to that point when she shall have just, for the first time, had to deny herself certain things.[34] When they two will divide up the berry juice, you shall use one thing only when you shall dip it up. You shall do thus when you dip up the juice of the fruit; each shall hold it, and at that time, each shall speak and say, "I greet you with thanksgiving, all you whom we are in the habit of greeting with thanksgiving. You also we greet with thanksgiving, all you of various ranks to whom he has assigned responsibilities. Now, then, we

31. The noise referred to is the noise made by those of each side to bring luck to their side and away from the other side.

32. An important rite in the Strawberry ceremony is the serving of the berry juice to all in attendance.

33. I.e., serve the drink to all.

34. I.e., begun menstruating. The reference is to menstrual taboos. Among the Iroquois and a number of other North American Indians, a menstruating woman should avoid certain kinds of contact with others and with objects they might use and was otherwise restricted in what she might do; see note 62, Chapter II.

greet you who dwells in the sky with thanksgiving, that still again we see what you have planted for us again bear fruit. I greet you with thanksgiving that now again I shall swallow the drink." Then, at that time, you shall drink the juice of the fruit. And it is the duty of each one of you, all, even to the least child, to speak. Should it so be that one is not able to speak, then all that is necessary will be that one shall speak specifically, saying, "I am thankful that still again I shall drink it. I greet with thanksgiving he who has completed our bodies." It is just the same if this is all that it is possible for one to do. If it so be that that one is not able to talk, let that one only think repeatedly, "I am thankful that I am alive in peace. Now, anew, I will drink it again. I greet you with thanksgiving who formed my body and who dwells in the sky." Thus shall you be in the habit of doing. When all will have drunk the juice of the fruit, then the Ceremony of the Great Feather Dance shall take place. All shall stand up and shall make a circuit of the fire and shall share in promoting the ceremony.[35] All shall continue to be happy, thinking, "I am thankful that I am alive in peace. Now again I see the time and place where he has placed this ceremony among the ceremonies that he has marked out, that still it is possible that I am able to take part in the Ceremony. Now, then, I greet you with thanksgiving who dwells in the sky. You have completed our lives." Thus you shall again do this in the future days.

I have assigned to a certain kind of tree the duty that it shall exude a sap, which shall be called sugar. It is that, then, that shall be put into it, when one shall prepare the juice of the fruit.[36] I have appointed to this duty what will be called the Maple. So then, this matter will be marked at the time and place when the days are beginning to be warm again, and also the earth. At that time, it will then be possible that it shall exude sap, which will become sugar. That, too, will result in good that, in this instance as well, you shall do the same thing, that you shall continue to utter thanksgivings when you will

---

35. I.e., all should dance the Feather Dance, an important rite of the Strawberry ceremony.

36. As a drink.

again see it, and then you will again drink it anew. That shall be called the Gathering of One's Sugar.

Now, again, another thing. I will deliver that by which you shall continue to live. So, then, now shall begin that which will become hard labor for you. You shall put your hands to them, you shall care for them when the time comes that the soil of the earth shall again become hot. When that time will come, you shall place them in the ground. And there shall be the three kinds of that on which you shall live; one shall be called Corn, and the next shall be called the Bean, and the next shall be called the Squash. So, then, when the time comes when you should place it in the ground, you shall plant it. When you shall finish this, then the people shall assemble and you shall give thanks, and for this purpose you shall make use of the preliminary Ceremony of your usual custom.[37] At that time, the Ceremony of the Great Feather Dance will take place.[38] You shall continue greeting one another with thanksgiving, and me also you shall continue to greet with thanksgiving. When it will have sprouted and will have come forth out of the ground, then you shall begin to care for it. Do you not spoil it in attending to it. Thus, again, next you shall do when you have finished this task. The people shall assemble themselves and you shall employ all the ceremonies you are accustomed to use. So then, when there is putting forth of beans, these shall be gotten, these be gathered, and a kettle of these cooked shall set there, and that will support the entire body of assembled people.[39] Then one shall be chosen by unanimous voice, and he shall speak. When he speaks, he shall follow the prescribed course, beginning with the matters such as they are in the preliminary Ceremony of Thanksgiving; he will begin below with the manifold things that give pleasure to your minds, and he shall carry his discourse upward to the manifold persons who assist you and protect you.[40] Now, then, also, you will

---

37. The reference is to the Planting ceremony.
38. The Feather Dance is one of the dances performed as part of this ceremony.
39. The reference here is to the green beans that are put into the soup that constitutes the feast of the Green Bean ceremony.
40. The reference here is to the Thanksgiving Speech.

continue to greet me with thanksgiving, that you will again newly partake of them. That shall be the first. Then, the Ceremony of the Great Feather Dance shall start and all persons shall continue to be happy. Everyone shall continue to be greeting with thanksgiving. Me, too, shall each greet with thanksgiving. Now, all shall take part in the Ceremony, and shall continue to go around the fire.[41] So, then, after this, you shall divide it[42] up into equal portions, and all shall share alike in what one swallows, the adults and the children as well. The same thing shall be done when the corn upon which you live puts forth grains and when the native squash puts forth fruit. So, then, as to that, these shall be combined in the ceremony marked when you shall again see all kinds of things, who are Sisters,[43] one to another, upon whom you live. At that place, where the ceremony is marked, you shall collect for yourselves the Grand Food.[44] At that place and time, the great rejoicing of the Four Ceremonies shall be performed. Now, then, I have completed the entire matter in the things that I have severally ordered that you personally shall have as customs here on the earth.

---

41. I.e., dance.
42. I.e., the soup.
43. I.e., the Three Sisters—corn, beans, and squash.
44. I.e., Green Corn ceremony.

IX. Southeastern Indian Formulas*

Among Southeastern Indians, perhaps more than among those to the north, ritual leaders tended to be priests, specialists who were trained by other specialists. Here, as in the north also, religion and medicine were not nearly as distinct spheres of belief and activity as they are in modern Euramerican societies. The same specialists usually supervised rituals and cured the sick, and their medical songs, spells, and procedures had many aspects that we would classify as religious. The major ritual dramas of the Southeastern Indians disappeared or were drastically simplified before they were adequately studied, and we have no suitable texts dictated by believers from which we could extract prayers or detailed ritual descriptions. But southern Indian folk medicine of a largely aboriginal sort, with native doctors using old procedures, has survived in places up to the present.

Among the Cherokees of both North Carolina and Okla-

---

* This chapter was written by William C. Hurtevant.

282

homa many doctors collected sacred formulas or charms for use in their medico-magical practice and wrote them down in the Cherokee language in the syllabary invented by Sequoyah and introduced in 1821. These manuscripts are very difficult for anyone but their authors to understand and translate—they are elliptical, couched in magical and sometimes archaic terminology, and often contain just reminders of the appropriate spells, usually without indication of the accompanying ritual or herbal procedures and frequently without statements of the specific purposes for which they were used. The charms have great power and importance for their owners, who have thus usually been unwilling to explain them to outsiders. The translations and explanations we have are usually from other Cherokees, knowledgeable about the belief systems and the general procedures but uncertain about the specific functions and meanings of the charms written by others for their own private use.

The following Cherokee formula for curing a toothache illustrates the frequent Southeastern Indian association of specific illnesses with specific animals and birds. Color symbolism is also a frequent element in these charms; while the significance is often obscure, in this case the whiteness of two of the disease-agents is said to indicate that they are contented to be where they are, in the patient's swollen tooth, while the redness of two of them indicates that they are victorious (but only temporarily) over the patient.

For Toothache[1]

Pileated woodpecker, very quickly you have just come to make it resound.[2]

---

1. A formula from the collection, originally written in the Sequoyah syllabary, of Adelaghdhiva Gansgawi, a doctor born about 1896 near Jay, Oklahoma, who died in 1938. The translation is by Jack Frederick Kilpatrick and Anna Gritts Kilpatrick, in *Notebook of a Cherokee Shaman*, Smithsonian Contributions to Anthropology vol. 2, no. 6 (Washington, 1970), p. 123. The notes are based on the Kilpatricks' commentary.

2. A reference to the vigor with which the insect-eating bird will work to remove the insect spirit from the affected tooth.

You have just come by to get out the white insect.[3]

Hairy woodpecker, very quickly you have just come to
make it resound.
You have just come by to get out the white insect.

Great crested flycatcher—ha!—very quickly you have
just come to make it resound.
You have just come by to get out the red insect.

Red-headed woodpecker—ha!—very quickly you have
just come to make it resound.
You have just come by to get out the red insect.

The following text was sung by a Creek doctor to cure
sickness caused by the beaver; the symptoms were constipation
and pain in the bowels. The song was sung to give curative
power to the medicine, a tea prepared from two roots. The
verses illustrate the very common Southeastern magical se-
quences of four colors and four directions, which were sometimes concurrent (as here) and sometimes independent. The
otter, woodchuck, and ermine mentioned in succeeding verses
were considered by the Creeks to be related to the causative
agent, the beaver.

Beaver the Cause[4]

He was sitting above[5]
South, aha! Red, aha! Beaver, aha! He kills, aha! It dies,
aha!

---

3. Translates a Cherokee term for small insects, larvae, and worms, whose ghosts
often take revenge for their continual destruction by humans by settling in their bodies
where they cause ulcers, blisters, and swellings.

4. This was sung in 1905 by Laslie Cloud, Kapichimathla, of the Creek town of
Tuskeegee, in Indian Territory (now Oklahoma), and recorded by Frank G. Speck on a
wax phonograph cylinder, from which it was transcribed and translated with Cloud's
help. The translation, arranged slightly differently, is from Speck, *The Creek Indians of
Taskigi Town*. Memoirs of the American Anthropological Association vol. 2, pt. 2
(1907), pp. 130-131, and Speck, *Ceremonial Songs of the Creek and Yuchi Indians*, Univ. of
Pennsylvania Museum Anthropological Publications vol. 1, no. 2 (1911), pp. 216-217.
The music is transcribed in the latter publication.

5. According to Speck (p. 217), this line here and in each case below was
"repeated a number of times"; four seems likely and evidently corresponds to the
pattern of the musical score.

He was sitting above
West, aha! Yellow, aha! Beaver, aha! He kills, aha! It
dies, aha!

He was sitting above
North, aha! Black, aha! Beaver, aha! He kills, aha! It
dies, aha!

He was sitting above
East, aha! White, aha! Beaver, aha! He kills, aha! It
dies, aha!

He was sitting above
South, aha! Red, aha! Otter, aha! He kills, aha! It dies,
aha!

He was sitting above
West, aha! Yellow, aha! Otter, aha! He kills, aha! It
dies, aha!

He was sitting above
North, aha! Black, aha! Otter, aha! He kills, aha! It
dies, aha!

He was sitting above
East, aha! White, aha! Otter, aha! He kills, aha! It dies,
aha!

He was sitting above
South, aha! Red, aha! Muskrat, aha! He kills, aha! It
dies, aha!

He was sitting above
West, aha! Yellow, aha! Muskrat, aha! He kills, aha! It
dies, aha!

He was sitting above
North, aha! Black, aha! Muskrat, aha! He kills, aha! It
dies, aha!

He was sitting above
East, aha! White, aha! Muskrat, aha! He kills, aha! It
dies, aha!

He was sitting above
South, aha! Red, aha! Ermine, aha! He kills, aha! It
dies, aha!

He was sitting above
West, aha! Yellow, aha! Ermine, aha! He kills, aha! It
dies, aha!

He was sitting above
North, aha! Black, aha! Ermine, aha! He kills, aha! It
dies, aha!

He was sitting above
East, aha! White, aha! Ermine, aha! He kills, aha! It
dies, aha!

The Cherokee frequently use tobacco in curing, often "re-making" it with a formula or spell such as the following, for treatment of an arthritic or neuralgic pain in any part of the body.

To Make Tobacco When They Are Hurting Somewhere[6]

Listen![7] Brown Person![8] You and I have just come
together to unite our efforts.
You and I are Great Wizards.
You and I are to fail in nothing.
Each of the Seven Clan Districts[9] is not to climb over
you and me!
Listen! Brown Whirlwind[10] itself! You and I have just
come together to unite our efforts.

---

6. Another formula from Adelagdhiya Gansgawi, translated by the Kilpatricks (see note 1 above), p. 90. The notes are based on their commentary.
7. An inexact translation of an attention-getting ejaculation.
8. This refers to the spirit of the tobacco that is being remade.
9. A figurative expression for the whole Cherokee nation, and occasionally for the whole world.
10. The translators are uncertain here. If Brown Whirlwind is correct, it refers to the spirit of the smoke of the remade tobacco. But perhaps this line should read: "Listen! Brown One! You have indeed just blocked them, You and I have just come together to unite our efforts."

SOUTHEASTERN INDIAN FORMULAS

You and I are Great Wizards.
You and I are to fail in nothing.
Each of the Seven Clan Districts is not to climb over
   you and me!

Procedures similar to those used in curing serve other purposes. The following Cherokee formula is for "remaking" tobacco to be used to win at gambling. If smoking tobacco is remade, the smoke is blown upon the opponent in the game; remade chewing tobacco is chewed to apply to the fingertips in small amounts in saliva.

For Remaking Tobacco For Use in Gambling[11]

In the deep forest I was in the treetops.
In the deep forest I just came to descend from a
   treetop.
Until I finish with them they are not to be stingy with
   their wealth.
All of you have just come to bring it to me in front of
   the Seven Clan Districts.
You[12] have just come to put the money in my hand!
The peewee just came and went.
He observed the insect![13]

Many Cherokee sacred formulas are for love magic. Some of these, such as the following, were used by a young husband to fix the affections of his wife (or, with appropriate changes, by a wife to fix her husband's affections). As the instructions at the end of this text imply, the husband must perform the ceremony at night while his wife is asleep. He sings the first verse, very softly, moistening his fingers with saliva (the vital fluid, according to Cherokee belief) and rubbing them on his

---

11. Another formula from Adelaghdhiya Gansgawi, translated by the Kilpatricks (see note 1 above), pp. 112-113. The title was supplied by the Kilpatricks. The notes are based on their commentary.
12. I.e., the spirit of the bird mentioned next.
13. I.e., the stakes to be gambled.

wife's breast. This is repeated on the three following nights, using the next three verses in order. The final song, on the fourth night, is followed by a spoken prayer or spell addressed to the Ancient One, also called Ancient Red (as in the last verse), that is Fire, an important deity. The final verse of the prayer indicates the successful accomplishment of the purpose of the spell.

To Fix the Affections[14]

Yu! Ha! Now the souls have come together.
You are of the Deer clan.
Your name is Ayasta.
I am of the Wolf clan.
Your body, I take it, I eat it.

Yu! Ha! Now the souls have come together.
You are of the Deer clan.
Your name is Ayasta.
I am of the Wolf clan.
Your flesh I take, I eat. Yu!

Yu! Ha! Now the souls have come together.
You are of the Deer clan.
Your name is Ayasta.
I am of the Wolf clan.
Your spittle I take, I eat. I! Yu!

Yu! Ha! Now the souls have come together.
You are of the Deer clan.
Your name is Ayasta.

---

14. From James Mooney, *The Sacred Formulas of the Cherokees*, Bureau of American Ethnology 7th Annual Report (Washington, 1891), pp.301-397, at pp. 382-383. The text was written in the Sequoyah syllabary by a prominent North Carolina Cherokee doctor (and Baptist preacher) named Gadigwanahsti, who died about 1870. In the original the personal and clan names are omitted, with X's and O's indicating where they should be inserted; Mooney added the appropriate names and clans for Gadigwanahsti and his wife Ayasta. The translation is here slightly rearranged. The notes and introduction are based on Mooney's commentary and explanation.

SOUTHEASTERN INDIAN FORMULAS

I am of the Wolf clan.
Your heart I take, I eat. Yu!

Listen! "Ha! Now the souls have met, never to part,"
 you have said, O Ancient One above.
O Black Spider, you have been brought down from on
 high.
You have let down your web.
She is of the Deer clan; her name is Ayasta.
Her soul you have trapped in your web.
There where the people of the seven clans[15] are con-
 tinually coming in sight and again disappearing,
There was never any feeling of loneliness.

Listen! Ha! But now you have covered her over with
 loneliness.
Her eyes have faded; her eyes have come to fasten
 themselves on one alone.
Whither can her soul escape?
Let her be sorrowing as she goes along, and not for
 one night alone.
Let her become an aimless wanderer, whose trail may
 never be followed.
O Black Spider, may you hold her soul in your web so
 that it shall never get through the meshes.
What is the name of the soul? They two have come
 together. It is mine!

Listen! Ha! And now you have hearkened, O Ancient
 Red.
Your grandchildren[16] have come to the edge of your
 body.[17]
You hold them yet more firmly in your grasp,
Never to let go your hold.

---

15. See note 9 above.
16. "Your grandchildren" is often used in addressing the more important deities.
17. This phrase, addressed to Fire, indicates that the performer has warmed his hands over a fire.

O Ancient One, we have become as one.
The woman has put her soul into our hands.
We shall never let it go! Yu!

[Directions:] And this also is just for the same purpose [as the preceding love charm in the original manuscript]. It must be done by stealth at night when they are asleep. One must put the hand on the middle of the breast and rub on spittle with the hand, they say. The other formula is equally good.

The medicine and magic of the Florida Seminole are similar to those of the Cherokees and especially of the Creeks. The following is the text of a Seminole song used to give power to a medicine prepared by boiling the ashes of four different kinds of tree. This is used, along with other procedures, to "clean the body" of someone who gossips and whose wife threatens to leave him. The patient's temperament is thereby changed, and his wife will again treat him properly. The words refer to the singer as a young otter, because the aquatic habits of that animal keep its body clean.

Washing the Body[18]

Go in the water
Go in the water
Go in the water
Go in the water

My body is dark, it is dark; my body is dark, it is dark.

Yellow otter
I am a young man; where is my water?

---

18. From William C. Sturtevant, "The Mikasuki Seminole Medical Beliefs and Practices" (Ph.D. diss., Yale University, 1954), pp. 250-252. The formula was recorded on wire in 1952, as sung by Josie Billie, the most renowned Seminole doctor of the period, and was transcribed and translated with his help. Although Josie Billie's language is Mikasuki, the words of the song, like those of most Seminole curing songs, are in the Creek language.

Go in the water
Go in the water
Go in the water
Go in the water

My body is dark, it is dark; my body is dark, it is dark.

Red otter
I am a young man; where is my water?

Go in the water
Go in the water
Go in the water
Go in the water

My body is dark, it is dark,; my body is dark, it is
    dark.

Black otter
I am a young man; where is my water?

Go in the water
Go in the water
Go in the water
Go in the water

My body is dark, it is dark; my body is dark, it is dark.

White otter
I am a young man; where is my water?

Fishouk, fishouk.[19]

Much of Southeastern aboriginal religion must have been
related to success in warfare, a very important activity; but
very few texts on this subject have survived. One of these is the
following, used by a North Carolina doctor to prepare the

---

19. A reference to the sound a frightened otter makes as it dives.

Cherokees who served in the Civil War. It was recited on four successive nights, while the warriors faced east, standing in the waters of a stream. Cherokee color symbolism is especially evident in this formula. Red signifies success, and in this and other magical procedures is associated with the person to be benefited. Black refers to death; here the soul of the enemy is beaten with a black warclub and enveloped in a black fog. Blue is associated with failure and spiritual depression. The ancient Cherokee cosmology is also reflected here: the souls of the enemy are placed in the underworld, while those of the Cherokee warriors are raised to the seventh and highest of the successive abodes of the spirits.

What Those Who Have Been to War Did to Help Themselves[20]

Hayi! Yu! Listen!

Now instantly we have lifted up the red warclub.
Quickly his soul shall be without motion.
His soul shall be under the earth where the black
    warclubs shall be moving about like ballsticks in the
    game, never to reappear; we cause it to be so.
He shall never go and lift up the warclub; we cause it
    to be so.
There under the earth the black warclub and the black
    fog have come together as one for their covering.
It shall never move about; we cause it to be so.
Instantly their souls shall be moving about, there in
    the seventh heaven.

Their souls shall never break in two, so shall it be.
Quickly we have moved them to the upper world,
    where they shall be going about in peace.

---

20. From Mooney, *Sacred Formulas*, pp. 388-391. The original was written in Sequoyah syllabary, for Mooney, by Ahwanita in 1888 (Mooney, p. 316). Mooney's translation has been slightly recast and arranged in a different form, guided in part by comparison with the Cherokee text. The notes and introduction are based on Mooney's commentary.

With the red warclub you have shielded yourselves.
Their souls shall never be knocked about; cause it to
be so.
Their souls there in the upper world, they shall be
going about.
Their souls, with the red warwhoop[21] let them shield
themselves.
They shall never become blue; instantly grant this.

---

21. The original text has "white warwhoop," which Mooney considered an obvious careless error of the recorder, since white denotes peace and happiness whereas the context calls for red.

Bibliography

Selected Studies

Fenton, William N. *The Iroquois Eagle Dance, An Offshoot of the Calumet Dance.* Bureau of American Ethnology Bulletin 156, 1953.

Hallowell, A. Irving. *The Role of Conjuring in Saulteaux Society* (Philadelphia: University of Pennsylvania Press, 1942).

Harrington, M. R. *Religion and Ceremonies of the Lenape* (Indian Notes and Monographs, Museum of the American Indian, Heye Foundation, vol. 19, 1921).

Hoffman, W. J. *The Midewiwin or "Grand Medicine Society" of the Ojibwa* (Bureau of American Ethnology Annual Report 7, 1891).

Hudson, Charles. *The Southeastern Indians* (Knoxville: University of Tennessee Press, 1976).

Landes, Ruth. *Ojibwa Religion and the Midewiwin* (Madison: University of Wisconsin Press, 1968).

_____. *The Prairies Potawatomi: Tradition and Ritual in the Twentieth Century* (Madison: University of Wisconsin Press, 1970).

Murdock, Gorge Peter, and Timothy J. O'Leary. *Ethnographic Bibliography of North America*, 4th ed., 5 vols. (New Haven: Human Relations Area Files Press, 1975).

Radin, Paul, ed. *Crashing Thunder: The Autobiography of an American Indian* (New York and London: D. Appleton, 1926).

Shimony, Annemarie Anrod. *Conservatism among the Iroquois at the Six Nations Reserve* (Yale University Publications in Anthropology no. 65, 1961).

Skinner, Alanson. *Associations and Ceremonies of the Menomini Indians* (American Museum of Natural History Anthropological Papers, vol.13, no. 2, 1915).

_____. *Social Life and Ceremonial Bundles of the Menomini Indians* (American Museum of Natural History Anthropological Papers, vol. 13, no. 1, 1913).

Speck, Frank G. *Midwinter Rites of the Cayuga Long House* (Philadelphia: University of Pennsylvania Press, 1949).

_____. *Naskapi* (Norman: University of Oklahoma Press, 1935).

_____. *Oklahoma Delaware Ceremonies, Feasts and Dances* (American Philosophical Society Memoir 7, 1937).

_____. *Penobscot Shamanism* (American Anthropological Association Memoir 6, pp. 237–288, 1919).

_____. "Penobscot Tales and Religious Beliefs," *Journal of American Folklore* 48, pp. 1–107, 1935.

Spindler, George, and Louise Spindler. *Dreamers without Power: The Menomini Indians* (New York: Holt, Rinehart and Winston, 1971).

Sturtevant, William C., and Bruce G. Trigger, eds. *Handbook of North American Indians*, vol. 15: *Northeast* (Washington, D.C.: Smithsonian Institution, 1978).

Swanton, John R. *Religious Beliefs and Medical Practices of the Creek Indians* (Bureau of American Ethnology Annual Report 42, pp. 473–672, 1928).

Tooker, Elisabeth. *The Iroquois Ceremonial of Midwinter* (Syracuse: Syracuse University Press, 1970).

Wallis, Wilson D., and Ruth Sawtell Wallis. *The Micmac Indians of Eastern Canada* (Minneapolis: University of Minnesota Press, 1955).

Witthoft, John. *Green Corn Ceremonialism in the Eastern Woodlands* (Museum of Anthropology, University of Michigan, Occasional Contributions 13, 1949).

Selected Texts

Chafe, Wallace L. *Seneca Thanksgiving Rituals* (Bureau of American Ethnology Bulletin 183, 1961).

Foster, Michael K. *From the Earth to Beyond the Sky: An Ethnographic Approach to Four Longhouse Iroquois Speech Events* (National Museum of Man Mercury Series, Canadian Ethnology Service Paper 20, 1974).

Hewitt, J.N.B. *Iroquoian Cosmology: First Part* (Bureau of American Ethnology Annual Report 21, pp. 127–339, 1903).

————. *Iroquoian Cosmology: Second Part* (Bureau of American Ethnology Annual Report 43, pp. 449–819, 1928).

Johnston, Basil. *Ojibway Heritage* (New York: Columbia University Press, 1976).

Michelson, Truman. *Fox Miscellany* (Bureau of American Ethnology Bulletin 114, 1937).

————. *The Owl Sacred Pack of the Fox Indians* (Bureau of American Ethnology Bulletin 72, 1921).

Mooney, James, and Frans M. Olbrechts. *The Swimmer Manuscript: Cherokee Sacred Formulas and Medical Prescriptions* (Bureau of American Ethnology Bulletin 99).

Parker, Arthur C. *The Code of Handsome Lake, the Seneca Prophet* (New York State Museum Bulletin 163, 1913). (Reprinted in William N. Fenton, ed. *Parker on the Iroquois.* Syracuse: Syracuse University Press, 1968.)

Radin, Paul. *The Road of Life and Death* (New York: Pantheon Books, 1945).

————. *The Winnebago Tribe* (Bureau of American Ethnology Annual Report 37, pp. 35–550, 1923). (Reprinted 1970, University of Nebraska Press, Lincoln.)

Speck, Frank G. *A Study of the Delaware Indian Big House Ceremony* (Publications of the Pennsylvania Historical Commission vol. 2, 1931).

INDEX TO PREFACE, INTRODUCTION, COMMENTARIES AND NOTES

INDEX TO TEXTS

71, 221, 260; of war, 87; Water-, 237, 239.
Sweat house, 223, 224-226.

Thunder, 37, 46, 47.
Thunderbirds, 89, 98, 99, 153-155, 158, 160, 224, 226, 227, 229, 234, 235, 246, 247, 256, 261.
Thunderers, 64, 99, 108, 153-158, 161, 162, 243.
Tobacco, 148; gratitude for, 134; incense of, 37, 47; as medicine, 286-287; offering of, 46, 47, 75, 77, 96-103, 126-129, 133, 135, 136, 152-154, 157-160, 168, 171, 173, 175, 186, 191, 197, 198, 207, 208, 218, 219, 221, 223-225, 227-237, 240, 243, 245, 246, 248-251, 253, 254, 257, 259, 260-266; sacred, 35.
Toohkaana, 203.
Transformation, 93-94, 177.
Trussed Thing, 274.
Turtle, 37, 51.

Visions, of buffaloes, 174; and bundles, 159; of Club-in-his-Hand, 154; and curing, 88-89, 239; and fasting, 84-85, 147, 153; fulfilling of, 48; recitation of, 109-117; and war power, 87-88.

Wampum, 118-120, 122, 123, 157, 159.
War, and blessings, 72, 73, 142, 240; bundle, 81, 83, 88, 152-163, 223-267; chiefs, 71; club, 227, 292, 293; -fare, 71, 72; and fasting, 82, 83, 87, 215; and myth, 152; -party, 83, 86, 161, 203, 211, 212, 243; path, 71-73, 80-82, 87, 88, 126, 178, 202, 213, 215, 227, 228, 240, 254; power, 71, 87-88, 219, 230-232, 234, 236, 238, 240, 246-249, 252-255, 258, 262, 263, 265, 266; of Thunderbirds, 246.
Warriors, 61, 72, 86, 152, 160, 161, 172, 178, 201, 208, 211, 214, 216, 227.
Warty One, 39.
Who-Bring-Day, 230.
Winnebago, advice to, 70-83; blessing of, 85-87; rituals of, 96-98, 217-267; visions of, 87-89.
Witchcraft, 53, 74.
World, sky-, 35, 36; under-, 47, 74, 84; up-above-, 35, 37, 67, 74, 84, 292, 293.
Worship, of buffaloes, 198, 207, 208; of Delaware, 107, 100-114, 116, 117, 120-124; of Fox, 187; of manitou, 189, 193, 194, 200, 204-206, 208, 210, 211, 213; of spirits, 247.

You-Who-Come-At-Night, 231.